PROFESSIONAL PRAISE FOR OUR CULTURE ON THE COUC

"Our Culture On The Couch is the right book at the right time. Employing a systems approach, Dr. Miller leads us through the blind spots of cultural denial to understand the underlying causes and cure for our global malaise. Using his considerable scientific skill, psychological experience, compassion and wisdom, he reveals how each of us can participate in our personal and global healing. Humor, ancient teaching stories, and personal revelation, make this book as readable as it is profound. Read this book and learn how to turn our personal and global stress to success! I recommend it highly."
– **Kenneth R. Pelletier**, PhD, MD(hc), Clinical Professor, University of Arizona School of Medicine and UCSF, Author of *New Medicine*.

"Our Culture on the Couch: Seven Steps to Global Healing is an original and practical guide which provides a systems approach to how the current paradigm of separation and opposition can shift to one that focuses on cooperation and unity. Dr. Miller offers a blueprint for a new type of leadership that incorporates universal values that can provide for personal, family, community, cultural, national, global and ecosystems healing. An invaluable and relevant book for our times!"
– **Angeles Arrien**, **Ph.D.**, Cultural Anthropologist and award-winning author of *Working Together: Producing Synergy by Honoring Diversity*.

"Dr Miller has assembled an amazing compendium of facts, resources and creative suggestions for healing our world. You owe it to yourself, your friends and family, and the world to be informed and begin to take action."
– **Jack Travis, MD, MPH**, *Author of The Wellness Workbook*, and pioneer of the wellness movement.

"In this book, Dr Emmett Miller, the closest person to a genius I know, applies his groundbreaking, cutting edge work in healing the human psyche to the formidable task of healing the planet. It's a brilliant approach filled with the wisdom that is desperately needed at so many levels if Spaceship Earth is to survive."
– **Robert Kriegel Ph.D.** Author of *If It Ain't Broke...BREAK IT!*

"Emmett Miller, M.D. is a man of extraordinary talents – a clinician, teacher, folk singer, group leader, and community activist. In this book, stimulated by the occurrence of 9/11, he has become an America activist! His presentations on how to heal ourselves as well as heal our country are carefully and colorfully presented in this reader-friendly book. Dr. Miller's goal is to

reshape how we, our communities and our country, can work together and create a safer and healthier 21st Century."
– **Richard H. Rahe, M.D.,** Professor of Psychiatry, University of Washington School of Medicine and Creator of the Holmes-Rahe Social Readjustment Scale.

"Through personal storytelling, the compelling medical metaphor offered in a new systemic framework, great visual images, summaries of core messages at the end of each chapter, and opportunities for individual reflection, Dr. Emmett Miller creates a compelling narrative of today's malaise and introduces powerful tools for individual and collective transformation. I hope this book will serve to stimulate collaborative dialogue across the nation around the critical issues raised by Dr. Miller. Our mutual survival may depend on it."
– **Juanita Brown Ph.D**., Co-Originator, The World Café; Consultant in strategic dialogue and large systems change.

"Dr. Miller's book is infused with wit, wisdom and lucidity. By merging scientific medical diagnosis and treatment with the profound techniques of deep healing, a new paradigm emerges; the way we think about ourselves and others is changed forever. Dr. Miller gives meaningful, actionable solutions to unite and heal a world that is in deep crises and conflict. This is the right book at the right time…"
– **Janice Dorn, M.D., Ph.D.**, Neuropsychiatrist, Financial Futurist, Author of *Personal Responsibility: The Power Of You.*

"With this book, Emmett Miller continues his important work of helping us to break out of our cultural denial, helping us to heal, and helping us to stop this destructive culture."
– **Derrick Jensen**, Author of *Endgame, What We Leave Behind*, and many others.

"A real wake-up call! It draws you in and shines a light on what is truly important in life. All of us often worry about what the future holds. This book will fill your heart and soul with the wisdom to deal with these life's challenges. Not only should everyone read it, they should study it and then pass it on to everyone they know!"
– **Jim Britt**, *Author of Rings of Truth.*

"Doctor Miller clearly paints the picture of our entry into the narrows, where it obvious we are all going to have to make a shift to successfully evolve through the next few years. The imponderables are there. He makes them clear. The choices then are to look at our own inhabited being state and then prototype ourselves into the most aware and adaptive vehicle we can manifest and from there, he coaches, we have the best skill set and being

to surf the wave through the narrows into the next most promising world we can imagine. Its up to us."
– **Jim Channon**, Lt. Colonel (Ret.), Founder, US Army First Earth Battalion

"With his heartfelt, wide-ranging, highly attuned intelligence and the huge, healing skill sets at his command, our uniquely inspired, brainiac physician/psychologist, Emmett Miller MD, puts contemporary culture on the couch and analyzes the dysfunction clean out of it. This book shows us where change must occur and what those changes must look like if we are to survive. Both a scary wake-up call and a hopeful blueprint for the future, this book is a must read."
– **Belleruth Naparstek**, LISW, Author of *Invisible Heroes: Survivors of Trauma and How They Heal*; and creator of the Health Journeys Audio Series.

"Taking on modern culture as a patient, Dr. Miller applies his finely honed clinical skills to diagnose our condition and, with compassion and clarity, prescribes a course of treatment that is deeply transformative. Hopefully we will be courageous enough, individually and collectively, to take it. It is a gift that offers real hope."
– **Martin L. Rossman, M.D.**, Clinical Associate, Dept. of Medicine, University of California Medical Center, San Francisco

"Since cofounding the fields of Holistic and Mind/Body Medicine in the 1970s, Dr. Miller's contributions to the healing arts and to education have been legend. The theories and practical applications presented here may well create global transformations equal to those he has already set in motion in the healing arts."
– **Anees Sheikh, PhD.**, Professor, Marquette University.

"I believe that all human beings are merely tiny symbiotic creatures living with the body of, and interconnected by the Earth. Dr. Miller has written an important new book, Our Culture On The Couch; Seven Steps to Global Healing. Let me say that this is an important book. This is a crucial book. This is a necessary book if humanity is to find a way forward.
Dr. Miller is a physician, a physicist, a former Officer in the Armed Forces, and the father of some of the finest children on our planet. He is a man who can be trusted. Read his book and take it seriously, for the sake of the Earth and for the sake of our survival!"
– **John F. Callahan**, consultant, Environmental Attorney (Ret.), formerly of US Environmental Protection Agency

OUR CULTURE ON THE COUCH
SEVEN STEPS TO GLOBAL HEALING

DR. EMMETT MILLER

LIMITED MANUSCRIPT EDITION

Other titles by Dr. Miller

Selective Awareness, Self Published 1973

Feeling Good; How to Stay Healthy, Prentice Hall, 1978

Self-Imagery; Creating Your Own Good Health,
Celestial Arts, 1978

Software For The Mind, Celestial Arts, 1987

Opening Your Inner "Eye", Celestial Arts, 1987,1991

Living In Hope, Celestial Arts, 1991

Deep Healing, Hay House, 1997

For more information regarding other writings and
products by Dr. Miller, visit www.DrMiller.com

Limited Manuscript edition printed April 2009
published by Lightning Source

TABLE OF CONTENTS

DIAGNOSIS

T R E A T M E N T

HEALING

DEDICATION

To the children of the world, to whom its future belongs, that their trust, innocence, and honesty might guide our choices.

ACKNOWLEDGMENTS AND GRATITUDE

It is, of course, impossible to individually thank all those who have, during the seven years' gestation of the book, given me valuable advice, information, and support. Some very special thanks and warm regards are in order, however, especially to Beth Landi for her wise editorial guidance and support; to Tom Durkin for copy and idea editing; to Jesse Churchill for formatting and design; to Tabatha Jones for transcribing my spoken notes and editing copy; and to Nancy Margulies and Jessica Slack for cover design; and to Juanita Brown for moral support and guidance. I am also deeply indebted to my family, patients, and friends for putting up with my seven-year obsession with this project.

I would like to thank all those wise and brave members of my human family who have braved abuse and tyranny to preserve and nurture the spirit of healing; those Healers who have walked and still walk among us, guiding people and peoples through challenging rapids; to those families, tribes, and races that have suffered that we might have the right to the lives and the prosperity with which we have been gifted; to the wise men and women who have shared their wisdom and works with my teachers and me; and to all those who have sacrificed, even to the point of giving their lives, so that mankind might survive. If I can see far, to borrow Sir Isaac Newton's turn of phrase, it is because I am standing on the shoulders of giants.

I would like to thank, as well, my patients who, for forty amazing years have contributed to my knowledge, maturity, and personal growth, whose stories and suffering have taught me compassion, and the ability of Love to heal body, mind, spirit, and family. And I want to thank you, dear reader, for taking your precious time to experience healing yourself and your world more deeply.

FOREWORD

In this remarkable book, Dr. Miller diagnoses the cultural pathologies that ruin our lives and threaten to destroy civilization as we know it. That bold assessment stimulates us to look in the mirror and assess the enemy we see. What systems run our lives, what concepts have we bought into, and where are we heading? If we can understand the nature of the illness, see where it's leading, and connect cause and effect, we might be able to intervene, forestall, or actually redirect the flow of events. Miller both lays this out clearly for us and shows us the tools at hand we can employ to assist in the work. This how-to manual can inform and ignite a broad community in ways that multiply the effectiveness of efforts to heal our society.

Miller's knowledge of relevant subjects, from medicine to global warming, from systems analysis to religion, seems broad and expert. But what's truly amazing is how he brings all of those perspectives and teachings to bear on one simply stated question: *What exactly do we need to do to clean up the mess before we literally destroy ourselves and our planet?* The answer can't be stated in just a simple mantram, but perhaps the closest hint to it comes from what he calls the "Systemic Healing Principle," which requires us to recognize that we are in the same boat with our neighbors, where cooperation and empathetic relationships provide the only plausible course of action.

The American experiences of 9/11, Katrina, and the world financial meltdown would each, by itself, be a wake-up call for the national psyche. But what do we do when we have such nightmares? Miller says: Learn from them, face the truth, and get to work changing our behavior before time runs out. That's a message that really does need to be heard 'round the world. We might actually be able to take the good Doctor's advice, rid our society of lethal pathologies, and go on to thrive. Can a book do all that? This one just might!

– Frederick Hayes-Roth, Ph.D., Professor, Information Systems, Naval Postgraduate School, Monterey, CA; Author: _Radical Simplicity: How Intelligent Organizations Attain Supremacy through Information Superiority

PREFACE

PREFACE

GLOBAL ECONOMIC CRISIS EVEN WORSE THAN EXPECTED

In moments of crisis, my nerves act in the most extraordinary way. When utter disaster seems imminent my whole being is instantaneously braced to avoid it. I size up the situation in a flash, set my teeth, contract my muscles, take a firm grip on myself and, without a tremor, always do the wrong thing ...
– George Bernard Shaw

Economists Predict Economic Collapse

As a headline, that is a real attention-getter, even better than "War Declared." The economic implosion we have been experiencing of late has gotten everyone's attention. Most of us will suffer, and the acute wounds of this debacle certainly need to be addressed post haste. But we must avoid being "headline junkies;" there is great danger, as we engage in the usual righteous search for someone to blame for the most recently revealed crisis, and the rooting around in congressional pork barrels for the ever elusive "quick fix." If we are characteristically unwise, and respond only symptomatically and reflexively, we might miss the golden opportunity this most recent challenge offers us.

That opportunity is what this book is about – the opportunity to wake up. But this is by no means our first chance to do so. Having witnessed a number of global crises in my lifetime, I have noticed a pattern is becoming clear (one of the advantages of growing older, I guess). Although there are many "special interests" whose continued wealth and power depend upon their continuing to keep us asleep, each crisis offers an opportunity to come out of our drunken slumber.

The Brief Awakening of the 1960s

We had a chance to awaken in the '60s when Chaney, Goodman, and Schwerner, were murdered – and many people did wake up. I was in college and medical school at the time. Suddenly people began to act like they really cared. Incredibly, they suddenly had the nerve to stick flowers in the barrels of rifles and date the brown-skinned kid.

Equality, spirituality, ecology, diversity, community celebration – and the arts – all flourished. "Negroes" actually gained the freedom to vote and the ability to sit in the front of the bus, and the rights of women expanded enormously. We moved against the Vietnam War, and in so many ways began to see the world differently – and act differently.

But the forces of reaction were strong. Soon the overclass

drew the cultural wagons into a circle, and voices for change were all but silenced. We moved into the Greed is Good period with Milton Friedman as its prophet, and Ronald Reagan as the Sir Galahad of deregulation. Lower taxes, less oversight, a "deficits don't matter" attitude, less government "intervention" – the "Me Generation" took hold, suppressing the awakening that had begun, and planting the seeds of destruction we see bearing their bitter fruit around us now.

> *Reagan proved that deficits don't matter. We won the mid-term elections, this is our due...*
> *– Vice President Dick Cheney* [1]

September 11, 2001

Another opportunity to wake up took place on September 11, 2001, the real "Y2K." Responding to the devastating terrorist attacks in the U.S., people from all over the globe felt a sense of unity, pride in being human, a sudden awareness of what might be called our "oneness." People were smiling at each other as they passed on the streets of Manhattan! (I thought I'd never see the day!) But it seems those qualities that so impressed me were not held in such high regard by the "deciders" of our world.

As a result, little was done to capitalize on them, and as national power consolidated, we gradually morphed from the America that the world loved into preemptive invaders, an America that thumbed its nose at the world, imprisoned citizens for years on mere rumor, and shipped prisoners to torture camps around the world. The symbol that represented the United States to the world gradually shifted from being the Statue of Liberty to the brown man receiving electric shock torture at Abu Ghraib!

---

[1] Ron Suskind, *the Price of Loyalty* (New York, Simon and Schuster, 2004) Suskind is a former reporter for the Wall Street Journal.

Face the Danger, Seize the Opportunity, Enjoy the Challenge

Once again, our actions have brought us to a crisis point – and once again we have choices to make. History, as we know, always repeats itself – and each time the price goes up. The opportunity, as I see it, is for us to address our problems at a deeper level than we have in the past. The question is whether or not we have yet learned the importance of treating the source of our problems, not just the symptoms. Will we be able to see past our blind spot this time? This book was written with the fervent hope that we are finally ready, that we will see the opportunity and seize it, that we will let this serve as the whack on the head that will awaken us to our potential and stop the madness. It is dedicated to those who are ready to look at the world and at themselves, to look deeply and honestly – and to respond to the truth with wisdom, integrity, passion, and inspired creativity.

This book is about change, deep, profound, radical change – indeed, well beyond what is usually considered radical – an invitation to transformation. And even though the steps to this needed transformation are gradual, we still face a challenge; people generally prefer a problem that is familiar to a solution that is not.

Yes, these are crisis times – yet the greater the danger, the greater the opportunity – or so say the sages. If this book is successful, the result will be more than simply another cosmetic "fix." Instead of rearranging the deck chairs one more time, this time, let's repair that gaping hole in our hull.

You may well ask, "What gives you access to this special knowledge or wisdom? What makes you think that you can see something so clearly that eludes so many others?" I have often asked myself that question, and I suspect the answer is that I have seen the world from a different perspective.

Certainly, every physician who has witnessed human healing take place right before their eyes, or who has wielded scalpel and suture, or held the hand of a dying patient, has been granted the opportunity of a very special insight into human nature, indeed.

iv

I have to give credit also to my fascination with science, computer science, psychology, and theoretical mathematical and logical systems. For four decades I have applied these learnings to human health and behavior, using powerful tools such as hypnosis, meditation, and cognitive behavioral therapy, with the goal of understanding the process of healing transformation.

Yet perhaps the most significant determinant of my unique perspective, strangely enough, is the result of an "accident" of birth; I have had the opportunity to look at the world from "out of the box" since early in my childhood. My ticket to this view from this vantage point was the color of my skin.

I thought it long before Jim Morrison sang it: "People are strange, when you're a stranger." For much of my youth I would, from time to time, imagine that I was actually from another world (Heck, it was true about Clark Kent), one that sees things very differently from how most folks here on this planet see them. It was hard to understand the behavior of the people around me.

As a kid I watched in amazement as people intentionally injured others for the *purpose* of giving them pain. As an "only child" who had always wished he had a brother with whom he could play and share his life, I watched in utter disbelief as even brothers and sisters seemed to enjoy hurting each other. People said, "You're an only child, and you don't understand about sibling rivalry." I nodded my head, but secretly thought, "I don't think I want to understand why that kind of behavior is permissible."

By my teens, my questions about the whys of abusive behavior became a lot more personal. The Brooklyn, New York neighborhood where I grew up was rife with thugs from local African-American street gangs – high school dropouts who were greatly intent upon attacking and trying to "kick my ass." Yet at school, my good friends, with one exception, never invited me to a single party, or any other event – even when most of the class was invited.

In time I heard that it was because I was "different" from them; I learned the problem was due to the fact that a few of my ancestors were African and Native American. That's why nobody invites me into his or her home? At first I thought it was a joke.

Soon I came to learn that there was a theory – a belief held by most people of the Caucasian persuasion – that the people whose forefathers were from Africa were somehow inferior, a kind of human subspecies. Therefore, there was no need to treat them with the kind of respect and dignity you were expected to display when dealing with someone of your own race. Yet, at the same time, they called themselves "Christians" or "Jews," and said they felt that they truly believed in the tenets of their faith, such as the Golden Rule. And they were telling the truth – they did think they believed in these maxims – yet their behavior (subtly in the North, not so subtly in the South) towards me quite clearly did not bear this out.

They came by their worldview also by accident of being born to a culture of people who could write the stunning words: "All men are created equal and endowed by their creator with certain unalienable rights, including Life, Liberty, and the Pursuit of happiness." Yet, without flinching they had imported slaves from Africa, forbidden them to marry, and claimed to believe they were saving their souls. Even after slavery was abolished, they created segregated schools, nightclubs, bathrooms, and even water foun-

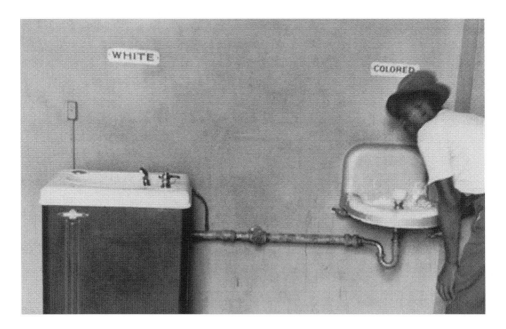

tains. And in the North, they effectively excluded the one kid in the class who is of African or Native American descent.

I have no doubt that most of these folks would have sworn on the proverbial stack of Bibles that they were not bigoted, that they deplored the segregationist attitudes of the South – yet I am sure it never occurred to them to make me feel welcome in their white world. These were not bad people. They had high family values, were often quite religious, and were active members of their community. Yet they somehow did not see my pain, my disappointment, and my confusion.

They were my good friends, but at a certain point I stopped being fully human in their eyes. "Some of my best friends are Negroes" is a line I heard uttered, straight-faced, countless times. What remained unspoken but true were the words, "but I wouldn't want my sister to marry one." During my college experience in the '60s, (when one third of the states had laws forbidding me to marry a white woman), the insults continued. I was an ideal fraternity pledge, and would ordinarily have been courted by at least half the groups on campus; I was an A student, a successful athlete, and a good dancer. Shamefully, not one of the 15 fraternities on campus ever even considered inviting me to a "get acquainted" dinner.

The impact of this discovery was more devastating than you might imagine. Here I was, an energetic, passionate young man in an all-male college, where women were not allowed on campus. There were lots of parties, of course, but they all took place in the fraternity houses located across the street from the campus. It was a painful four years, watching the others walking hand in hand with girls who would refuse to even make eye contact with me. My friends could only shrug and say, "The national charter of all the fraternities excluded blacks and Native Americans."

I want to emphasize that throughout my life the people at whose hands I experienced such abuse were, actually, very good people; many were friends and colleagues who were very supportive in many ways. Yet there existed a fundamental assumption about the world at a deep level within them, a way of looking at the world that limited the range of choices available to them. The result was that, somehow, I was invisible to them. They had a blind spot, and I was in it. It seemed that nothing I could say or do could shatter their denial.

You may have had this kind of experience in a milder (or more severe) form, and you are well aware of how illogical, harmful, and cruel this kind of attitude can be. And you may be aware of it in a particularly excruciating way if you have had the experience of being a minority living within an abusive majority. It happens over and over, yet each time you are struck in the face by it, it hurts anew. You are forced to see how very pervasive this kind of thinking is, and how destructive it is.

It is hard to imagine the pain of being reminded several times a week that you are considered less than equal to those who are supposed to be your peers. The wounds are still healing.

What does not kill me makes me stronger.
– Friedrich Nietzsche

Yet these same wounds would turn out to be the source of great energy and creativity, as they provided me with great compassion for others who have suffered even more. I became aware that my suffering was just a special case of a more widespread phenomenon.

The Wounds of Cultural Blindness

When treated as defective by a large part of their world, most people begin to believe that they actually are inadequate. African-Americans and Native Americans were widely believed to be less intelligent and less creative than White Americans – and under the pressure of all the propaganda, many began to believe it.

The uniqueness of my experience lies in the fact that I was virtually always at the top of my class in school, yet I was still treated as if I were inferior. The facts were clear to me – they were wrong. I could see that I was as good as they, in fact, in many ways, better!

What baffled me was: how so many people manage to not see *me*, and later, how some could not see other people if they were women, Asians, Jews, and so on. And why were they not embarrassed at how inaccurate and ridiculous their projections were.

Fascinated, I started studying this phenomenon, this ability to not see what is obvious. I came to see this most remarkable tool as the cognitive process of *denial* [2]. It became clear that simply showing people was not enough; people need to actually "see the world with new eyes," to actually accept a new model of the world, one that would enable them to really see others (like me).

This gave me purpose, and inspired much of my work through the next decades. I was determined to discover why it was that people could be so blind.

I had seen mathematics, logic, and science at work, and I fervently believed that there was a solution to this amazing situation – and a solution was sorely needed; beyond the personal suffering, these cultural cruelties were at the base of the conflicts and wars that had exacted such a toll on the human race since time immemorial.

Clearly the cost to society of racism, nationalism, and religious bigotry was huge, both in terms of the personal tragedy, the wholesale destruction, and the loss of creativity. Surely science could solve this problem. It seemed like a worthy mission for my life. For guidance in how to transform thinking, I turned to one of my personal heroes, Albert Einstein.

---

[2] First referred to by Freud, denial is a defense mechanism used when a fact is too uncomfortable to accept. The person in denial will insist it is not true even in the face of overwhelming evidence. He or she may either deny the reality of the unpleasant fact altogether (simple denial), admit the fact but deny its seriousness (minimization), or admit both the fact and seriousness but deny responsibility (transference).

Thought Experiments

My earliest studies were in science and mathematics. Like most scientists I had the highest respect for the mathematician and quintessential genius, Albert Einstein. In the mid-1950s the world was still reeling at how he had, almost single-handedly, transformed our concept of our universe and the science we use to try to comprehend it.

One thing that particularly impressed me was the unique way Dr. Einstein approached science, especially his "thought experiments." One of his most famous was his imagining he was riding on a beam of light, traveling in one direction, at the speed of light, passing another beam traveling in the opposite direction, also at the speed of light. He knew that if he measured his speed relative to a stationary object, he would find his speed to be, of course, "c," the speed of light.

"But," he asked himself, "how fast am I going relative to the particle coming toward me?" Common sense tells us it must be "2c," or twice the speed of light – impossibility, since the speed of light is the maximum speed any object can travel. Out of this seeming contradiction came the Theory of Relativity, and a whole new era of science ensued! People woke up to a new world. Einstein had given the world new eyes.

The real purpose of scientific theories is to open the doors to the scientific advances that propel civilization forward (guns, medication, steel, etc.). For example, the theory that many diseases are the result of infection with living organisms invisible to the naked eye opened the door to modern sanitation and medical treatment, and the societies that have become possible as a result.

We mathematicians are familiar with "thought experiments," but the fact that Dr. Einstein had brought such stunning insight to the field of science fascinated me. I practiced this technique in my own research, and found that it has been extremely fruitful. In fact, my contributions to psychology and Mind-Body Medicine are based on the application of this powerful tool to "reprogramming" the biocomputer that is the unconscious part of the mind.

The Nine Dot Problem

Here is a little thought experiment, a challenge for your mind. Below there are nine dots arranged in a square shape. Copy them on a piece of paper, then take a pencil and draw four straight lines in such a way that every point has at least one line passing through it.

Now comes the kicker. You must be able to draw all four lines without lifting your pencil from the paper!

Most people, when they encounter this problem for the first time, find it frustrating, most do not solve it in any reasonable amount of time. If you're familiar with this problem, then perhaps you can recall your frustration at first, and the "aha" experience when you discovered, or were shown the solution.

If you already know the solution to this problem, then perhaps you can recall your frustration while struggling to figure it out (or try it on some friends and watch their reaction). It's uncanny!

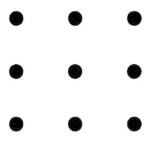

You go through the process of being stumped for a while – even thinking it is impossible – then suddenly see the answer, and realize that it has always been right in front of you. You hadn't even considered going outside the imaginary box in which your creativity was trapped. *(The solution can be found at the end of this chapter.)*

Thinking "Out of the Box"

The experience you have going through this process demonstrates some important qualities of the unconscious part of your mind. The first is its tendency, without your permission or knowledge, to impose imaginary limits on a situation – limits that are not part of its essential nature. When this happens, you are unaware that you are limiting *yourself*; instead you *project* the limitation onto the situation itself, with the unfortunate result that the easily attainable solution lies unseen right before your eyes.

We *hallucinate* limitations where there are none, imagine we must stay within a box, and *yet have no idea we are imagining the box*. The unconscious part of the mind has created a rule that works against our true goals. In many cases, the solutions, or the path that leads to the solutions, of the most vexing of human problems also lie right in front of us.

A human being is a part of the whole, yet he experiences himself, his thoughts, and his feelings as something separated from the rest – a kind of optical delusion of consciousness. This delusion is a kind of prison, restricting us to our personal desires and to affection for a few persons nearest to us. Our task must be to be free from this prison by widening our circle of compassion to embrace all living creatures and the whole nature in its beauty.
– Albert Einstein

The second thing to notice is that particular inner experience you have at the moment of seeing the solution – the experience of discovery, of watching as your world expands to include a part of the universe that had been invisible to you. This is a most important and useful feeling; it is the result of the neurons of your cerebral cortex excreting a special blend of neurotransmitters, producing a "rush" of positive feelings that are associated with the experience of creation, of awakening a significant truth. Suddenly you have discovered a new vantage point, one from which you can see the world from an important new perspective.

This book, like my life, is about discovery, the expansion of awareness to encompass a world not previously envisioned, a new universe where problems that formerly seemed intractable suddenly begin to melt away. Its highest goal is to enable us to see that there is a way to proceed in which we can maximize what it is that we all really want and need. I have become convinced that learning to open ourselves to the possibility of having these "Aha!" moments is crucial, not only for resolving our personal issues and relationships, but for successfully addressing the challenges of today's world.

One of our most valuable skills for doing this is the ability to understand and produce those internal cognitive states that enable us to quickly move from a stuck place (like the Nine Dot Problem), to a place where we can quickly see what to do, a move that is accompanied by that joyful little feeling of discovery. It is kind of like watching your team win a big game, or suddenly recalling where you left something you were searching for. Remember? It is also a place in which you feel truly free. We will explore the way these breakthrough moments can be intentionally created, and how they can enable us to transcend the blind spots that are key aspects of the problems that plague us all.

Blind Spots

Psychologists and practitioners of mind-body medicine are well aware of the tendency of people to have blind spots. Much of therapy is devoted to finding the relaxation and the courage to go beyond one's blind spots to see the simple solutions that have been eluding them. The result of this is the ability to choose a different set of behaviors (thoughts, emotions, speech, or physical actions), behaviors that are more appropriate and successful.

When you have this kind of limitation on your perspective, the behaviors available are insufficient, and even though the intention behind these behaviors is to resolve your problem, they do not. They simply lead to increasing frustration, and an unfortunate tendency of these behaviors to actually make the problem worse!

One only has to think of the alcoholic deciding to go drinking to relieve some inner stress, promising himself that he is going to have "just one." Or think of the obsessive person, making him or herself physically sick by spending every free moment worrying about something that could never be solved by worrying. Or about the man verbally abusing his wife, as if somehow he actually thought that being abusive was a good way to solve the problem and create a better life for both of them. As we look on and shake our heads, we can easily see a much better way to proceed, yet it is invisible to them.

In a similar way, it is not uncommon to find families continually getting stuck in the same dysfunctional loops – sometimes for generations. They repeat the old patterns, somehow expecting different results, blind to creative solutions that are right there in front of them.

Continuing up the scale, we can see the same fundamental pattern at the level of communities, cultures, and nations. The Arabs and the Israelis have, for an unimaginable number of decades, been fighting an "eye for an eye, tooth for a tooth" war – where each side justifies its attack by calling it a reprisal for a previous attack by the other side. How many lives have been lost, how many children orphaned, how many wounded, how much global instability has resulted from this pattern? This pattern has been repeated countless times throughout the world! And it is always blamed on the *other guy.*

As you read you will notice that I refer to concepts of psychology that are generally only spoken of when speaking in reference to a person who has an illness such as anxiety or depressive disorder. It is important to remember that these concepts may apply to traits that all of us have, to one degree or another. The difference is that the person who needs clinical evaluation and attention is one in whose life the imbalance is creating a much greater degree of pain and dysfunction in his or her life. But we all have our blind spots – and people in the outside world can often see them in us as easily as we can see them in others. But usually, like the naked emperor, we are in denial of this fact (an attempt by the unconscious to help us feel more comfortable).

Our success in life, our health, creativity, and happiness are all improved when we discover and transcend such imaginary limitations, and those who are wise seek to discover them, and welcome the observations of anyone who can help us find them. The best way to understand what I am trying to share with you is to remain open to the possibility of expanding your sense of the world, and of yourself. You and I are both aware that you have the power, if you choose, to remain completely closed to these thought experiments, and as a result, experience little or none of what I suggest. On the other hand, you will find that, to the degree you can permit this openness, this *beginner's mind*, you can make rapid leaps in your ability to heal yourself and your world.

The Central Role of Denial

One of the remarkable facts about the human brain is that when it finds itself faced with two equally valid but seemingly incompatible interpretations or perceptions, it tends to suppress one of the interpretations – to make it invisible – then take the other interpretation as the "truth." Then, rather than deal with the cognitive dissonance, it will rationalize and defend its position to the point of absurdity.

To the left, I have drawn the well-known "optical illusion" of the stairs. Are the stairs going up or down? Are the treads black or

white? When you first look, it appears they are going up. But soon you see them going down, and the other interpretation becomes *impossible* to see. It is a property of the brain itself that you cannot see both at the same time. Figure becomes ground, and ground figure, and you see a different world.

Likewise, in the following picture, you have to see the archway as having either two columns or three. In order to see one interpretation, you have to suppress the other.

This is a kind of *denial*, an *unconscious*, usually *unintentional* suppression of alternate interpretations of the world, when an easy synthesis is not found. Denial also takes place on a regular basis in our everyday lives; it is the basis of much prejudice and conflict, when there is insufficient commitment to knowing and acting in harmony with the truth.

Obviously, these little experiments are very simplistic, and are being used only to present some of the principles and approaches we will be exploring in much greater depth, and in much

more complex systems. The basic idea here is that what you do is conditioned by what you view, and that by shifting to a more expansive viewpoint we can often turn stumbling blocks into stepping stones. Here is another example, in a somewhat more "real world" form.

The Sisters and the Orange

Two sisters happened to arrive in the kitchen at the same time, where they found an orange sitting on the kitchen table. They both reached for it at the same moment, and a fight broke out, each claiming they had seen the orange first. Hearing the racket, their father came in and stopped the argument.

"You are sisters," he told them, "and sisters should share equally." He then cut the orange neatly in half with a sharp knife, and gave each their fair portion.

This mollified the girls to some degree. They stopped fighting, but each still eyed the other's portion longingly.

At this moment the mother happened to come into the kitchen. "What did you want the orange for?" she asked the first girl. "I wanted to use the flesh of the orange for a fruit salad," she replied.

"And you?" she asked the second.

" I wanted the rind to make some marmalade," she answered. The mother then took the orange, divided it differently, and each sister got twice as much as before, and was completely satisfied.

In this little story, the father resorted to the standard solution, a good one, given his understanding of the situation. The mother, on the other hand, had a deeper, more systemic view of the problem. The problem was not how to divide the orange; it was how to give both sisters the maximum benefit from the orange. Her solution was invisible to the father, who saw the problem merely as how to be fair to both his daughters. This different perspective transformed the situation. The shift in the mode of looking at the problem made it go away! The mother understood the systemic nature of the situation, and could thus address it from a different level of system.

Healing Our Planet

I found that the systemic healing approaches I had discovered and developed in my practice of Mind-Body Medicine were remarkably effective in my work with families [3] as well as with individuals, and with teams, companies, and communities. The high-functioning community is like a high-functioning, healthy individual:

- All the parts of the system are healthy,
- They all relate to each other in a healthy, productive way,
- The system utilizes the highest possible levels of wisdom to govern and guide its behavior.

So it was only natural that I would carry out a thought experiment in which the planet as a whole would be the "patient." I imagined myself as an interplanetary consultant, a cosmic doctor, an interstellar physician, who had arrived on Earth to find things in shabby shape indeed. So, for the next three decades, like a good doctor, I set out to:

---

[3] I am most grateful to Virginia Satir, the "Columbus of Family Therapy," for her guidance in applying these principles with families and communities.

1. Investigate and document the chief complaints and the history of the problem
2. Perform a physical examination
3. Make a diagnosis
4. Develop a treatment plan
5. Present the findings and suggested plan to the patient, just as I would if it were a person or a family.

A Book is Conceived

The spark that occasioned this book came a few weeks after September 11, 2001, when a friend asked me what message I would want to send if everyone in the world were listening. My response was that I would ask people to avoid acting precipitously and to examine the current situation as carefully, scientifically, and honestly as they would want their child examined if she were to have seizures and a fever of unknown origin.

Likewise, if we are to go beyond the *crisis de jour* mentality, if we are to transcend the old reactions, habits, and prejudices, we must use the formidable tools we have available to us. I have been aware for many decades, that the world is facing the possibility of unimaginable catastrophe. Since September 11 and the economic meltdown of 2008, many more people are beginning to understand. Given the extreme complexity and globalized nature of our finances, diseases, pollution, food supply, and weapons of mass destruction, our only hope for survival is to carefully and honestly examine the entire situation carefully – and use logic and the scientific method to reach the true roots of our problem.

Strange as it seems, here in the age of computers and space flight, people are not accustomed to approaching the stressors in their lives using the scientific method. They are impatient, impulsive, and tend to be acting out of fear. Few really understand the scientific process of examining, diagnosing, and intervening in most situations. Indeed, recent years have seen the wholesale rejection of the findings of science in fields such as evolution, global warming, pollution, peak oil, and so forth.

We can no longer afford the luxury of remaining in denial. The methods the good doctor uses are ones we approve of, and trust our lives to. So why not use the same principles that guide the physician in treating the human patient as we approach our current global situation? It can't hurt, and it *could* be enormously helpful.

And that is the way this book was conceived. My goal is to present my findings, as I would to a patient or to a group of doctors at grand rounds – to enable as many people as possible to experience the essence of what I have learned about the process of healing, becoming more whole, and achieving optimal performance – and to present it in a way that it can be applied at every level, from relaxing a tense neck, to bringing peace and love to a family, to acting decisively on climate change.

I know that if enough people allow themselves to have the experiences I suggest in these pages, we have an excellent chance of reaching critical mass, and creating the transformation that we and our world desperately need. But we must act soon, time is running out.

A Living Document

I began writing this book in the weeks following the attacks of September 11, and continued to write it over a period of nearly six years, during which the world continued to change. As I was writing, we invaded Afghanistan, then Iraq. Hurricane Katrina pounded us, the cost of oil skyrocketed, and our economy all but collapsed. Time and again the inadequacy of our problem-solving skills was painfully demonstrated.

As we learn more facts about the condition our world is in and the people and behaviors that created this condition, some of my illustrative examples may seem a trifle long in the tooth, and facts may need a little updating. Do not let this distract you. You can probably think of even better examples from your own experience – please feel free to do so. Though the names and details may change from event to event, I think you will find that the underlying pattern we are examining stays the same.

To get the most out of this book, start at the beginning and follow through the development of the ideas, all the way to the end. To really receive what it has to offer you must go beyond merely a cognitive understanding of the principles and ideas – to truly let its wisdom in, you must experience it. Throughout, you will find important questions to ask yourself, imagery to create, and connections to be made that will help you discover what it is that you need to bring forth to bring about the transformation you want. In spite of how fast the world is moving around you, please take the time to experience.

On the other hand, I realize that some people will choose to move quickly through this work, at least the first time. So I have constructed it in such a way that you can flip through the pages, reading only the quotes, subheadings, italicized text, and the "Take Home Messages"; this will give you an excellent glimpse of the heart of some of the subject matter. Or you can begin at essentially any place that interests you, read on from there, and go back to earlier sections when the time is more appropriate.

The purpose is of this book is to help catalyze global transformation, and to that end it is designed as a living, evolving work that will continue to be in flux – just as we all are, and as is the world we live in. For that reason, I am open to and invite your comments, constructive criticisms, more effective illustrations, inspirational stories, powerful quotes – and especially, better and newer statistics and documentation.

Our goal is to discover and embody the truth, and the wisdom that can enable it to bring about the healing and transformation we need.

Thank you in advance for sending me your thoughts and contributions: DrMiller@DrMiller.com.

Emmett C. Miller, M.D.

Solution to the Nine Dot Problem

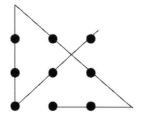

CHAPTER 1

A PLANET IN PERIL

*We know the challenges that tomorrow will bring are
the greatest of our lifetime – two wars, a planet in
peril, the worst financial crisis in a century.*
– Barack Obama Presidential Acceptance Speech 2008

How poignant the story of our planet, as it slouches toward Armageddon – her surface pockmarked with bomb craters, her skies browning with smog, her once stately rainforests being reduced to dry scabs, her black and white penguins adrift at sea on her melting glaciers, her once crystalline waterways poisonous and choked with sludge, her people starving, enslaved, and fearing each other.

Sometimes in my darker hours, I imagine I can actually hear the cries of species vanishing by the thousands, the starving millions, the teenage girls kidnapped and raped into a short life of sexual slavery, and the mothers as their infants are dashed against stone walls or hacked into pieces with machetes.

I can hear their cries as keenly as I heard the cries of that

1

woman being brutally examined by my professor at the start of my clinical training in medical school[1]. Until then, I had been an innocent, drawn into the study of medicine by heroic tales of physicians who volunteered to brave battlefield bullets to operate on soldiers, who went out into blizzards to treat a feverish child, or who personally tested an experimental medication on himself before prescribing it to a patient, lest the patient be harmed by it.

I was in for a rude awakening. Instead of a healing garden, the world of Medicine proved to be more like a battlefield. Our job was to fight the foe, the illness, which was imagined to be an enemy to be destroyed with scalpels and poisons. Patients were, to a large extent, simply the host, there to deliver the disease to us so we could destroy it.

With important and valuable exceptions, patients were far too often treated with indifference, callousness, and even cruelty.

Moreover, as medical students, we too were often treated with disdain. Our working conditions and on-call schedule promoted ill health and impaired decision-making, sometimes with disastrous consequences. We were encouraged to avoid responding emotionally to patients, so that we would not become attached, lose objectivity, and be unable to take some of the drastic and life-endangering steps we might need to take in battling their illness.

It was surprising to me to discover that, although we were well aware that there were many behavioral changes patients could take that would prevent disease (diet, exercise, relationships, for example), we were not given the tools or the encouragement to pass them on to those who had entrusted their health to us. Instead, we were pressed to make hurried decisions to treat disorders that could have been prevented. And always, circling like sharks, were the scheming malpractice lawyers, forcing us to perform unnecessary and health-impairing tests and procedures for "medical-legal reasons," rather than medical need.

And hard as it may have been on us as physicians in training, our patients suffered even more, for the essence of the healing

---

[1] See Dr. Harrington excerpt in the Appendix, page 353.

response, which lies within the patient, was usually ignored – or even actively inhibited.

Changing Medicine

Believing the words of Andrew Jackson, that "One man with courage makes a majority," I chose as the first very important goal of my life's work to change the way medicine is practiced. Even before leaving medical school in 1967, I had begun to realize that the healing response of the patient is central to the improvement in their health. I had seen, with my own eyes, that there were things I could do as a doctor to encourage the healing response of my patients – and that there were things I could do to inhibit it. Somehow, incredibly, it seemed that this aspect of treatment was usually not addressed in our healthcare system. How could this be, that what often turns out to be major factors in recovery and healing – the thoughts, feelings, and beliefs of the patient – were so often ignored?

In the ensuing years, I was to discover that the roots of our blindness seemed to be located in our culture itself, from the family and local community to global village. Critically important aspects of human healing, the essential components of traditional folk and tribal medicine, have been leached out of the doctor-patient relationship by the negative inroads of our increasingly materialistic, power-based approach to life.

Through the years, I have witnessed the continuous attrition of compassion, integrity, and respect, as advertising, stress, overspecialization and the lack of awareness of our spirituality took their toll. As few others seemed to see the disastrous effect this was having on the healthcare system, I made it my goal to try to create a way to re-establish the sacrosanct doctor-patient relationship.

At the time I began my work in medicine, Western and Eastern approaches to healing were seen as incompatible; most medical practitioners had essentially no knowledge of such things

3

as acupuncture, meditation, yoga, or herbology, to say nothing of exercise, physiology, or nutrition. Only a few "fringe" practitioners actually studied these other systems sufficiently to discover that they were not only compatible, but actually different aspects of the same thing: the healing process.

My discoveries and explorations were aimed at finding a "third way" to bring our minds and emotions into balance and enable us to heal ourselves. This work, that I and my colleagues began to refer to as **holistic medicine**, has helped bring about many changes in the way the world now thinks about healthcare.

Nowadays, yoga studios are commonplace, acupuncturists abound, and exercise gyms are everywhere. We all have at least a passing knowledge of the consequence of stress in our lives, as well as the central role our thoughts and feelings play in maintaining our health and peak performance. Yet most people are unaware of the most important and profound information about how to successfully manage their thoughts, emotions, images, behavior – and the impact they are having on our health and our world. Nevertheless, the healthcare industry, driven as it is by the medical-pharmaceutical complex, is breathtakingly slow in realizing the profound importance of completing the transformation of the field we ironically call "healthcare."

Understanding the principles of healing is
crucial to understanding and
transforming society and our world.

The Source of Suffering

In the process of discovering the third way – as presented in my book *Deep Healing: The Essence of Mind-Body Healing* – I realized that the stressors I was teaching people to manage and transcend were being generated, to a large extent, by their interaction with their environment (both current and past). In fact, these stresses, presenting themselves as physical and behavioral imbalances, were the direct result of their relationship with their families and communities, their jobs, their culture, and their physical surroundings.

Simply treating the symptoms was only producing temporary relief. Failing to address those parts of the system that were out of balance was like placing Band-Aids on cancers. As I studied the healing process, I began to realize that in order for the physician or the patient to address the true cause of illness and dysfunction, we needed to expand our concept of treatment – so that we can see that we are dealing with a system, examine the entire system, discover the fundamental imbalance, and address the issue from a *higher level of system* than just symptoms would point us towards.

Remarkably, the way imbalance, dysfunction, and illness are produced in an individual patient is closely analogous to the way dysfunction is created in our families, our society, and the culture of our planet as a whole. And the feckless way we usually go about addressing these issues is by merely reacting to crises, rather than proactively preventing them. Here, too, we need to expand our concept of treatment to address a more global level of system.

In my healing practice I have found it very common to discover that several different symptoms very often can be traced to a single internal source – and the source is often in the mind, the emotions, or the relationship to what might be called the spiritual level. This is why deep healing can be obtained only by holistically addressing that complex system of body, mind, emotions, and spirit.

Seeing the profound changes initiated by the application of the concept of holism to individual health, it seemed reasonable to me to ask: "What would happen if we applied the holistic paradigm to the problems of our planet as a whole? Could there possibly be – as there often is when an individual displays a set of symptoms – a single source that is expressing itself as symptoms at the societal, national, and cultural levels of our global system?

"Could the nature of the source of our distress – whether we examine the case of an individual, a partnership, a family, a community, or a nation – be something as simple as a set of out-of-control emotions, or an outmoded paradigm? And if so, is there still time to heal ourselves? And how might we do that?"

Is there still time to heal ourselves?

Putting Our Culture on the Couch:
A New Sense of Urgency

Humanity's greatest power is the ability to clearly record the events of the past, to write them down, to study them, and to learn lessons from them – and in this way, chart a new course into the future, building on strengths and releasing outmoded patterns of thinking and behaving. Perhaps, then, it would be of value to study our response – or better, our reaction – to the disastrous attack on **civilians** in New York City and the Pentagon on September 11, 2001.

One very clear reaction within myself was a distinct increase in my urgency to discover and clarify those deep healing principles that might enable our global system to heal at all levels, from that of the individual to that of the planet as a whole. The bombing of the World Trade Center made it quickly clear to me that our planet – and especially the United States – would soon be displaying symptoms of post-traumatic stress disorder (PTSD). Indeed, the repeated televising of the harrowing footage of the planes hitting the buildings, the fireballs, and the final collapse of the towers virtually guaranteed a PTSD response.

The extreme reactions – the shock, denial, anger, anxiety, suspicion, and near-paranoia – so visible during the year following the 9/11 atrocity are perhaps less stark and apparent now. But what if the underlying disease is still with us, dividing us into sharply contrasted camps, fueling animosity, and leading us ever deeper into the quagmire?

How dangerous would it be to react to all this with officially condoned denial, thus effectively maintaining the status quo? Could there be a better answer to our challenges than our polarized electorate and our ongoing reaction formations – defensiveness, obsessive-compulsive self-abuse, impulsive military responses, prejudice, and ethnic violence – and harmful kinds of competition?

If so, it seems to me to be incumbent upon us to be certain to leave no stone unturned in our search for the **truth**. After all, when we know the truth about a situation, we discover its unique ability to help us successfully deal with the obstacles and challenges we face. As most of us know, an honest examination of ourselves very often leads us through some uncomfortable realizations on the way to real self-knowledge. Similarly, any honest history and examination of our familial, cultural, and planetary dysfunctions must also inevitably reveal many unpleasant realities. But, please, bear with me as I touch on some disturbing issues. I learned long ago that an excellent physician must do a complete and thorough exam in order to reach the correct diagnosis.

This is especially important when the patient (in this case, our community, our culture, and our planet) has a life-threatening disease. Our goal is to examine and explore the common elements of the various ills that plague us in the hope of clarifying the nature of our syndrome, and leading us to a more profound understanding of the underlying source – and revealing effective ways to treat it.

For most life forms on our planet, including the vast majority of human beings, the quality of life and quality of the environment we all live in (including the economic and social as well as the physical environment) have been steadily diminishing. To a huge majority of us, the geopolitical situation appears to be deteriorating at an ever-faster rate. The threat of terrorism, and our reaction to it, fills the morning and evening news, creating stress and polarizing attitudes, leading to further divisiveness, dysfunction, and widespread suffering.

7

The Law of Unexpected Consequences

Perhaps what most amazed me about the economic collapse of 2008 was how totally surprised people were when it happened. We were like the drunk explaining to the policeman that he did not see the brightly lit storefront he had just crashed his car into. The truth was there, in plain view, and yet most were blind, either to the obvious bomb ticking away, or they were blind to how big the explosion would be. Again! If so many people and so many big companies with so many high-powered financial experts could invest their money in a 50 billion dollar Ponzi scheme such as Bernard Madoff seems to have perpetrated, one is left to ponder the two most obvious possible explanations – that they could not see that it was a pyramid scheme or that they knew it was, and were hoping to cleanup and clear out before the suckers at the end of the chain could figure it out. Either way, they sawed off the branch they were sitting on, and lost the entire company. And as the tale is unraveling, more and more such stories suggest the enormous degree to which we have all been blind to the obvious truth.

What I, and others, have found is that the real culprit in these recurring social and cultural disasters is the lens through which we are examining the problem. The startling truth is that it may be our very method of approaching the issue that is guiding us unfailingly to a head-on collision with the Law of Unexpected Consequences: Many of our "solutions" appear to be actually increasing the number of our problems.

An illuminating metaphor can be found in the sad tale of the sugarcane growers of Hawaii and their battle against the rats who were gobbling up their sweet plants. They imported and set free hundreds of mating pairs of carnivorous mongooses, an enemy of rats. Unfortunately, their strategy was more than inadequate – it was disastrous. Their examination and understanding of the system was inadequate, for they failed to realize these rats feed only by night, and spend their days well hidden in their burrows. The result was that the mongoose, a daytime hunter, turned for sustenance to the eggs of Hawaii's beautiful ground nesting songbirds, driving them quickly to extinction.

More to the point, in the U.S. our healthcare system continues to create new and better ways to treat the symptoms of illness – with the negative result of convincing people that they can get away with taking even poorer care of themselves, overworking, overindulging, and overspending. Similarly, the "Coalition of the Willing" invaded Iraq, ostensibly to counter terrorism, yet the number of terrorists increased tenfold.

Could it be that such apparently counterproductive actions as these examples all reflect the same mistake, the mistake of failing to realize the true nature and the full extent of the system we are confronting? We are like Charlie Chaplin shoving a pendulum away from us, only to be knocked over on its return swing. An effective resolution, when dealing with a systemic issue, requires us to step back from the apparent problem and view it from the perspective of the whole. In other words: living systems thinking.

A sensible way, then, to approach our challenge is to:

• Find – through systematic evaluation, thinking, and inductive reasoning – the underlying source or systemic dysfunction at the core of the problems generated by "human activities" on Planet Earth.
• Sweep away denial, realize our true power to overcome our helplessness, and wisely address our problems.
• Discover that set of fundamental principles that underlies the healing process.
• Apply these principles at every level of system (individual, family, community, culture, nation, and global ecosystem) to the end of achieving profound healing.

Seeing With New Eyes

Much of what I will present here may not be completely new

9

information to many of my readers; in many cases, I will simply be presenting familiar information from a new and different perspective. So feel free to skim over familiar issues, especially in the opening chapters. What is important is how they all fit together and relate to the whole.

For example, during the 18th century, God-fearing Americans used the Christian Bible as a justification for enslaving other races of people. People who deeply believed in Jesus Christ supported the laws that permitted masters to whip and kill their slaves as a means to "save their souls." Derrick Jensen documents this admirably in his book *The Culture of Make-Believe* [2].

Now, however, the majority of those who call themselves Christians use exactly the same book – which they, too, believe is the word of God – to condemn the utter wrongness and un-Christian practice of slavery. Same situation, same reference book, but clearly, a new way of seeing.

None are so hopelessly enslaved, as those who falsely believe they are free. The truth has been kept from the depths of their minds by masters who rule them with lies. They feed them on falsehoods till wrong looks like right in their eyes.
– Johann Goethe

What if we are currently engaged in the same kind of self-delusion? What if there are important truths hidden right out there in front of us – truths that can enable us to effectively address the challenges of our time? What might we find if we honestly:

• Examine the current state of affairs through a specific lens, a specific frame of reference, and discover the fundamental principles at work within the different levels of our system?
• Present the Deep Healing approach in such a way that it

---

[2]   Derrick Jensen, *The Culture of Make Believe* (New York, Context, 2002).

can be applied at every level from the individual to the community to the cultural to the planetary level?
• Develop specific interventions, and establish a deeper kind of **knowing** that can enable us to embody these interventions at every level of system?
• Use the World Wide Web and other communications media of our high-tech society to disseminate this information and understanding to as much of the world's population as possible?

Intellectuals solve problems; geniuses prevent them
– Albert Einstein

Let There Be Light

No issue of this size can be handled by a single person, or even a single group. Healing deeply at all these levels requires many minds and many hearts. What we now need is an approach that will facilitate the development of a "critical mass," one that can result in a transformation, a healing, at every system level up to the planetary.

Therefore, after analyzing the chief complaints, taking a history of the present illness, reviewing past treatment failures, conducting a physical examination, and coming to a set of diagnoses, I'll discuss a proposed treatment.

The treatment plan will focus on both individual and global transformation. My mission is twofold: to find and to distribute wise guidance. Put another way, it is to:

1. **Seek and find wisdom** to reveal the deepest and the wisest information about healing, optimal performance, and positive change at every level of system, from the personal to the family to the hospital to the community to the nation to the planet.
2. **Develop portals and vehicles** to conduct easily learned principles of wisdom and deep healing, for application at all levels of system, to people in all walks of life, to be used for the purposes they choose.

The early chapters will focus on the gathering of information, a necessary prerequisite to making an accurate diagnosis. Our attitude will be receptive and attentive, as it should be; clear seeing is of the essence. When we arrive at the treatment phase, our explorations will become more experiential, as we learn to apply these tools within to create focus, balance, healing, and optimal performance. In addition, products and programs are available online for instant download, to enable you to more fully integrate positive learnings into your life. They will be described in the footnotes.

Let there be Peace on Earth
Let it begin with Me and Thee.

Questions to Ponder

1. What do you sense is the source of our suffering, individually and as communities?

2. Are there issues you believe urgently need to be addressed in our world? What are they?

3. When have you experienced the sense of "seeing with new eyes?"

Notes to Self

Planet in Peril: Take Home Messages

• A holistic living systems approach is necessary for healing individuals as well as for transforming society and the world.

• Treating symptoms only produces temporary relief for a distressed culture or for a sick person.

• Our recurring social and cultural disasters are the result of our failing to consider the whole system.

• Only through careful scientific evaluation of the entire system can we discover the underlying source of the problems facing our world.

• A proper approach to treatment must involve gathering the most accurate information and the wisest responses that lead to healing on all levels of system, from the person and family, to the community, nation, and planet – then developing ways to distribute that information.

CHAPTER 2

OUR PLANET AS A PATIENT
A Living Systems Approach to Global Healing

The Fighting Wolves

An old Cherokee was teaching his grandson about life. "A fight is going on inside me," he said to the boy. "It is a terrible fight and it is between two wolves. One is evil – he is anger, envy, sorrow, regret, greed, arrogance, self-pity, guilt, resentment, inferiority, lies, false pride, superiority, and ego."

He continued, "The other is good – he is joy, peace, love, hope, serenity, humility, kindness, benevolence, empathy, generosity, truth, compassion, and faith. The same fight is going on inside you – and inside every other person, too."

The grandson thought about it for a minute and then asked his grandfather, "Which wolf will win?"

The old Cherokee simply replied, "The one you feed."

A Crisis of Global Proportions

> *Unless we change our direction, we're likely*
> *to end up where we're headed.*
> – Chinese Proverb

Many would argue – most persuasively – that the human race is headed, disaster by disaster, towards extinction. As our global crises grow ever more catastrophic, we must learn from history and develop wise and effective new ways to deal with our crises. There is much we can learn from the recent past. Consider:

The 9/11 attack on the United States was more devastating than Pearl Harbor – perpetrated, we are told, by Islamic terrorists hell-bent on killing as many of us as possible – in the name of Allah, the Merciful.

Likewise, in the name of ridding the world of "Evil-Doers," the U.S. has invaded and occupied two sovereign nations on the other side of the world and is currently considering further preemptive military strikes on other countries.

Much of the world hates and fears us. Incredibly, repeated worldwide polls reveal that the United States is seen as the greatest threat to world peace! Even our allies have been estranged. For our part, we took the word "French" off the menu in the Congressional Dining Room, because the French did not believe there was ample evidence of WMDs in Iraq.

And here in the homeland of the world's only superpower, we the people are bitterly divided over whether our government is doing the right thing. The real Y2K disaster, some say, was our preemptive engagement in a transnational holy war that could very well escalate into World War III ... into the Apocalypse. It could happen any time now, they say – even right now. Here's why:

Our most cherished institutions are failing us.

It doesn't take much effort to see how our news media, instead of protecting our freedoms by revealing the truth, are biased, inaccurate, and often merely purveyors of corporate and government-sponsored propaganda. Comedy Central's "The Daily Show" now rivals "60 Minutes" and The New York Times when people are asked where they go for credibility and incisive analysis of the news.

Political dialog has degenerated into near-paranoid suspicion and name-calling, legislators belong to the highest bidders, and dishonest commercials are the prime form of campaigning. Soulless multinational corporations are cheating us, bribing our leaders, and polluting our planet in what often seems to be a mindless frenzy to enrich the few at the expense of the rest of us. Rapacious 21st-century robber barons literally get away with murder. War is as good for business as ever.

Some say business is just "war without bullets." If so, then abused employees, stockholders, and customers are the "collateral damage." Enron commits unarmed robbery of its own employees. Wal-Mart hires illegal immigrants, pays substandard wages, wipes out local businesses – and glosses it all over with a public relations campaign.

Arthur Anderson collapses under evidence that it conspired to obstruct justice by destroying Enron-related documents. Dupont cuts employee pension plan by two thirds (sic!) in order to raise stock earnings by three cents per share and provide retiring CEO with a 2.1 million dollar a year retirement income. Fortune 500 CEO salaries have ballooned 51% in four years, the top 1% of the population owns nearly 60% of the wealth, and the 150 million folks at the bottom own less than 3%.

And Martha Stewart goes to jail for insider trading. Martha Stewart? Et tu Brute!

The World Wide Web has made the "global village" a clear and present reality. The multibillion-dollar pornography industry has harnessed the awesome power of the Web to exploit women, children, and emotionally disturbed individuals. Pederasts and child molesters lurk in chatrooms, and there's blood in the streets of the global village. Terrorists wage worldwide psychological warfare with TV broadcasts and Web postings of medieval beheadings. Now any Muslim extremist can learn to build a suicide bomb from detailed,

Oh, can't complain.

explicit postings on the Web.

Ignorant and deliberate disinformation undermines the truth. High-tech criminals steal money and identities in virtual muggings. Biological viruses have gone digital. And Big Brother is watching. You. Right now.

The natural course of evolution is being altered as global warming, insidious pollution, and unrestrained overpopulation growth threaten preternatural consequences. We're already witnessing extensive loss of biodiversity, and climactic changes portend an uncertain and unnerving future.

Indeed, human beings are finding the "beingness" of being human evermore difficult. Stress and depression are more common than the common cold – and so much more debilitating. Too many of us are living lives of barely controlled chaos and unquiet desperation. Our lives, our families, our communities, our institutions, our ecosystem, and our very perception of reality are becoming exponentially dysfunctional. We are at war with the world and with ourselves.

Or, as Walt Kelly's cartoon character Pogo so aptly put it:

We have met the enemy, and he is us.

It is a corollary of this that nobody can save us from us but us.

The Possibility of Hope

In the face of all these challenges I, for one, still believe we do have the power to save our culture, our planet, and ourselves. But saving ourselves from ourselves won't be easy, and there are no guarantees.

We cannot cure what ails us with the current crazy quilt of patchwork remedies. Medicine cannot cure our highly inadequate healthcare system. Psychotherapy cannot cure our society's neuroses. Neither religion nor politics seems likely to unite our communities and nations. War will not solve our global geopolitical differences. And science cannot bargain with Mother Nature. And a house divided against itself cannot stand.

What we need is a holistic, systemic diagnosis of what's really wrong with us at all levels. We must look beyond the symptoms and palliative treatments. We must search deep within ourselves and look outward to the universe to find the cure.

> *The world is a dangerous place to live;*
> *not because of the people who are evil,*
> *but because of the people*
> *who don't do anything about it.*
> – Albert Einstein

Our Planet as Patient: Why Use the Metaphor?

The notion of looking at our entire culture, the culture of humanity on Planet Earth, may seem to you, at first, as overreaching, maybe even a bit bizarre and farfetched. Soon, however, I think that you will see that using this metaphor is particularly appropriate, and that it offers an unparalleled opportunity to look more deeply into the situation from a unique perspective.

The "Medical Model" is actually a very powerful one to use in examining an issue. I am well aware that there has been some significant erosion of the automatic respect afforded physicians over the years. I think much of this is the result of the compartmentalized bureaucracy of today's medical management system.

So let me make it clear, however, that the medical model I am referring to is fundamentally different from the unfortunately superficial and symptomatic approach found in many mainstream clinical settings. Such an approach typically involves all-out antibiotic assaults and "surgical military strikes," against the *symptoms* of disease. My goal, on the contrary, is to carefully employ the theories that gave rise to modern holistic (integral, complementary) medicine, and look at not just the symptoms, but at the deeper sources, to see if we might find a single etiology, and thence, an ultimate, elegant remedy.

You may already have noticed the widespread use of the medical metaphor when discussing social issues; policy analysts "diagnose" the problem with our economy, we seek "remedies" for injustices, the tax hike is called "bitter medicine," and so forth.

This makes sense – one's health is very serious business, and physicians are held to the highest standards. Their *raison d'etre* is fundamentally different from those of politicians, the media, talk radio hosts, and "soft science" pop pundits who get away with reasoning and behavior that no self-respecting physician would ever allow him or herself.

If you are going to confront a truly serious crisis (such as one's health), you want to use the most reliable and scientific approach available. Thus, regardless of how natural and organic you are, if you are stricken with a serious cancer or glandular disease, you will probably choose to be examined by a careful, experienced physician. You know that the most dependable way to discover the cause of illness is to submit to the physician's careful history-taking, examination, ordering tests, developing a differential diagnosis, and prescribing (and monitoring the progress of) treatment.

When you are coughing up blood, have a huge lump growing in your breast (or testicle), or have crushing substernal chest pain, you don't want to rely on "old wives' tales," wild guesses, or some TV huckster's slick exhortations. At such times, you want a systematic scientific investigation, a thoughtful generation of possible causes, and wise decisions regarding diagnosis, treatment, and follow-up.

You don't want makeup to hide the smallpox lesions, or pain relievers to cover the warning signs of a rupturing appendix. Moreover, you are willing to bear the pain of confronting the possibility of deep problems; after all, it's your life we're talking about here.

Though you might "feel fine," you listen when the doctor tells you only a diet change will prevent serious disease. Instead of staying in denial and thinking, "That lump is probably just a cyst," you are willing to consider the alternative he presents, and even let him/her invade your body with a scalpel to check it out. Or at least you should be willing.

Our current global situation too, all the way from the personal to the international, is truly serious. Politics, patent medicine, snake oil, and sound bites are not good enough – real science is needed. We need a treatment that does not just alleviate the symptom, but goes to the root of the imbalance to treat – and cure – the source.

There is no sharp boundary around the individual – the imbalance that creates headaches, alcoholism, and depression continues into higher levels of system. We see it vividly in the burgeoning dysfunction of our families, the social and political strife that increasingly dominates our headlines, and corporate and government corruption – right on up to the international level, where we have a situation that may deal a death blow to civilization (and even life) as we know it. We need a good global doctor.

All I am saying is NOW is the time to develop the technology to deflect an asteroid.

Practicing Good Global Medicine: Beyond Symptomatic Treatment

The poor physician treats the symptoms.
The good physician treats the disease.
The excellent physician treats the patient.

Far too often, in our culture, we are exposed to poor physicians. In addressing an individual's health problems, we frequently stop at treating the symptoms.

We often approach interpersonal problems in similarly superficial ways. In our interactions with our family and co-workers, we often abuse them with guilt, anger, intimidation, blame, coercion, humiliation, contempt, emotional blackmail, or outright threats – instead of respecting, accepting, acknowledging, and trusting that we have common purposes, and that working together as a team is the best choice. Likewise, at the international level, we resort to propaganda (spin), economic sanctions, threats, covert operations, and military invasions to treat the symptoms of discord. Whatever happened to Abraham Lincoln's trick of getting rid of enemies by turning them into friends?

Short-term relief may appear to work, but as in the case of treating illness, the untreated deeper issue usually worsens. These superficial, quick-fix solutions are often marked by destructive results, and offer very little assistance in rebuilding and rehabilitating. And the worst thing about history, it has been said, is that

It's been moved and seconded that we fly the company to Geneva, divvy up the bank accounts and go our merry way.

every time it repeats itself the price goes up.

What seems to be needed – for the individual patient, the family, the community, and the planet as a whole – is a "systems approach," an approach that recognizes that the individual human being, as well as the human society as a whole, is not just a collection of parts. Human beings are social animals. They form, when in groups, a system consisting of a complex array of dependent and independent subsystems and organs whose careful coordination and choreography give rise to qualities and abilities not found in any individual person.

What Is a Systems Approach?

> *When one tugs at a single thing in nature,*
> *he finds it attached to the rest of the world.*
> – John Muir

David Sobel defined a system as: An organized set of components that is conveniently regarded as a whole, consisting of interdependent parts. If one part or a subcomponent is replaced by a different but similar one, the system functions as before; if the organization among the parts is changed, however, the system's function is altered even though the parts remain.

A brief introduction to the history of the systems approach can be found in the Appendix on page 343.

A mobile hanging from the ceiling offers an instructive model of a system. Left alone in a quiet room, it will come to rest in a certain configuration. If you then move one part of it (a symptomatic intervention), all the other parts of the mobile begin to shift around in reaction to this. Left undisturbed for a few hours, however, the mobile will return to stillness, with its parts in exactly the same configuration as before it was disturbed. To get it to rest in a different configuration, the very "infrastructure" of the mobile must be altered. This would be a "systemic" level of intervention.

Another example: Consider the all-important white blood cells that circulate through your body, protecting you from disease. Each is alive, but the life of each is pretty meaningless unless the animal in whose bloodstream it exists is also alive. The white cell gains its meaning and value only in relationship to the body of which it is "part."

Your body, likewise, is meaningless all by itself. Its true value is as an aspect of a person – you. So "you" are best conceptualized as consisting of a collection of subordinate systems and subsystems, comprising body, mind, emotion, beliefs, habits, and behaviors. You are all this, and more – for there are certain "emergent" qualities you experience in your body that cannot be found in any of its component parts. These are qualities such as love, joy, attitude, personality, and values. Indeed, you are more than merely the "sum of your parts." This is why, in treating an illness, you as a whole must be taken into account, as well as the well-being of all these parts.

Similarly, you are the product of your family, and one's family has a pronounced and major effect upon every aspect of one's beliefs, attitudes, and behavior. Likewise, the community has a powerful effect on your family, shaping it by the kinds of language, religion, and culture it imposes. In turn, the community is affected by higher orders of system, such as the nation and the planet as a whole. Imagine, for example, how the character of Jewish, African-American, Native Americans, or Gypsy societies might have developed differently, had the dominant cultures in which they lived treated them with respect and appreciation!

Applying a Systems Approach

As we work our way through, in order, the history of the illness, the diagnosis, and suggested treatment, I will discuss the principles I develop and how they relate to all these levels of system. I want to emphasize the systems nature of our investigation by showing how these principles have similar application at every level of system – a fact that should be obvious to anyone familiar with modern psychobio-social approaches to healing[1].

Russian dolls as an example of internested systems

A systems approach examines the presenting symptoms, while keeping in mind fundamental principles concerning how systems function. An understanding of how these principles operate allows us to apply them to treat deeper causes, not just symptoms. At the level of the individual patient, for instance, when we finally understood the role of insulin in the body, we could find a treatment where before there was none. Until then, the many symptoms and dysfunctions in many organs and systems of the body were completely baffling. Until insulin was given, all that symptomatic therapy could do was to hide the continuing worsening of the disease. Another example of how understanding of the system leads to a better treatment – people whose behavior became more and more bizarre 150 years ago might be chained to a wall in a mental institution until they died. Today we would perform an MRI and do lab tests. We would discover their brain tumor or syphilis, and thus have a far better chance of saving their lives.

---

[1]   For others, I recommend the relevant sections of my book, *Deep Healing*.

A Systemic Examination of The Cultures of Planet Earth

Our goal in this paper is to examine, using a systems approach, how some of our typical cultural beliefs and behaviors might be giving rise to many, if not all, of our physical, political, and environmental issues. As with an individual patient or a dysfunctional family, we see certain symptoms at each higher level of system (abuse, family fights, wars, pollution). And just as the physician or therapist must examine the underlying, unconscious, psychic mechanisms to find the true source of the problems, our examination of the global situation must look beyond the surface symptoms – regardless of how dramatic and urgent they may seem.

Another task of the therapist is to discover the purposes, goals, or secondary benefits to/of the patient. Most of the time, these symptomatic reactions have an underlying purpose or intention, and these must be addressed in order for a complete healing to occur. Along the way, we might expect our careful exploration to uncover deeper, unexamined assumptions that are creating ever-more imbalance. From the personal to the planetary, assumptions are the termites of relationships.

System imbalances that present as physical symptoms (soma) in an individual may have, as part of their etiology, the mind (psyche). In a similar manner, the physical problems that a group of people, or a planetful, suffers may be the result of a subconscious psychological imbalance, a cultural neurosis, so to speak. Thus, it makes sense to put our culture "on the couch."

The Meaning of "Global"

One additional clarification: In this document, when the word "global" is used, the intention is to refer to all levels and sublevels of the system. In other words, "global" implies that the issue under discussion applies at every level, not simply at one level. In other words, it applies at the level of an individual, but also at the level of the cells of the person (a subordinate level), at the level of the family and community (superordinate levels), and as well, at the level of the planet as a whole. So global doesn't just mean the planetary globe, it means everything that we know, at all levels of system.

It can be done. It must be done. My best wishes for this opus are to awaken and empower you to see a new perspective – a vision of how an ever-growing global community can transcend politics, religion, medicine, science, technology, and the human tragicomedy to achieve a new level of humanity and harmony.

I know of no safe depository of the ultimate power of society but the people themselves; and if we think them not enlightened enough to exercise their control with a wholesome direction, the remedy is not to take it from them, but to inform their discretion by education.
— Thomas Jefferson

Questions to Ponder

1. Which of the "systems" that you are familiar with demonstrates the Russian Doll effect, and what kinds of properties emerge are possessed by higher levels of system, but not lower ones?

2. What do you see as the major crises you and the world face today?

3. When have you seen merely symptomatic treatment allow an issue to get worse?

4. In what way do you think the metaphor, "Planet as Patient" works? In what ways is it inadequate? Can you think of a better model?

5. How would you describe what is meant by "The Systems Approach?"

Notes to Self

Planet Patient: Take Home Messages

• Corporate and government corruption, global warming, and overpopulation head the huge list of ailments threatening the existence of humans and the health of the planet.

• A scientific approach, employing the theories that gave rise to modern holistic medicine, is necessary to find a true remedy for what ails the world.

• Treatment should go to the root of the imbalance to treat — and cure — the source.

• Just as imbalance creates symptoms of illness in an individual, imbalance can be seen to be the root of our problems at higher levels of system: family, community, even up to the international level.

• Attacking our problems with wrong-headed quick-fix solutions often creates bigger problems than it solves, and rarely offers assistance in rebuilding and rehabilitating.

• Cultural beliefs and behaviors appear to be giving rise to many of our physical, political, and environmental issues.

CHAPTER 3

CHIEF COMPLAINTS: WHAT THE [BLEEP] IS GOING ON HERE?

Man is a strange animal. He doesn't like to read the handwriting on the wall until his back is up against it.
– Adlai Stevenson

The first question the physician asks the patient is, "What brings you to my office?" Next he/she records, carefully, the patient's Chief Complaints. This gives us clear insight into what disturbs the patient enough to make him/her willing to give up a day's pay, wait for an indeterminate amount of time in the waiting room, put on that embarrassing little gown, and be poked and prodded. It tells us what symptoms the patient most wants to relieve, and how the patient views those symptoms. It helps with the diagnosis, and will be important in organizing the treatment later on.

Our Chief Complaints

The global question that parallels "What brings you to my office?" is, "What most ails the world right now?" Recall that by "global" we include not only the relationship among nation-states and the environmental impact on humanity (i.e., "global issues"), but also the more local struggles at the level of the community, the family, and even what are the most significant personal stressors and imbalances.

Asking different people and different societies, or even asking on different days, would produce different answers. Yet, I think they fall into several overlapping categories, which I will address.

There are far too many complaints to mention them all. Still, along the way, I hope to lasso the great majority of what we see as the main problems of our time. We will then go on to explore their deeper roots. I will start at the personal level and move towards the global, for the sake of clarity. Again, this is by no means a complete list. Feel free to add to it.

Chief Complaint 1: Stress, Fear, Hopelessness

As individuals, our stress levels are at dangerously high levels. The dysfunction in our families and communities is off the charts, and there is no indication it will go down. Even the most conservative physicians now acknowledge that most physical illnesses are the result of, or made worse, by stress. People are working longer and harder than ever at tenuous, tedious, uninspiring jobs. Most families now need both husband and wife – and sometimes their older children – working to survive. Less than half of our children have the benefit of two parents.

Our world has become a frightening place, economically, geopolitically, and socially. Even our identities and cherished institutions are threatened (e.g., the threats of school and workplace violence, loss of Social Security, inability of our government to protect and serve us, easily accessible Internet pornography). Paranoia, perceived loss of personal liberties, and suspicion of authority, and fears of corporate and political corruption all run rampant in this post-9/11 world.

This is future shock. The levels of fear, stress, frustration, and rage have reached the point that neologisms such as "road rage" are widely known and understood. Friendships and marriages disintegrate with breathtaking ease. Relationship failures lead, in turn, to depression, alienation, hopelessness, violence, addiction, and anxiety. Our stress has spun out of control, and the diseases it causes are giving rise to the bankruptcies, deterioration, and chaos in our health care system. The control of what constitutes good medical practice is inexorably slipping out of the grasp of dedicated physicians and into the hands of anonymous investors, uncaring administrators, and Wall Street Machiavellis, none of whom has the ability to really responsibly protect and care for our health.

The role of a loving, devoted family – the traditional support for individuals – is eroding. Children have become a net financial liability, instead of net assets as in families of yesteryear. As a result, they are receiving less love and guidance. Disenfranchised young people skulk through the malls and video arcades, baffled as to what to look forward to in life. Alienated high school kids shoot up their families

and schools even as disgruntled workers assault their coworkers and workplaces. I tend to agree with George Fowler, that "all these problems are caused by a race asleep and thrashing about in its panicked nightmares ... as long as people dream that they are inse-cure and needy and in some sort of eternal jeopardy, there will be atrocities."

People suffer from a lack of love and an inability to handle conflict. Children are dispossessed, lost, and hopeless. Elders are not respected or cared for. Thousands of our precious young men and women are having their emotions and psyches permanently maimed and scarred, and many thousands will die in Iraq, Afghani-stan (and perhaps Iran and North Korea). They will be unable to return to a normal life, their plight ignored by the government, and not counted as a cost of the war.

The news regularly reports on the increasing tendency of our kids to physically abuse themselves (tattoos, piercing, self-cutting, anorexia, and bulimia). The viciousness of the music they choose reflects their mood (compared, for example, to the "All You Need Is Love" music of the '60s youth, and the "Mairzy Doats" of the '40s). And then there are the reports of child abuse and neglect, gang drive-by murders, drug-related violence, and date rapes.

I could go on and on, and I'm sure you could as well. The challenges to our serenity and our balance are clear, and the stress they produce in each of our lives grows greater by the year. And although most medical professionals acknowledge global warming, the medical system has not fully recognized the centrality of stress in human suffering and don't provide adequate means for treating and preventing the diseases and disorders it brings about.

Chief Complaint 2: Social Disintegration

Chesterton pointed out that "When people begin to ignore human dignity, it will not be long before they begin to ignore human rights." Families, social patterns, and cultures are all composed of individuals, and, especially, the connections among them. Consider the following news items:

• A van veers out of control and smashes into a group of people sitting on a porch in Chicago. Neighbors rush out, grab the driver and passenger from the truck and beat them to death with bricks and clubs.

• In Ohio, a deranged man shoots and kills a heavy metal guitarist in the middle of a performance in a nightclub. He kills three other men before he is killed by the police. A man is dragged behind a pickup truck until he is dead as punish-ment for the sin of being black. Another man, in another town, is nailed to a fence and allowed to die there because he was "gay." And a physician is gunned down by a pro-life "Christian" anti-abortion zealot.

• Gang members attack a man and his pregnant wife stopped at a traffic light in San Diego, and then later, they beat a 15-year-old boy unconscious with a piece of lumber.

• In Wisconsin, a Hmong (a S.E. Asian hill tribe) man fatally shoots six White deer hunters, fueling racial tensions.

• "You'll never get away with this," says the kneeling Jewish woman in Schindler's List. "You're probably right," the Gestapo replies laconically as he off-handedly shoots her in the head – and a crowded Oakland, California theater erupts in laughter.

• Perverted Catholic priests rape more than ten thousand of our children. Islamic priests strap plastic explosives on the backs of Arab children to further their own twisted ends. Re-ports of genocide (often under the euphemism "ethnic cleans-ing") appear in the news far too often.

• Doctors perform unnecessary surgeries to pad their bank-books, while angry patients shoot up emergency rooms after waiting 12 hours to be seen (not an unusual wait, with our crumbling medical system).

• With amoral atheism on one hand and intolerant fundamentalism on the other – racism, religious strife, nationalism, intolerance are becoming the rule again, as the advances of the '60s are reversed (e.g., the Alabama State Legislature recently voted to not remove racist language from their state constitution; how "retro" is that?)

• The news media fairly revel in their all-too-often reports of children being kidnapped, raped, and murdered in our own neighborhoods (even those who live in gated communities). And spurring it on is the child pornography on tap at the laptop of the local pervert.

• Illegal drugs are glamorized in the movies, and sold on street corners, creating two sets of victims – the users themselves, and those they rob and injure to get drugs.

• First, there were the Enron, WorldCom, and Merrill Lynch scandals, then there was Martha Stewart (Martha Stewart no less?) and now Bernard Madoff. Boards of directors vote themselves obscene salaries and bonuses, while their companies go bankrupt, robbing workers of their jobs and their pensions. And remember when Arthur Anderson was the most trusted name in accounting? All these were but harbingers of the disastrous financial debacle of 2008.

• Disinformation has replaced the words of wise elders, and there is a widening gap between rich and poor, the gradual disappearance of the middle class (e.g., more than 40 million U.S. citizens with no health insurance). Fancy advertising lies to people that true happiness can be bought. And in the absence of family, religion, schools, or wise elders to teach them otherwise, they believe it.

• For years, while most

incomes have been flat, or decreased, the number of million-aires and billionaires has multiplied enormously. The financial "overclass" has done very well, but regarding the rest of us, financial insecurity has become an unwelcome companion. For the first time, our children can expect to experience a substan-tially lower standard of living than their parents, unable even to afford to live in the same neighborhood.

• The workplace is brutal and unrewarding. People are uncom-mitted to their work, resentful of the behavior of their corporate overlords, overworked and underappreciated. Moreover, they are being driven out of work by the relentless creep of technol-ogy, massive corporate layoffs, economic decline, outsourcing jobs to foreign countries, and the stark reality of job obsoles-cence.

• The entertainment industry, to which people have turned to for solace in the absence of healthy human relationships, panders to the lowest common denominator. It strives for ev-ermore shocking blood and pulp, served up over commercial advertisements designed to create dissatisfaction and anxiety (to boost sales). Sex and violence on TV and in the movies have morphed into blatant pornography and gore. Network sleaze garners huge audiences in the Bible Belt, while music soundtracks laced with obscenities glorifying the "gangsta" mentality throb hypnotically beneath the spattering of blood on screen at your local cineplex.

• At the current moment, over 37,000 homeless people stay in shelters in New York City every night and there are now over 70,000 homeless people just in the Los Angeles area. 33% of homeless are families with children, many of which are new to the streets. Veterans who've served our country constitute 40% of the homeless population.

A pandemic of social disintegration is easy to recognize when you connect the dots.

Chief Complaint 3: Disunity and Corruption: Corporate, Political, and Governmental

> *The death of democracy is not likely to be an assassination from ambush. It will be a slow extinction from apathy, indifference, and undernourishment.*
> – Robert Hutchins

Franklin Roosevelt warned us that:

> *The liberty of a republic is not safe if the people tolerate the growth of private power to a point where it becomes stronger than their democratic state itself. What, in its essence, is fascism, but ownership of government by an individual, by a group, or by any controlling private power?*

"We have the best government money can buy," goes an oft-repeated cliché these days. Sarcasm about our government and its agencies is rife, and who can blame us? Never before have we witnessed, up close and personal, such lurid displays of dysfunction, cynicism, and corruption.

Our current financial and economic woes are testaments to both the monumental incompetence of those who claimed to be so wise and knowing on one hand, and the breathtaking dishonesty of so many individuals and organizations on the other. How strange the spectacle of the three largest automobile manufacturers asking Congress for handouts.

We trusted and were led into a war based on falsified evidence of weapons of mass destruction (WMDs). It is hard to ignore the indications that information has been suppressed; officials simply refused to answer questions they are bound by law to answer. The prisoner abuse debacle in the Abu Ghraib prison, the condoning of torture, and imprisonment for years on mere suspicion only added to the public disenchantment with the war. Administration officials expose the identity of a CIA agent and then drag their feet to thwart the investigation. A large portion of our population suspects our leaders are in bed with less than honorable business interests.

The votes of our elected representatives are being purchased by lobbyists. In today's world, the biggest bankroll usually determines who will be elected to office. Liberals are panicked over what they see as the rise of an American Fascist Party controlled by a consortium of evangelical right-wing Christians, corporations, and political puppets. Republicans are equally frightened of what they call "The Atheistic, Antifamily, Liberal Agenda." A new Mason-Dixon Line weaves through our nation, sharply demarcating highly polarized Red and Blue states. And, although bitter enemies, Christian fundamentalists and Muslim fanatics are both preparing themselves for Armageddon – a potentially self-fulfilling prophecy.

All national institutions of churches, whether Jewish, Christian, or Turkish, appear to me no other than human inventions, set up to terrify and enslave mankind, and monopolize power and profit.
– Thomas Paine

Megacorporations are systematically wiping out small businesses, the "Mom and Pop Shops" that are the backbone of our American economic infrastructure. Many people are up in arms at those corporations, who are owned by anonymous investors around the world, and guided by hired, highly paid executives. They accuse corporations of using advanced technology and sinister strategies to decimate communities and lay waste to the social and physical landscape. After defeating their competition with low prices and a huge treasury, they are free to raise prices. The corporation wins, we lose.

These corporations, unlike Mom and Pop, have no real commitment to the community, but they do have high-powered PR agencies to make it *look* like they care. They play to our greed – our wanting more and cheaper products. They manage to be held unaccountable for their actions as they destabilize their workers, families, and communities, and pollute our planet.

These relentless corporate machines, they say, destroy the environment, dumping waste into rivers and oceans (Love Canal), irreversibly damaging the Earth (Exxon Valdez) and threatening human survival. They exploit underpaid laborers in Third-World countries, and sow terror to silence protestors. Increasingly in our own country, they violate basic human rights in illegal sweatshops (from New York to Los Angeles), and abroad, they make deals with nations that are known enemies of the U.S., finance and support assassinations and death squads, and perpetuate totalitarian regimes. The unchecked rise of corporatism is clearly a chief complaint.

In the councils of government we must guard against the acquisition of unwarranted influence whether sought or unsought by the military industrial complex. The potential for the disastrous rise of misplaced power exists and will persist.
– President Dwight D. Eisenhower

Chief Complaint 4: Global Political Instability and Terrorism

We have seen right here in New York the tragic consequences that can result from failed states in faraway places. The Western world is getting too rich in

relation to the poor world. We're looked upon as being arrogant,
self-satisfied, greedy, and with no limits ... misery breeds hatred ...
fanatics use people who are the products of misery.
– Canadian Prime Minister Jean Chrétien

After we got rid of the "Soviet Menace," many thought it was supposed to be fun and games forevermore. Then, on that fateful day in September, 2001, a deeply rooted problem emerged as a very painful symptom, one that got all of our attention. By striking the Twin Towers, terrorists thus announced that they are perfecting ways of using our cherished freedoms against us, that they are so disturbed by something that they are willing, nay eager, to sacrifice their lives to kill and cripple us. Our reaction to that was to declare war on a concept, "terrorism," or more precisely, "radical Islamic terrorism."

The Department of Homeland Security has advised us to stock up on plastic tarps and duct tape to seal up our houses in the event terrorists attack us with nuclear, biological, or chemical WMDs. In anticipation of a possible nuclear "dirty bomb" detonation, plans have been drawn up to evacuate cities by alternating the days people would be allowed to leave based on odd and even-numbered automobile license plates. I must admit I was struck by the inadequacy, even the silliness of these measures.

Meanwhile we seem to be doing nothing to address the concerns of the millions of Muslims who are angry with the West, especially the U.S., the "Great Satan." Certainly not all those who hate us are terrorists, but they form the silent majority that gives money and support to the terrorists. And on top of this, anti-Americanism has been spread

ing throughout Europe. Much of this negative sentiment has been laid at the feet of what many see as the seeming arrogance of the United States, in the wake of the enormous outpouring of warmth and support from our allies following 9/11.

And all around the world there are dozens of armed conflicts, often genocidal in nature. The victims who are not killed violently are herded into refugee camps to slowly die of starvation. Between 2000 and 2002, in Sudan alone, tens of thousands have been killed and nearly two million survivors are homeless and starving. And the situation in the Congo is worse. And that is just the beginning.

Several years before 9/11, on April 19, 1995, mass-murder domestic terrorism had already made its formal debut with the bombing of the Alfred P. Murrah Federal Building in Oklahoma City. A little more than a year later, a bomb was detonated at the Olympics in Atlanta, killing one woman and injuring dozens. With political polarization increasing, private ownership of assault weapons expanding, and Internet bomb-making instructions as near as your computer, the eruption of a new breed of homegrown terror is highly likely to "surprise" us in the near future.

Chief Complaint 5: Environmental Destruction

*It isn't pollution that's harming the
environment. It's the impurities in our air
and water that are doing it.*
– Vice President Dan Quayle

With fears about global warming leading the way, our planetary environment is being challenged in myriad ways. The vast majority of inland waterways are now polluted, the smog of cities now spreads far and wide, and the worldwide shortage of water is threatening to trigger water wars in the near future.

The gradual warming of the planet, and the pollution of our air and water, according to our most experienced scientists, is contributing to global ecocide – the wholesale destruction of millions of years of evolution, as evidenced by the many vanishing species of fish, animals, and plants. Every day entire species are being lost forever because of how humankind is mistreating nature. Coral reefs are disappearing, as are amphibians and the great apes. Overfishing and overgrazing are taking their toll, rainforests are disappearing at the rate of one acre per second, and the wild salmon is approaching extinction. Soon, wars will be fought over water.

The global population of human beings, on the other hand, is increasing at a totally unsustainable rate, and the huge numbers of those starving are expected to steadily increase. Strangely, in the face of the continuing spread of AIDS and the unrestrained population growth in underdeveloped countries, our government is removing support for teaching birth control and prevention of sexually transmitted diseases (STDs) in favor of teaching abstinence.

Power demands of developing economies are increasing at 2.5 or more percent per year. If these demands are met by burning fossil fuels, greenhouse gases, global warming, rising seas, fiercer storms, severe droughts, and other climatic disruptions are likely, if not inevitable.

Our oil-based economy seems headed for disaster as more and more factories come online in the face of diminishing global reserves of petroleum and the looming *Peak Oil Crisis*[1]. We in the U.S. are consuming energy at several times the rate of other countries, and making little investment in changing that. With only 5% of the population, the U.S. consumes 25% of the energy and produces 25% of the pollution. Perhaps the most oft-mentioned example is that of the gas-guzzling SUVs (our response to the Arab Oil Embargo of the '70s), that pollute and consume at an extraordinary rate.

And then there is the "sleeping giant", China, who already uses more coal than the United States, the European Union, and Japan combined. No wonder, since it has increased its coal consumption 14% in each of the past two years, and every week China opens another coal-fired power plant big enough to serve all the

---

[1]   http://www.hubbertpeak.com/

homes in Dallas or San Diego. Meanwhile, India is following suit, stepping up its construction of such plants, to serve a population due to exceed that of China by 2030. The deterioration of our environment to the point that a cataclysm occurs is almost a certainty if something is not done, and soon.

> *Only after the last tree has been cut down, only after the*
> *last river has been poisoned, only after the last fish has*
> *been caught, only then will you find that money cannot be eaten.*
> – Cree Indian prophecy

Questions to Ponder

1. Which of the Chief Complaints seem most important to you?

2. Can you think of other major categories that you would add to the list of chief complaints? Write them down.

Notes to Self

Chief Complaints: Take Home Messages

• Stress is rampant in today's world, leading to depression, hopelessness, violence, addiction, and anxiety , all of which tend to lead towards social disintegration.

• We've never before witnessed such lurid displays of dysfunction, cynicism, and corruption with regard to corporations, politics, and government.

• Terrorism looms and we seem to be doing nothing to address the concern of millions of Muslims who are angry with the West.

• Armed conflicts, many genocidal in nature, go on all around the world.

• The likelihood of homegrown terrorism is growing with the increasing political polarization, expanding private ownership of assault weapons, and easy-to-find bomb-making instructions on the Internet.

• The planetary environment is being challenged by pollution, global warming, overpopulation, and the overconsumption of resources.

CHAPTER 4
PREVIOUS ATTEMPTS
AT TREATMENT

When I think of the ways mankind has attempted to deal with our global illness, I am reminded of a story, "Sifting Through Straws," that was popular back just after the Soviet Union collapsed.

It seems there was a farmer who, every day, would show up to cross the border out of Russia sitting atop an old wooden cart filled with straw, pulled by a donkey. Suspicious, the border guards searched ever more diligently each time, but though they sifted through, straw by straw, they could never find anything.

Some years later, as the story goes, after the fall of the Soviet Union, one of the border guards happened to meet the old farmer on the streets of Moscow. The farmer's natty clothes attested to his financial good fortunes.

The former border guard couldn't resist. "The Soviet Union is no more. I no longer work as a border guard, but I know you were smuggling something. Please tell me what it was."

"Of course," replied the farmer, with a mischievous twinkle in his eye, "donkeys and carts!"

Before going on to the History of the Present Illness, let us take a brief detour and examine some of the attempts people have made to address these critical issues. This will probably help us as we decide on what kind of story we want to write.

Since 2001 we have been living in a climate of terror created by such threats as "dirty" nuclear bombs, poison gas, and biological warfare. And how have we responded to it? Ever more invasive searches at airports, laws restricting foreigners' entrance into the U.S., American suspects are imprisoned for months and years, incommunicado, and denied legal representation on "suspicion." And the "Patriot Act."

Not long ago, newspapers reported that our new, beefed-up airport security missed 40 to 80 percent of the dummy bombs and guns brought on board by federal agents testing the system. The authorities in Washington built a fence around the White House in preparation for the Fourth of July, just as Israel built a fence around Jerusalem. *Tout ca change, tout c'est la meme chose.*

Meanwhile, quite a few voices are suggesting that the obsession with infiltrators, national identity cards, witch hunts, and the building of ever more expensive (and annoying) ways to sift through straws is the wrong response. Perhaps we should figure out what kind of horses and carts are being smuggled!

After all, as technology continues to develop, terrorists will be supplied with ever smaller and more powerful weapons. Continuing our present reactive solutions to terrorism will, in all likelihood, result in still more and more loss of civil liberties. Many are beginning to believe that the ultimate result may be a police state.

They that can give up essential liberty to obtain a little temporary safety deserve neither liberty nor safety.
– Benjamin Franklin

Toward a Fuller Understanding

Any careful, honest examination of our responses and re-actions to today's challenges quickly reveals that we are missing the point on several scores – and that by continuing to pursue our current policies, we may be creating far more problems than we are solving. I have addressed very similar issues as they appear in the lives of individuals in *Deep Healing* [1], and it is worthwhile to examine to what extent the principles involved in these individual cases are also applicable at the level of the family, community, and at higher levels of systems.

Consider terrorism, for instance, perhaps the most frighten-ing of the issues we now face. What if we are dealing with a Hy-dra-headed monster? If you cut one head off, two will grow back. Supporting this viewpoint are reports that the number of Islamic radicals seeking to become suicide bombers has increased ten to twenty-fold since the preemptive strike on Iraq by the "Coalition of the Willing."

Advocates of preemptive war subscribe to the belief that we must launch attacks on any nation we strongly (even if wrongly) suspect of harboring terrorists. Conceivably, they argue, we must learn to live with the collective guilt of so-called "collateral dam-age" – the deaths and maiming of thousands, tens of thousands, hundreds of thousands, possibly even millions of children and unarmed civilians in those countries we attack. Fight the war in their backyard so it won't be fought in ours. Better them than us. Right? Maybe . . .

It may be that the sponsors of The Patriot Act are right that we just have to get over those quaint notions of civil rights, lack of censorship, and privacy, and get used to having our phone calls, purchases, mail, e-mail, Web surfing, library books, and physical whereabouts spied upon by government agencies. Other sugges-tions have been a national ID card, or even having a tracking chip

---

[1]   Emmett Miller, *Deep Healing* (Hay House, 1997). www.ShopDrMiller.com

implanted in every citizen? Illegal aliens could then be detected by a simple hand-held device. Maybe ...

On the other hand, to my way of thinking, before we surrender our privacy and hard-won civil rights, it seems only prudent to examine the arguments of those who suggest there may be another, more appropriate, less destructive approach. There is an increasingly vocal group of people who feel, strongly, that we are laboring under erroneous assumptions, and headed in a dangerous direction.

Some of their arguments are:

1. The current global system of government may be unsustainable, based as it has been, on "aggression abroad and repression at home."

To suggest that "war can prevent war" is a base play on words and a despicable form of warmongering. The objective of any who sincerely believe in peace clearly must be to exhaust every honorable recourse in the effort to save the peace. The world has had ample evidence that war begets only conditions that beget further war.
–Ralph Bunche (as quoted by President Jimmy Carter)

2. The behavior of our government, both at home and abroad, although it may benefit a privileged few, often seems to not be in the interests of the vast majority of our citizens. If this is so, it represents a danger, not only to our global political position, but also to our domestic situation (economy, environment, social stability).

As Ariana Huffington points out, "The economic game is not supposed to be rigged like some shady ring toss on a carnival midway. Yet it has been, allowing corporate crooks to bilk the public out of trillions of dollars, magically making our pensions and 401(K)s disappear, and walking away with astronomical payouts and absurdly lavish perks for life. Tyco's Dennis Kozlowki, Adelphia's John Rigas, the inimitable Bernard Madoff, and the Three Horsemen of the Enron Apocalypse, Ken Lay, Jeff Skilling, and Andrew Fastow, are not just a few bad apples. They are manifestations of a megatrend in corporate leadership – the rise of a callous and avaricious mindset that is wildly out of whack with the core values

I don't see how this is any different than the million dollar bonus you got from AIG after the government bailout.

of the average American. WorldCom, Adelphia, Tyco, AOL, Xerox, Merrill Lynch, and the other scandals are only the tip of the tip of the 'corruption iceberg'." And she said this even before the economic debacle of 2008!

3. The corporate-controlled media often seem to be hiding relevant facts from us. And more often than we would like to admit, we receive more disinformation than truth, to the benefit of advertisers, politicians, and those shadowy figures manipulating the economy and public policy from behind the scenes. It is an accepted truism that democracy can flourish only where citizens are informed, and the primary organ of such information is a free press. Without it there can be no true democracy.

Still, according to John Swinton, former Chief of Staff, The New York Times, "There is no such thing, at this date of the world's history, in America, as an independent press. You know it and I know it ... The business of the Journalist is to destroy truth; to lie outright; to pervert; to vilify; to fawn at the feet of mammon, and to sell his country and his race for his daily bread. We are the tools and vassals for rich men behind the scenes. We are the jumping jacks, they pull the strings, and we dance. We are intellectual prostitutes." Although penned in 1880, there are many who feel things have become, if anything, worse.

4. North Americans consume and pollute at several times the rate of most other countries. The non-U.S. world is beginning to protest and there is increasing domestic discontent. As Bill Moyers said, once he believed people would "... protect the natural environment when they realize its importance to their health and to the health and lives of their children. Now I am not so sure. It's not that I don't want to believe that – it's just that I read the news and connect the dots."

5. It is quite possible that the president was mistaken, perhaps even disingenuous, to suggest that terrorist attacks such as September 11 are the work of "evildoers," "suicidal" extremists who "hate us" because "we stand for freedom and equality." An alternative view is that the terrorists represent the extremist fringe of a deep reservoir of discontent resulting from centuries of what they feel has been disrespect and contempt by the West, and aggression by our corporations, our government, and our cultural attitudes. The Crusades, though they occurred centuries ago, represent a genocide that is still vivid in the minds of many in the Middle East, while we in the West have only romantic Hollywood depictions of that era. Some people, including Zbigniew Brzezinski[2], are convinced of an even more sinister and intentional plot. He said, "World events since the attacks of September 11, 2001, have not only been predicted, but also planned, orchestrated, and – as their architects would like to believe – controlled. *The current war is not a response to terrorism, nor is it a reaction to Islamic fundamentalism.* It is, in fact, in the words of one of the most powerful men on the plan-

---

[2]   Zbigniew Brzezinski, served as National Security Advisor to President Carter, was a member of President Reagan's Foreign Intelligence Advisory Board, and co-chairman of the Bush National Security Advisory Task Force.

et, the beginning of a final conflict before total world domination by the United States leads to the dissolution of all national governments. This will lead to nation states being incorporated into a new world order, controlled solely by economic interests as dictated by banks, corporations, and ruling elites concerned with the maintenance (by manipulation and war) of their power." (italics mine)

6. Money, sex, and power are far too often the goals of our leaders, and these corrupting goals often distort their morals and ethics. Their abuse of the privileges of office, historically, has not worked to the greater good of the American people.

> *This office is a sacred trust, and I'm*
> *determined to be worthy of that trust.*
> – President Richard Nixon

7. It is becoming easier and easier to create weapons of mass destruction. It is almost (but not quite) child's play to create organisms never before seen on the planet – organisms whose sole purpose is to infect and kill millions. The makings of "dirty" nuclear bombs are available on the world black market, and the instructions on how to build them are on the World Wide Web. At the same time, our borders are quite porous, and it is proving impossible to fully protect ourselves. Smaller, more powerful weapons, and indefensible borders means that we continue to alienate large constituencies of people at our peril.

> *War has become not just tragic, but preposterous. With modern*
> *weapons there can be no victory for anyone.*
> – President Dwight D. Eisenhower

Mask the Symptom, Miss the Source

Not infrequently, in the practice of medicine we have the means to relieve pain and other symptoms in a patient, even though we have not yet accurately diagnosed the underlying condition. The problem is that if we remove the symptom, we may not be able to complete the diagnosis.

Generally, it is considered very bad medicine to do this – even if there is only a 1 or 2 percent chance that treating a symptom would prevent the discovery of a deeper, life-threatening disease. Attacking the symptom would be tantamount to killing the patient, a particularly disturbing outcome. Relieving the excruciating abdominal pain of a person with appendicitis could allow it to burst without our ever knowing it, thereby producing a condition that is seriously life threatening.

The possibility that there is a deeper cause to all our symptoms forces us to suspend judgment and temporarily refrain from excessive symptomatic treatment. Failure to do this could obscure deeper issues, and the reaction to our ill-advised intervention could worsen the problem.

Sure, we can remain in denial and make ourselves feel more comfortable by hiding the symptom – but it should be clear to most of us that the dangers of remaining in denial are enormous. Our failure to use our intelligence, our wisdom, our eyes, and our ears resulted in September 11. That same failure led to the current financial mess. Are we going to be wiser this time? I hope that our examination of the Present Illness that follows will help stimulate the kind of thinking that can lead to the kind of questions and solutions we need to explore in our quest for a more complete cure.

Questions to Ponder

1. What attempts at solving problems, at a personal, community, or global level have you seen go awry due to poor understanding of the system?

2. What current "solutions" to the financial crisis promise to be similarly misguided?

Notes to Self

Previous Attempts: Take Home Messages

• Continuing our present reactive solution to terrorism will most likely result in more and more loss of civil liberties.

• Our government's behavior, at home and abroad, has often been quite opposed to the interests of a vast majority of its citizens.

• The corporate-controlled media are often guilty of hiding relevant facts from us.

• The rest of the world is beginning to protest the fact that North Americans consume and pollute at several times the rate of most other countries.

• Failure to use our intelligence, wisdom, eyes, and ears has resulted in crises ranging from the terrorist attacks of 9/11 to the current financial meltdown.

CHAPTER 5

HISTORY OF THE PRESENT ILLNESS

Facts do not cease to exist because they are ignored.
– Aldous Huxley, novelist (1894-1963)

Once the physician has elicited the patient's Chief Complaints, the next step is to gather information that will enable him/her to understand how the signs and symptoms of the deeper illness have made their appearance in the person's life. As the physician listens, he/she begins with a completely open mind, open to all options. Gradually, while listening, he/she begins to eliminate certain possibilities and assign a certain weight to others that are consistent with the story he/she is hearing. Soon a clear picture of the fundamental issues is obtained, and our knowledge of pathophysiology and our clinical experience can be used to look past the symptoms to the deeper cause of the imbalance that has created them.

Our Present Global Illness

Even a passing knowledge of world history convinces us immediately that the kinds of issues we are examining are not the exclusive property of today's world. We have always had headaches and infections, wives have cheated on their husbands (and vice versa), and depression, anxiety, and anger have always plagued individuals; genocides, crusades, inquisitions, witch burnings, wars, and racial hatred are older than history itself. If we really want to go to the beginning, we may need to go back to the beginning of Life itself.

Two most fundamental qualities of Life are continuous activity (such as the constantly flowing protoplasm of a living cell) and a concerted effort to hold together the parts of that which is known as "self." A paramecium protects itself by swimming away from water that is too acidic, a lioness feeds herself and her pride of cubs by killing a zebra, and a father works three jobs to keep his kids in good schools. These actions support and protect the life of the individual and the family by sustaining wholeness. Without wholeness[1], life ceases.

To a one-celled animal, like a paramecium or an amoeba, a most important aspect of wholeness is the integrity of the cell membrane. If it is ruptured it must be immediately repaired (healing) just as we must put pressure on a wound to prevent life threatening hemorrhage. More than this, the membrane needs to have functional integrity, so it can carry on its crucial tasks of bringing oxygen to the interior of the cell, expelling wastes and the toxic products of metabolism, ingesting food, and so forth.

The community of cells that comprise a multicellular animal

---

[1]   When we examine any system, we discover that all the properties of that system can never be determined or explained by its component parts alone. Instead, the system as a whole determines in an important way how the parts behave (holism – from the same Greek root as whole). Wholeness reflects the integrity and coherence of the system's function.

must carry out all these same functions, but, since it is composed of many individual cells, must succeed in a number of other ways as well. Among other tasks, there must be a way to hold all the cells together, to organize their functioning, and to provide for their support and defense. In addition, every creature must figure out how to exist in a world full of other creatures, many of which want to eat it, or compete with it.

Competition and Conflict

For better or for worse, the way life has evolved on this planet has led, ineluctably, to an ongoing state of competition and conflict – conflict among organisms and groups of organisms for scarce resources. Attack and/or defense become necessary for survival ... and survival is the name of the game—in the jungle, in the streets of the ghetto, in the corporate boardroom, and on the battlefield.

Multicellular animals had to develop ways to continue to maintain the wholeness of the separate cells comprising them, as well as of the individual as a whole. Likewise, as individual animals began to band together, they needed to define themselves not only in terms of their own individual survival, but also in terms of the survival of the hive, pack, or tribe. How utterly futureless is a honeybee that flies off to save itself while the others of the hive perish.

Still, within the group, each individual must find a balance between serving its own needs (Grrrr ... this is MY bone, go away), as well as those of the group, "us" (our gang, family or pack). Sometimes this may mean competition, and even battle, against "them" as a group (their gang).

At the level of human beings, this instinct translates into "that's my rattle", "this is our surfing wave," "you're an infidel," "you're a foreign er," "you're the wrong color," "you're not cool," "you're too stupid," "you're too old" ...

In far too many cultures and communities the following is accepted as appropriate: Once a person or group has been defined as "other," we have permission (indeed, it is often praised) to criticize, exclude, treat unfairly, abuse, attack, injure, maim, or even kill. You can even become a hero this way. Yet in the wake of such behaviors lie terrible destruction, wars, concentration camps, atomic bombings, child molestation, racism, torture, rape, beheadings, and other brutalization of "them."

It is forbidden to kill; therefore, all murderers are punished unless they kill in large numbers and to the sound of trumpets.
— Voltaire

Survival of the Fittest

Charles Darwin's theory, often summarized as "Survival of the Fittest," has been updated in recent years to reflect our increased understanding of ecology. This primitive paradigm of "survival of the fittest" occurs in the early stages of maturation of an ecosystem. Evolution biologist, *Elisabet Sahtouris* has presented convincing evidence that this is, in actual ecological systems, followed by a later stage of cooperation, which presages long-term stability of the ecosystem, and produces health and longevity of the species within it.

The competitive paradigm (to the winner go the spoils, second place is just first loser, he who dies with the most toys wins, more is better, winning is everything) is responsible for an enormous portion of our own inner pain. To it may be attributed many of the diseases of stress[2].

---

[2] See <http://www.drmiller.com/news_library/book.html> for a more complete description.

At the level of the individual:

Our inability to treat ourselves with love and kindness results in violence to the (internal) system that may show up as heart disease, cancer, chronic fatigue, obesity, substance abuse, or even suicide. We all know the statistics.

At the family/community level:

Lack of love, nurturance, and human compassion have led to the acceptance of, and even participation in, all kinds of injustice to other human beings, including members of our own families – the very ones to whom we should give and receive the most love and support! Women are beaten and raped, often by their spouses or partners. A woman is beaten by her partner every six seconds in the United States.

During recent decades, we in the United States have witnessed the gradual dissolution of the family (the fundamental unit of human society), the neighborhood, and the community. Our homicide rate is several times that of any other industrialized country – and all too often, the murder victims are spouses, partners, or other family members, including the children.

Advances in technology (computers, violent video games, cars, online shopping, and the "unreality" of commercial television) have allowed us to isolate and insulate ourselves from others to the point where many people lack even the most basic interpersonal skills, including empathy, sympathy, and intimacy.

Sadly, our culture tends to have a blind spot, making us blind to the tragedies of broken homes, socioeconomic inequality, sexism, racism, all the other 'isms, and the myriad kinds of verbal and physical violence we perpetrate against each other – and ourselves.

At the global level:

In the last 100 years, we've fought two World Wars, and seem to be inching towards a third. We've seen the detonation of atomic bombs and the horror of radioactive fallout. We've witnessed brutal "ethnic cleansings" by gas chambers, guns, artillery, machetes, and starvation.

We saw the fall of communism in the Soviet Union, and the rise of communism in China. We all are affected by worldwide pollution and the depletion of natural resources.

We read about the pandemic of AIDS, biological terrorism (anthrax) via the U.S. mail, and after 9/11, the invasion and occupation of two Third-World nations.

Yet, as frightening as the current global situation, it's nothing new. This fundamental struggle of "us" vs. "them" has gone on for millennia – feuds, wars, crusades, pogroms, witch burnings, inquisitions, slavery, genocide ...

> *The thing that hath been, it is that which shall be; and*
> *that which is done, is that which shall be done; and*
> *there is no new thing under the sun.*
> *– Ecclesiastes*

Grass

Pile the bodies high at Austerlitz and Waterloo.
Shovel them under and let me work –
I am the grass; I cover all.

And pile them high at Gettysburg
And pile them high at Ypres and Verdun.
Shovel them under and let me work.
Two years, ten years, and passengers ask the conductor:
What place is this?
Where are we now?

I am the grass.
Let me work.
– Carl Sandburg

A History of Violence

*The need is not for more brains, the need is now for a gentler, a more
tolerant people than those who won for us against the ice, the tiger,
and the bear. The hand that hefted the ax, out of some old blind
allegiance to the past, fondles the machine gun as lovingly. It is a
habit man will have to break to survive, but the roots go very deep.*
– Lauren Eisley

The history of humankind can be measured in wars and conflicts. The map of Europe changed dramatically every century, and
soon the competition and wars spread beyond Europe during the
Age of Empires and Colonization.

During this time, the "Americas" were "discovered" – and
then invaded. The European invaders, through clever media advertising, convinced themselves the indigenous non-whites were savages. Therefore, they viciously attacked the peaceful natives, with
the eventual total destruction of their nations – a genocide exceed-
ing twice the number of people slaughtered in the Nazi concentration camps.

The penetrance of this war
becomes clearer when we consider
our own country. Although we believe
in peace, we find ourselves repeatedly fighting wars. Consider the fact
that, currently, with the U.S. invasion
of Afghanistan and Iraq, many Americans fear our country is embarking on
a reckless course of global imperialism. Historically, the U.S. government,
often using the CIA for covert action
(e.g., death squads), supported the
capitalistic corporate invasions of other
countries (Chile, Iran, Nigeria, Guate-
mala, to name but a few).

Consider the effect of the adversarial position the U.S. has taken against the Islamic world, presenting itself as a defender of Israel, often quite pugnaciously. That stance, whether or not we believe it to be appropriate, nevertheless antagonizes the national pride and sensitivities of many Muslims. The submerged anger surfaces in the suicide bombers that emerge from the radical fringe of the anti-America movement.

Try as we might to focus on peace, war seems to be inevitable – we continue to keep our primitive "dog-eat-dog" reflexes alive. Their roots go very deep, and only profound change can affect them.

> *Gandhi was once asked what he thought about Western Civilization. He replied, "It would be nice."*

Questions to Ponder

1. What else would you add to the Present Illness?

2. How have competition and conflict shaped your personal life? In what other ways have you seen it impact the world?

3. In what ways have you abused yourself through shame, lack of compassion, or blame? When have you witnessed others harm themselves?

Notes to Self

Present Illness: Take Home Messages

• Life on this planet has evolved to an ongoing state of competition and conflict; the history of humankind can be measured in wars and conflicts.

• Our inability to treat ourselves with love and kindness results in violence to the internal system that can show up as disease, substance abuse, and suicide.

• We are often blind to the myriad verbal and physical violence we perpetrate against each other daily.

• The fundamental struggle of "us" vs. "them" has gone on for millennia, and produces some of the most tragic stories for people and the earth.

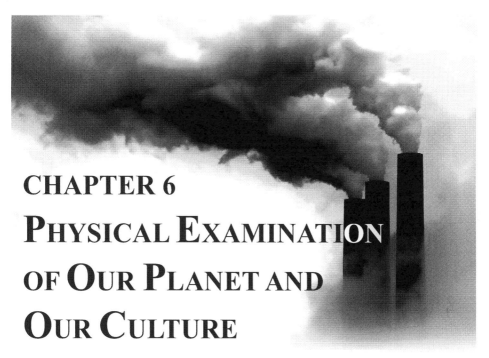

CHAPTER 6

PHYSICAL EXAMINATION OF OUR PLANET AND OUR CULTURE

Just as a physician would conduct a physical examination of a patient – complete with lab tests, X-rays, MRIs, and so forth – our next task is to examine the current physical condition of our world.

Although the history of the present illness alone, taken by a competent historian, is sufficient to diagnose 80 percent or 90 percent of human illnesses, the physical exam is valuable. It confirms suspicions, reveals the extent of the illness, and sometimes the information is essential to the diagnosis and prognosis.

Because we cannot place an actual stethoscope to the heart of our patient, we must rely on the laboratory tests and surveys done by scientists concerned about the planet's health.

You have probably already seen or heard of most of the findings listed here – and this list is far from complete. Still, it is compelling to see all these facts, estimates, and predictions at once to appreciate the gestalt, the overall picture. (Remember, in seeking the deeper source, we are searching for the common factors among all these symptoms.)

Physical Examination

> *To cherish what remains of the Earth and to foster*
> *its renewal is our only legitimate hope of survival.*
> – Wendell Berry

The patient is a 4.5-billion-year-old, well developed, moderately anemic, blue-green planet in acute and chronic distress. Born of a supernova, it dwells in the Orion arm of the Milky Way Galaxy, which is part of the Virgo Supercluster. A toxic brown-grey cloud covers portions of it, and its temperature appears to be rising. Vital signs and major findings include:

- Global warming
- Pollution
- Water crises
- Declining biodiversity
- Population pressures
- Disease and starvation
- Declining forests and farming
- Socioeconomic inequality
- Unfair use of prisons and "justice"
- Absence of adequate health Insurance and rising medical costs
- Disappearance of independent news media
- Increasing terrorist threats
- The slow drift toward nuclear proliferation

What follows are a few glimpses of some of the vital signs and major findings.

Global Warming

Geologically speaking, the Earth continues to evolve, and changes in the climate are natural and inevitable. However, scientists tell us they have detected "a discernible human influence on global climate." The influence on the climate comes in the form of anthropogenic greenhouse gases. Some of these gases are natural, like carbon dioxide, but others, like chlorofluorocarbons, are man-made.

The burning of fossil fuels and deforestation has increased the amount of carbon dioxide in the atmosphere. Farming, industry, and transportation have also produced gases that

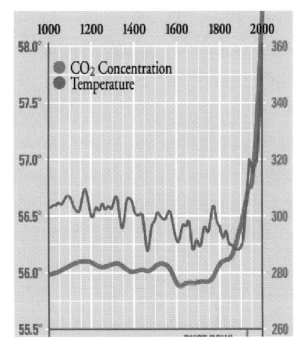

http://www.koshland-science-museum.org/exhibitgcc/historical03.jsp

contribute to the theoretical "greenhouse effect" – an increasingly less controversial hypothesis that human activities are causing the average temperature of the Earth to rise. Al Gore's film, *An Inconvenient Truth,* presents plausible arguments in favor of the theory. Regardless of whether we believe in the theory or not, the geological facts are these:

• Glaciers are melting, plants and animals are being forced from their habitat, and the number of severe storms and droughts is increasing.
• In the Arctic Sea, the ice averaged 5.8 feet thickness from 1958 through 1976. That dropped to 5.6 feet between 1993 and 1997, and today the situation is even worse.
• Since 1945, the Antarctic Peninsula has experienced a warming of about 4.5 degrees Fahrenheit. The annual melt season has increased from two to three weeks in the past 20 years.

69

• At the present rate of global temperature rise, all glaciers in Glacier National Park will be gone by 2070.
• The number of Category 4 and 5 hurricanes has almost doubled in the last 30 years.
• Malaria has spread to higher altitudes in places like the Colombian Andes, 7,000 feet above sea level.
• The flow of ice from glaciers in Greenland has more than doubled over the past decade.
• At least 279 species of plants and animals are already responding to global warming, moving closer to the poles.
• The ice-covered period for New Hampshire's Mirror Lake has declined by about half a day annually for the past 30 years.

If the warming continues, we can expect catastrophic consequences[1].

• Deaths from global warming will double in just 25 years – to 300,000 people a year.
• Global sea levels could rise by more than 20 feet with the loss of shelf ice in Greenland and Antarctica, devastating coastal areas worldwide.
• Heat waves will be more frequent and more intense.
• Droughts and wildfires will occur more often.
• The Arctic Ocean could be ice free in summer by 2050.
• More than a million species worldwide could be driven to extinction by 2050.

Pollution

"It is horrifying to me that we have to
fight our own government to save the environment."
– Ansel Adams

---

[1]   For further, more current information see http://www.climatecrisis.net/thescience/

The most obvious evidence of pollution is the air we "see" and breathe – smog. Less obvious, and more insidious, are the pollutants found in our food, water, and bodies. Consider the following:

• Measurable levels of the mutation-causing chemical, dioxin, can be found in the milk of every mother on the planet.
• Human sperm counts are falling worldwide due to the effect of estrogen-like insecticide residues in our food.
• As much as 86 percent of Indonesia's coral reefs, home to thousands of marine species, are severely damaged by over-fishing, sedimentation, and pollution.
• There are about 176 toxic chemicals at measurable levels in the blood of the average person. Each individual chemical is below the "permissible" level, and no one has ever calculated what effect the combined levels may have.
• More than one-fourth of the nation's lakes have advisories warning consumers that fresh-caught fish may be contaminated with mercury, dioxin, or other chemicals. Eating fish that contain high concentrations of mercury, dioxin, PCBs, and other industrial chemicals can be especially harmful to children and to the fetuses of pregnant women.

Water Crises

Without water, there is no life. As humans, we require large amounts of fresh, clean water, but water shortages and polluted water threaten much of the world's population:

• About half the world's rivers are seriously depleted and polluted.
• By 2025, two-thirds of the world's population will be living in countries that face serious water shortages.
• An estimated 1.1 billion people will lack access to clean drinking water.
• About 2.4 billion humans will lack adequate sanitation.

71

Declining Biodiversity

Currently, careful examination suggests that Planet Earth is going through its sixth and probably most devastating period of mass extinction. Hundreds or thousands of species of animals and plants are dying out each year. But unlike the previous five extinction waves – which were the result of geologic cataclysms, such as the Ice Ages or a hypothesized asteroid collision – this time the culprit is another life form: Homo sapiens. According to a compendium of recent reports, some 11,046 species of plants and animals face a high risk of extinction. These include 1,130 mammals (24 percent of the total) and 1,183 species of birds (12 percent of the total).

The chart above shows how the total number of wild (woodland) bird species is dropping precipitously, in relation to the few species that have learned to coexist (so far) with the incursions of humans.

Scientists have also identified 5,611 species of plants known to be on the verge of extinction. They report the true figure is likely to be far higher, given that only 4 percent of the world's known plant species have been properly classified.

The following list shows the percentage of species already at risk for extinction:

- Birds – 11%
- Vascular plants – 12.5%
- Reptiles – 20%
- Mammals – 25%

- Amphibians – 25%
- Fish – 34%

Furthermore, about a third of all coral reefs are expected to vanish in the next 30 years. The number of wild orangutans has declined 50 percent since 1992. And the wild salmon is on the verge of extinction.

Among the serious threats to life on Earth are:

- Over-exploitation of natural resources
- Pollution
- Habitat destruction
- Introduction of alien species into local ecosystems
- Global climate change.

Massive extinctions have occurred five times during Earth's history. The last one was the extinction of the dinosaurs 65 million years ago. Scientists are calling what is occurring now, the sixth mass extinction. Most scientists believe the rate of loss is greater now than at any time in the history of Earth. Within the next 30 years as many as half of the species could die in one of the fastest mass extinctions in the planet's 4.5-billion-year history. Dr. Richard Leakey, co-author (with Roger Lewin) of The Sixth Extinction, believes that 50 percent of the earth's species will vanish within 100 years. The human species may become one of those lost.

Even if we manage, somehow, to survive, the problem is even greater than the loss of species; there is also the loss of the genetic diversity within species, as well as the loss of diversity of different types of ecosystems, which can contribute to or hasten whole species extinction. The preservation of the wider gene pool is crucial, for it provides the raw material for the evolution of new species in the future.

Scientists have identified and named about 1.5 million species of life forms, but they believe that between 5 million and 15 million species have yet to be formally classified. It is now generally assumed many unnamed animals, plants, and microorganisms are going extinct before they are even known to science.

Unless we change our ways, half of all species could disappear by the end of this century. Many of these provide food and medicine for humans.
– Edward O'Wilson, Harvard Biologist

Population Pressure

There are 2,220 million more people alive today than in 1972. The world's population is now estimated at 6.1 billion, and it is predicted to rise to 8.9 billion by 2050.

If India does not curtail its population growth by 2050, it will be home to a projected 1.5 billion people, surpassing the population of the vastly larger country of China. (China, foreseeing its own overpopulation risks, has instituted very strict population control, allowing only one child per family.)

Just 15 years ago, only 18 percent of the population in the developing world lived in cities. Now, it's jumped to 40 percent, and by 2030, it's estimated 56 percent of these countries' populations will be urban.

Interestingly, the population of the industrialized countries is estimated to remain constant through 2050 at about 1.2 billion. Virtually all human growth will occur in the developing world, where the population is expected to increase from the current 5.1 billion people to 7.7 billion. These developing countries bear the brunt of the earth's grinding poverty, desperate hunger, disease, illiteracy and unemployment. In fact, some developing countries, including Burkina Faso, Mali, Niger, Somalia, and Yemen, are likely to quadruple their population by mid-century.

Disease and Starvation

When will our consciences grow so tender that we will act to prevent human misery rather than avenge it?
– Eleanor Roosevelt, diplomat and writer
(1884-1962)

Due to overpopulation, climate changes, and genocidal wars, horrifying numbers of people on Earth face disease and undernourishment to the point of starvation:

- In the poorest parts of the world, most notably Africa, the spread of infectious diseases such as AIDS, malaria, cholera, and tuberculosis is out of control.
- Rural land degradation is pushing people into cities, where crowded and filthy living conditions create the perfect breeding grounds for sickness.
- Worldwide, at least 68 million people are expected to die of AIDS by 2020, including 55 million in sub-Saharan Africa.
- Up to one-third of the world's population is in danger of malnutrition and starvation.
- Two billion people lack reliable access to safe, nutritious food, and 800 million of them – including 300 million children – are chronically malnourished.
- Just 15 crops, such as corn, wheat, and rice, provide 90 percent of the world's food. Planting the same crops year after year strips the fields of nutrients, lowering the quality and quantity of crop yields.
- Of the Earth's land surface, 15 percent of it is now classified as "degraded by human activities."
- The amount of crops, animals, and other biomatter we extract from the earth each year exceeds what the planet can replace by an estimated 20 percent. In other words, it takes 14.4 months to replenish what we use every 12 months. This is deficit spending of the worst kind.
- A U.N. environmental report warns of the effects of a haze across all southern Asia. The report estimates the "Asian Brown Cloud" to be two miles thick, and it may be responsible (or at least a contributing factor) for hundreds of thousands of deaths a year from respiratory diseases.

75

Forests and Farming

Perversely, agricultural activities both feed us and hurt us.
Think about the following:

• Corporate agribusiness is driving family farmers off the good
land. These displaced farmers will either go to the cities to compete for low-wage jobs or attempt to farm marginal land.
• U.S. farmers in 1999 received 36 percent less for their products in real dollars than in 1984.
• During the 1990s, 84 percent of new jobs were created
in metropolitan areas. The income gap between metro and
non-metro workers has increased to $13,200 per worker from
$4,600 in 1985.
• The United States is losing two acres of mostly prime farmland every minute to development. This is the most rapid decline in the country's history.
• Worldwide, rain forests are vanishing at a rate of one acre
per second. This translates to a loss of 36 million acres of forest annually.
• According to the World Resources Institute, more than 80%
of Earth's natural forests already have been destroyed.
• As much as 90 percent of West Africa's coastal rain forests
have disappeared since 1900.
• Brazil and Indonesia host the world's two largest surviving regions of rain forest – and those forests are being stripped at an

alarming rate by logging,
fires, and land clearing
for agriculture and cattle
grazing.

Forests are one
of the planet's primary
sources of oxygen, liter-
ally, the breath of life.
Furthermore, without

forests to absorb carbon dioxide (and convert it into oxygen), the greenhouse effect of excess carbon dioxide is amplified.

Economic Inequality

> *Peace can exist only between equals.*
> – Guiseppi Mazzini

The income gap of the haves and the have-nots is expanding into an abyss:

- In 1980, the ratio of executive pay to that of a factory worker was 42-to-1. In 1998, the ratio had leaped to 419-to-1.
- In 1977, the disclosed wealth of the top 10 U.S. senators was $133 million. In 2001, it was $1.83 billion.
- In 1979, the top 1 percent of Americans possessed 21 percent of the household wealth; by 1999, this elite 1 percent had 39 percent of the household wealth.
- In 1982, the Forbes 400 richest people had personal wealth of at least $91 million and included 13 billionaires. Today, there are 268 billionaires on the list.
- Eighty-six percent of stock market gains between 1989 and 1997 flowed to the top 10 percent of households. During the same period, the top 1 percent of the well-to-do garnered 42 percent of the gains.
- Between 1973 and 2001, the income of the poorest 20 percent of our population increased 14 percent. The income of the 20 percent in the middle went up 19 percent. And the income of the richest 5 percent shot up 87 percent.
- Wages for the bottom 10 percent of wage earners fell by 9.3 percent between 1979 and 1999.
- In 1998, the top-earning 1 percent had as much income as the combined income of 100 million Americans with the lowest earnings.
- In 1982, U.S. foreign debt was less than 5 percent of the U.S.

Gross Domestic Product; now it's almost 25 percent.
• In 1998, only two-thirds of American households that were headed by a person between the ages of 47 and 64 had as much pension wealth in real dollars as they had in 1983.
• Almost 20 percent of all near-retiree households can expect to retire in poverty.
• For the second year in a row, a record number of companies went bankrupt in 2002. The value of the bankruptcies beat the previous record set in 2001 by 50 percent and included five of the 10 largest bankruptcies ever recorded. And the 2008 and 2009 bankruptcy rate is expected to dwarf these figures.
• The Federal Reserve has found that family wealth was "substantially below" 1989 levels for all income groups under age 55.
• According to Howard Zinn, "One percent of the nation owns a third of the wealth. The rest of the wealth is distributed in such a way as to turn those in the 99% against one another: small property owners against the propertyless, black against white, native-born against foreign-born, intellectuals and professionals against the uneducated and unskilled ... which obscures their common position as sharers of leftovers in a very wealthy country."

Prisons and "Justice"

As long as there is a low class, I am one of them.
As long as there exists a crime, I am in it. As long
as there is even one person in prison, I am not free.
– Kurt Vonnegut

78

Social inequality abounds. A poor person goes to prison for years for stealing $1,000. A corporate criminal steals $50 million – and gets off with having to wear an ankle bracelet and be confined to his/her mansion for a few months.

Meanwhile, prisons and jails are filled to capacity with minorities and people who have committed crimes of debatable severity (possession of marijuana, for example).

In "the land of the free," you can find the following statistics:

• With a prison population of more than two million, the U.S. has more people behind bars than any other country in the world.
• With one out of every 142 Americans incarcerated, the U.S. has the highest per capita number of prisoners in the world. In 1980, there were fewer than 500,000 people in prison in the U.S. By 2002, there were more than two million, according to the federal Bureau of Justice Statistics.
• In 1980, 8 percent of the prisoners were jailed for drug offenses; by 1998, 28 percent were.
• Between 1980 and 2000, the U.S. per capita spending on schools increased 32 percent. The per capita spending on prisons grew 189 percent.
• California built 21 prisons between 1980 and 1998. During the same time, the state built one college.

He who opens a school door, closes a prison.
– Victor Hugo

Health Insurance

More than 40 million Americans, many of them children, have no health insurance. The current costs of medical treatment, even of the most basic variety, are prohibitively expensive for the uninsured. Likewise, these people cannot afford the drugs that would be prescribed if they could get treatment.

In 1988, 71% of Americans were insured under fee-for-service plans. Ten years later, in 1998, only 14% were insured under fee-for-service plans. It's even worse now.

Health care issues loom ever larger in the weeks before elections, as they do in corporate boardrooms, where the health care costs facing companies are threatening to consume all the profits! There must be a better way.

The Vanishing Free Press

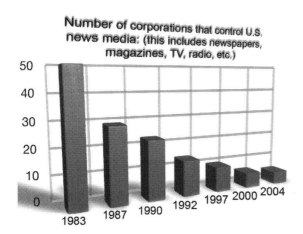

Number of corporations that control U.S. news media: (this includes newspapers, magazines, TV, radio, etc.)

In 1996, the top 50 corporations owned about 700 radio stations among them. Today, the top 10 corporations own 1,700 stations.

corporations.org/media/

Although Freedom of the Press is guaranteed by the Bill of Rights as are our other rights, this particular freedom is different from other liberties of the people in that it is both individual and institutional. It addresses not only an individual person's right to publish their ideas, but also the right of broadcast and print media to express political views and to publish news. It is a cornerstone of a truly democratic society.

*"A free press is not a privilege, but an organic
necessity in a great society."*
– Walter Lippmann

According to the Media Reform Information Center, 50 corporations controlled most of the news media in America in 1983. Today, just five corporations do. And as you can quickly see by watching the various newscasts, they are anything but unbiased. Those who work for these corporations are bound to present the news in the way that the corporations require them to. The result, as might be expected, is often quite skewed[2].

Patient Appears Gravely Ill, Perhaps Moribund

To cite all the symptoms of the present illness of humans, society, and the planet would go far beyond the scope of this work. Nonetheless, the findings of the above physical exam are more than enough to justify immediate and urgent intervention.

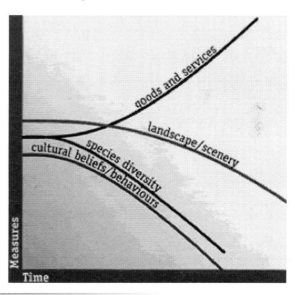

But first, as excellent doctors, we must attempt to diagnose the true source of the illness

---

2   See: David Korten, *When Corporations Rule the World* (Berrett-Koehler Publishers, 2001)

before applying the appropriate treatment. As we've learned, treatment of symptoms before diagnosis can actually harm – or even kill – the patient.

Questions to Ponder

1. What other physical evidence, or statistical evidence are you aware of that can shed even more light on the current state of affairs globally, nationally, and at the personal level?

2. Do you sense within yourself that there are an extraordinary number of ways our world is out of balance?

Notes to Self

Physical Exam: Take Home Messages

• Global warming, pollution, water crises, declining biodiversity, and overpopulation are among the planet's current ailments.

• Overpopulation, climate changes, and genocidal wars have left horrifying numbers of people facing disease and starvation.

• Farmland is vanishing.

• More than 80 percent of Earth's natural forests have been destroyed.

• The gap between the wealthy and the poor is expanding; in 1998, the top-earning 1 percent of the population in this country had as much income as the combined income of 100 million Americans with the lowest earnings.

• More than 40 million Americans, including many children, have no health insurance.

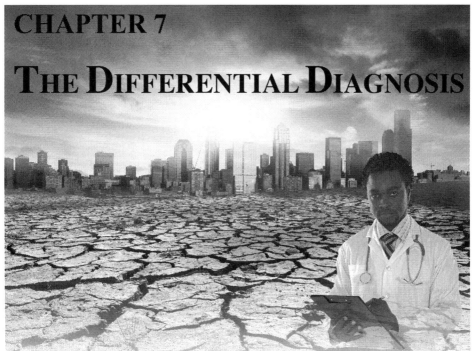

CHAPTER 7

THE DIFFERENTIAL DIAGNOSIS

After integrating the history, physical examination, lab tests, and other data and impressions, the physician makes a number of "educated guesses," thereby creating a prioritized list of deeper imbalances that might be at the root of the symptoms and signs with which the patient or family system presented.

High Index of Suspicion

Moreover, the physician must always have a "high index of suspicion," and consider the worst possibility first. Even if the symptoms are mild or appear to have no apparent connection to each other, the excellent doctor must suspect the worst first.

For instance, a patient reports extreme fatigue, the need for frequent urination, shortness of breath, insatiable hunger in the face of unaccountable weight loss, and near constant thirst. A poor doctor might treat each symptom individually, which might not necessarily be a bad thing – if there were no dangerous underlying process.

A good doctor with a high index of suspicion would recognize this diverse set of symptoms as possible evidence of a deeper imbalance. Routine lab tests would reveal that the patient has abnormal blood sugar levels, a sign that there has been a failure of the beta cells in the pancreas – and the diagnosis is made, Diabetes Mellitus. This doctor would prescribe a strict diet, appropriate exercise, and insulin if the disease is sufficiently advanced.

An excellent doctor would do everything the good doctor does, but would look even deeper to find cause(s) that might be exacerbating the progress of the disease, such as stress, overwork, and/or substance abuse. After talking with the patient, the doctor might also prescribe relaxation therapy (e.g., meditation or yoga), stress reduction medication, and mental health intervention (which might also include the patient's family and significant others).

A poor doctor treats symptoms – and the patient dies.

A good doctor treats the disease – and the patient survives.

An excellent doctor treats the patient – and the patient thrives.

Diagnosis Defined

We must remember at all times that a "diagnosis" is not a "fact." Rather, it's more like a hypothesis or a theory. And a theory is neither "true" nor "false." It is merely useful or not.

The scientifically established characteristics of a good theory are:

1. It is based on the accepted axioms and principles of science.
2. It is internally consistent with the rules of science and logic.
3. It explains the phenomena we observe.

4. It has high heuristic value – it leads to useful new discoveries and ideas.

Generally, when two theories equally explain a phenomenon, the simpler one is preferable (Occam's razor, aka the "Principle of Parsimony"). Our goal, then, is to come up with a theory, or a hypothesis, that will help us deal effectively with the many vectors present in our lives, from the individual to the global. We need a way to conceptualize and manage the confluence of phenomena and energies around us.

Of course, the diagnoses offered here are metaphorical in nature. When we discuss a "Global Cancer," we are certainly not referring to a certain type of living cell that has broken free of its growth-limiting genes, which would be what we were discussing in the case of an actual human cancer. Instead, by analogy, we are conceptualizing a part of the global system that has escaped from the modulating influence of the guiding spirit of the system as a whole. Remember, Dr. Einstein never actually rode on a beam of light, yet his ability to imagine it led to a transformation of the entire world, its entry into the Nuclear Era. What could potentially happen if we discover the "social $E=Mc^2$"

Remember, there is no Big Dipper in the sky. Its stars are not even close to each other – the furthest of its stars from Earth is nearly twice as far away as the nearest! Yet finding the "big dipper" has saved many a life, and guided travelers since time immemorial. All you have to do is to imagine a dipper when you look at the sky, and soon the North Star will show you in which direction you want to go.
– from a Joseph Goldstein idea

by using our imagination in a way that gets to the source that lies beneath all these symptoms? Just imagine!

Diagnosing the Root of Our Global Symptoms

Just as with our diabetic patient, we want to look beneath the superficial symptoms. As in the case of the human patient, the symptoms of our culture or planet as a whole should guide us to look deeper for the true source of the imbalance – and the course of treatment we must pursue.

Clearly, history shows us in vivid detail that we have been stuck with treatment by poor doctors. We have followed leaders (doctors) who urge us to attack (treat) the symptoms. And far too often, like those CEOs who got multimillion dollar bonuses as their companies and stockholders went bankrupt, those who have so assiduously misled us have walked away with huge profits.

The bad news is that in today's global village, complex and tightly networked, another round of treating symptoms just might kill us all. The good news is that we have the information and wisdom available via Web 2.0 to develop the leadership that can lead to healing – on the global as well as the individual level. But more on that later.

We will begin with the most acute diagnosis, because until we do something about it, it will be hard to focus on the others. ("When you're up to your ass in alligators, it's hard to remember your goal was to drain the swamp.")

Diagnosis #1 - Post Traumatic Stress Disorder (PTSD)

When a person perceives an external stressor – whether it be terrorism, crime in the streets, public embarrassment, or any other threat – the first reaction is alarm. In the body, this can be seen as tension, anxiety, racing thoughts, massive secretion of adrenaline into the bloodstream . . . the classic "fight-or-flight" defense response.

Not unusually, people make poor decisions at such times, so great are the haste and stress. "Road rage," "crimes of passion," and phobias represent common examples of this phenomenon. Families, organizations, and communities can fall prey to this phenomenon, too. Stress responses often cause individuals to act in ways that relieve the immediate pain, but may cause serious backlash later. The same is true of governments.

The Economic Crisis of 2008

At the moment this book is being written, the nation and the world are in a shock state, and the wide swings in the stock market only hint at the enormous emotional swings underway and yet to come in ourselves, our families, and our world. This is the very acute stage, and wisdom dictates calm, reasoned responses, rather than impulsive actions and rash decision. On the other hand, such a response is particularly difficult in a world that has not fully recovered from the PTSD resulting from the attacks on the World Trade Center.

The danger is that we will respond as is so often the case with all PTSD – not wisely and thoughtfully – but with precipitous decisions and impulsive, poorly considered actions that cause great harm to many innocent people. It is easy to see examples of this:

•After the attack on Pearl Harbor, Japanese-Americans, many of them native-born or naturalized citizens, were stripped of

WWII Japanese-American internment camp
http://www.dtman.com/images/internment.jpg

their property and civil rights, and herded into internment camps for the duration of World War II. No adequate reparations were made.

• In the early years of the Cold War, Sen. Joseph McCarthy led a witch-hunt against alleged Communists. He particularly targeted the entertainment industry, leading to the infamous Hollywood Blacklist, which destroyed the careers of many writers, actors, and directors.

• Presidents Adams and Wilson pushed through laws that were supposed to protect us from enemies in foreign places, but then turned around and used them to imprison newspaper editors and anyone else who too publicly advocated peace instead of war. Not only were the individuals harmed, but also the precious idea upon which this very country was founded.

I cannot and will not cut my conscience to fit this year's fashions.
– Lillian Hellman, letter to Committee on Un-American Activities of the House of Representatives, May 19, 1952

• During the Vietnam War, on May 4, 1971, National Guardsmen opened fire on peaceful antiwar demonstrators at Kent State University in Ohio. Four protesters were killed and nine wounded.

Tin soldiers and
Nixon's comin'.
We're finally on our own.
This summer I hear
the drummin'.
Four dead in Ohio.
– Crosby, Stills, Nash & Young

• In the last 20 years, the national panic over violent and drug-related crimes has sometimes led to legislation of dubious value, like "Three Strikes" laws and mandatory sentences for drug offenses. In California, third-strike felons are being sentenced to life in prison for nonviolent crimes. In federal courts, minor drug offenders (e.g., possession of a single marijuana joint) are sentenced to years in prison and their property – houses, cars, boats – are seized and sold at auction.

Conflict in the Middle East

In the wake of the 9/11 attack, we went to war in Iraq without carefully considering whether we were treating the symptom or the problem – in the process alienating our allies around the world. Most political analysts believe the retaliation against Afghanistan to be an appropriate and necessary response to 9/11. But many of these same analysts see the U.S. invasion of Iraq as a seriously flawed, dysfunctional, acute stress reaction that has provoked a volatile backlash in the Muslim world, in addition to destroying the lives of many thousands of American soldiers, and the lives of hundreds of thousands of Iraqis. They may be correct.

Indeed, in the wake of the "pre-emptive" invasion of Iraq, the ranks of Al Qaeda have swollen with the ingress of thousands of new fighters and suicide mission volunteers – and financial support for al Qaeda has poured in as well. In other words, it is not far fetched to read from this that perhaps our treating the "symptom" of Iraq with a full-scale military invasion may have actually increased the threat of international terrorism – the opposite of what we intended. The Law of Unexpected

coutesy of the Department of Defense

Consequences strikes again.

PTSD may be seen not only in our aggressiveness internationally following the terrorist attack; we can see evidence of this same harsh reaction here at home. In rapid succession there was the "Patriot Act", the dismissal of moderate voices like Secretary of State Colin Powell, "Patriot Act II", the polarization of our people, and the vigorous management and manipulation of the news. Certainly has the earmarks of an overreaction with self-destructive potential.

American citizens can, and are, being held for months or years, without being charged, and without access to a lawyer! We had a Bill of Rights that was supposed to protect us from such excesses as these, especially since these are exactly the steps that totalitarian and fascist regimes take in suppressing the rights of people and seizing power. Where is that Bill of Rights now, when we really need it?

Vast new powers have been given to government agencies to investigate (some would say "spy on") American citizens, powers that would make an old-time KGB agent salivate. Indeed, if one looks at the characteristics of a fascist regime, such as Nazi Germany, these current changes seem to be bringing us uncomfortably close to a fascist form of government. Whether the fears these reactions have generated are valid or not, the general level of stress and dissention has massively increased – both at home and abroad – as we became more divided and more fragmented, at a time when the highest level of unity would be most desirable.

A Hidden Agenda?

Continuing the medical model, could the invasion of Iraq be, metaphorically, a ploy of unscrupulous "doctors" looking to line their own pockets with an unnecessary operation that has actually done the patient (our world) more harm than good? The "revolving door" of government concerns many Americans; many of our lawmakers have formerly been (and will in the future) be on the payrolls of companies that will benefit from continued hostilities, and those companies fund their election campaigns. Could people really be so Machiavellian?

In today's world, no one will be surprised when today's administration officials, as soon as they leave office, take multimillion dollar "consulting" jobs with the corporate clients their in-office decisions have helped. No question, it may be legal – but is it ethical? How can people be blamed for not totally trusting?

There are also people who fear the "Patriot Act" could be used to "disappear" any "patients" who might want to cry "malpractice." This seems unthinkable to most of us – yet to those who recall the machinations that tricked us into the Spanish American War, the Vietnam War, and the Noriega debacle, it does not seem farfetched at all. Add in such governmental duplicity as revealed by Watergate, the Iran-Contra arms-for-hostages deal, the presidential election of 2000 and 2004, the "yellowcake uranium flimflam," and the Abramoff-Foley oil-for-votes scandal and it seems all too frighteningly believable.

Whatever – our reaction to 9/11 has produced social anxiety, a sharply divided citizenry, a hotly contested preemptive war that became a quagmire, a staggering national debt, and widespread fear at home, as well as anger, apprehension, and mistrust worldwide.

The world watched in awe as the U.S. abandoned the habeus corpus policy that has protected our freedom, and embraced the substitution of "torture-lite" in the place of our fifth amendment protections. And all the while, the flashback to the nightmare of 9/11 is replayed over and over in political speeches on the nightly news.

How can we allow the disintegration of our world in this way? This could be well explained by the well-known symptoms of PTSD-denial, emotional detachment, and numbing of feelings. Individuals with PTSD tend to avoid thinking about reminders of the traumatizing period, and exhibit extreme distress when exposed to images of the sensitizing events. Such images are triggers that may often produce a startle response (think "shellshock") in an individual, and in a culture – a fact used with remarkable skill by the PR agencies of political candidates and parties. And just as an individual with PTSD may suffer clinical depression and anxiety, our world, (at least all the folks I see out there), certainly expresses the helplessness ("we have no choice, we have to have the bomb, torture, fight against our pitiless, evil adversaries") and the hopelessness that characterize clinical depression.

In today's flagrantly opportunistic environment – where "winning is not everything, winning is the only thing," politicians make decisions on the basis of how to stay in power, not on the basis of what is best for the people. Our PTSD symptoms make us vulnerable to manipulation, especially since we are staying in denial about them. Corporations and the wealthy elite who have control of the media make excellent use of these symptoms, regardless of their source, to program us to buy their wares and ideas without recourse to rational, intellectual consideration. As we watch the world unfold around us, we cannot help but recall Adolf Hitler's words of gratitude, "How fortunate for those of us in power that people do not think."

Yet those who become too vocal about such questions run the risk of being branded "traitors," and punished (think Dixie Chicks). Not everyone would agree with such a policy. Even Thomas Jefferson, the conservative chief framer of our constitution, admonished us, "Dissent is the highest form of patriotism."

Given all of the above, the diagnosis of a counterproductive, highly dysfunctional, Post-Traumatic Stress Disorder appears worthy of consideration.

Diagnosis #2 – Global Autoimmune Disorder

In Diagnosis #1, we examined the acute and chronic dysfunction resulting from the external stressors of the 9/11 attack. In this Diagnosis #2, we look at dysfunctional behavior caused by internal stressors in our culture. The medical parallels here are represented by what are called autoimmune disorders, which are illnesses characterized by a dysfunction of the immune system in which antibodies are formed against cells of a person's own body.

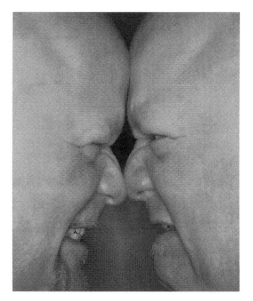

It is quite obvious one of the most salient aspects of the present illness is the way in which anger, violence, and abuse are destroying the fabric of our lives, quite like autoimmune agents. Do we, as a culture, and as a planet, have an autoimmune disease? Will it simply grow worse as the stress in the system continues to increase?

Probably.

The function of the immune system is to mount attacks against invading organisms and foreign material that could support infection. The reaction of the U.S. to radical Islamic terrorism involves the intelligence community and the military. We seek out terrorists who are trying to attack us, and launch attacks against them. Here we have humanity attacking humanity, each side certain that it is in the right, that "God/ Allah is on our side," and that the "Other" is the "Axis of Evil" (or the "Great Satan," depending upon your political persuasion.

Our autoimmune disorder is also clearly visible at domestic levels within our own culture. It seems every day there is another story about someone shooting up a school, or killing their estranged wife and kids, or sexually abusing a child.

Dysfunctional, Disintegrating Families

One of the basic laws of survival in social animals is that the family must maintain its integrity, and the members must protect each other. This theme carries on from the primitive beehive, through the wolf pack, to the level of the human tribe or community.

Good night, Mommy.
Good night, Daddy.

In our culture, we flagrantly disobey this law of survival. We abandon our elders, neglect our children, and fight our relatives. In a sense then, we as families are attacking ourselves.

We say we believe in marriage, but half of our marriages end in divorce.

We claim to love our children, but we embrace the philosophy of the 24/7 "work ethic." It's a bitter irony that many people end up sacrificing the core values of the family in order to support the family.

We say we love our parents, but only 9 percent of us are willing (or able) to make space for them in our homes.

Given the above, it's not very far-fetched to opine that we, as a species, have developed a kind of an autoimmune disorder. A crucial function of the immune system is differentiation. A healthy immune system has the capability to determine accurately what is friend and what is foe, what is to be nurtured and what is to be attacked. To a shocking extent, we have lost this capability to differentiate.

Abusive Relationships

The examples of "man's inhumanity to man" are pandemic. Race, color, age, gender, height, weight, nationality, income level, education, political affiliation, religion, even favored sports team – it almost seems that any time people can find differences between them, they find a way to turn this difference into a "reason" (excuse?) to abuse each other.

That abuse may take the form of thought, word, or unkind (even violent) deed. The travesties that take place in our professional sports arenas, involving abuse by both fans and athletes, are only the latest shameful form this tendency takes.

Many of our human institutions, from the "honor killing" of the tribal societies to the penal system of the United States, reflect how this abuse can become institutionalized and an accepted part of the culture.

Could it be true that our Western culture is based upon relationships that are fundamentally abusive?

For many years the U.S. was the model of freedom and fairness, the "leader of the Free World" – but much of the rest of the world sees our Western culture as aggressive externally and repressive internally. International polls named the president of the U.S. as the biggest threat to world peace!

And at home we repress minorities, yet as long as we will not admit to ourselves how repressive we are, we'll never be able to fix the problem – much less live up to the highest ideals of our nation. The failure of our government to respond to the needs of the poor, mostly black residents of New Orleans in the face of Hurricane Katrina was a dramatic underscoring of our lack of concern for them.

We are not caring for ourselves, but pursuing policies that hurt us. In a way, it is like an autoimmune process.

Diagnosis #3 – Global Cancer

Could it be that we are afflicted with a kind of cancer?

A cancer occurs when one group of cells within the body, or one cell on its own, decides it's going to "do its own thing," and ignore the needs of the body as a whole. It begins to grow, and its only goal is to consume more fuel and acquire more mass for itself. Freed of the regulation of the individual, it becomes virtually immortal. This malignancy saps life energy and produces dysfunction, disease, pain, and eventually death of the whole.

Metastatic Social Malignancy

Organizations, such as governments, corporations, and religions can act like malignancies too. Like most cells in the body, many organizations are (more or less) honest, fair, and promote the human health and well-being of their citizens, members, and those they interact with. But like some cells, certain groups may morph into selfish, aggressive, energy-sapping cancer-like growths.

Take governments, for example. The quality of government depends upon the quality of the administration currently in power.

Sometimes, a "malignant" administration comes into power in a country, and the character of the government changes drastically. As it grows, its destructive character metastasizes, spreading into the corporations, religions, the military, cults, PACs (political action committees), special interest groups, and even terrorists who find a way to create symbiosis with it.

Human Resources

Or consider the corporation that is expressing its intrinsic ability to become cancerous. A corporation is an immortal, nonhuman entity that has been given equal rights with living, feeling human beings. If its directors become greedy, it begins to behave like a cancer. Through lobbyists and campaign contributions, it begins to alter the decisions of our elected officials. Soon one of its former employees manages to become embedded in the government at a position where he can directly make decisions that benefit the corporation and its cohorts. And, as Mussolini taught us:

Business + Government = Fascism

Insanity in individuals is something rare – but in groups, parties, nations and epochs, it is the rule.
– Friedrich Nietzsche

Instead of being good, sharing entities like normal cells, cancer cells exhibit what looks like sociopathic behavior. People with what psychiatrists refer to as Antisocial Personality Disorder single-mindedly pursue their own wills and desires without any consideration for other people (or groups) and without reference to conventional morality. Cancers behave that way in the body, ignoring the rights of other cells and the organism as a whole.

It's easy to imagine what a sociopathic government, religion, or corporation could do. And it's hard to forget what they have done in the past [1].

The Metastasis of a Corporatocracy

Our global cancer has metastasized, spread, and appears in different forms in different places. We can see this pattern especially clearly when we

www.aiga.org/resources/content/4/9/0/0/
images/AIGA_Corporation_flag.jpg

---

[1]   See *The Corporation* (2004), which hits hard at the crimes and misdemeanors of the corporate world.

look at the behavior of corporations and governments.

For example, to the degree that our government serves corporations (oil and defense contractors come to mind), our government functions as an extension of corporations themselves. Elections are won disproportionately with legal and illegal bribes called "contributions," commonly from corporate interests. Subsequently, corporations hire surrogate sycophants (lobbyists) to remind our legislators: "Who's your daddy?"

Let's not just pick on big business. Religious zealots, PACs, labor unions, foreign governments (overtly and covertly), cults, and powerful NGOs (non-governmental organizations) use similar insidious infiltration tactics to gain control of governments to serve their own self-interests. But remember, no matter how much damage these cancers do, in the final analysis they are only the symptoms of a deeper systemic imbalance. We must find the source of these cancers so we can prevent, as well as eliminate them.

What Makes a Cancer a Cancer?

Currently, most scientists believe that cells become cancerous due to changes in their chromosomes. Located in the cell's nucleus, the chromosomes are part of the cell's "brain," its control center. Healthy cells submit to the wise guidance of higher levels of system, so that they continue to further the interests and life of the organism as a whole.

When complex and powerful systems begin to operate in the absence of this Wise Guidance, they begin to operate outside the limits set by the higher level of system. When this happens at the level of the family, or organization (Cosa Nostra), or nation, a virulent entity is created. And by presenting themselves through their PR and advertising agencies, as well as being friendly and helpful, they avoid detection by our societal immune system. When the body's immune system learns to identify the cancerous nature of a cell, it can react and heal itself. Perhaps we, as a culture, can do the same thing. The alternative is unthinkable.

Diagnosis #4 – Global Parasitic Infection

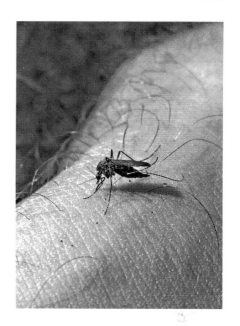

Looked at as a whole, over the past few centuries, our planet and its living things seem to be afflicted with a kind of "parasitosis." Although the actual nature of this parasite is not immediately obvious, its effects are. The quality of the air, the water, and the soil is gradually vanishing. Animal life around the world is suffering, and the quality and diversity of human culture is declining.

Parasitic Pleomorphism

Just as the symptoms of diabetes appear in different organs and in different forms, this global parasite expresses itself in many different outward appearances. We can see its expression in the usual suspects: corporations, governments, extremist religions, HMOs, cults, banks, trade unions and guilds, and NGOs.

Let me emphasize that I am not accusing all of the above organizations of being parasites. Far from it, indeed, many, if not most, of these entities enjoy symbiotic and harmonious relationships with humans, our cultures, and Earth. We must always remember that symbiotic good or parasitic evil is not an intrinsic property of the entity itself. My point is that any such entity has the potential of becoming malignantly self-righteous or mindlessly amoral when it is not under what I call the "Wise Guidance" of the human spirit.

"The Machine" as Parasite

I am not completely satisfied with the name I have chosen to represent this parasitic entity, but, for the purposes of framing the issue, let's call this theoretical global parasite "The Machine," whether we are talking about big financial institutions such as those that led to the economic crisis, big oil companies, or any such big "limited liability" entity. Here are three reasons for doing this:

- Many of the main "organs" of this parasite are real-world machines and computers.
- Even though they are managed by human beings, corporations, governments, and other organizations often behave like machines.
- The parasite "thinks" and behaves the way machines (and computers) think and behave.

Of course, there is an incredible variety of machines, and many perform very worthwhile and necessary functions. It is only when certain machines and machine-like entities work in concert to commit immoral or amoral parasitic acts against us, our culture, or our earth that I will refer to the global parasite as The Machine.

To understand what I'm talking about, consider this: There is a certain set of operating principles that constitute a virtual "mindset." That mindset is common to all machines. A machine does the specific tasks it was built to do, for as long as it can, for as long as it is turned on. And that is all it does; it doesn't adapt itself to any other jobs. (That's why we have landfills overflowing with computer equipment that cost billions of dollars. Because the equipment is "obsolete," it has no way to be recycled into the system. Anybody want to buy an Apple II computer?)

What's more, a machine doesn't care who's operating its controls, and it has no mercy for anything that gets in its way. It does not care about the feelings or well-being of any living thing. A machine does not care.

If I fall off my tractor, it may roll over me and go on to smash down the wall of my house – and it doesn't care a whit. It feels no pain, no remorse, no shame, no embarrassment. Nor does my chainsaw mind chewing off my index finger. I, on the other hand, am feeling all sorts of unpleasant things just imagining these events.

According to this nomenclature, a cellphone is a machine. Corporations are machines. Even the Catholic Church is a machine. The news media taken as a whole is a machine. Hollywood, Madison Avenue, and Wall Street are machines too. The government is a machine, as are its political parties.

A building is a machine. A TV is a machine. All human institutions – families, schools, laws, the military, charities, clubs, and prisons – turn out to function as machines, programmed to carry out certain activities and not others.

If you kill someone, rob a bank, or commit some other such crime, you will trigger certain mechanisms within that machine that we call "society." Police investigators and SWAT teams will hunt you down and capture or kill you. They do not evaluate whether or not you deserve to be killed or captured, they simply do as they are ordered, the same way a gun does when you pull the trigger. If you are captured, other machines will put you on trial, convict you, and place you in a barren room behind steel bars for a long time. Or asphyxiate you with cyanide gas. This is a social machine in action, presumably serving the greater good of the population.

In other words, a machine is just a mechanical system, and a mechanical system is just a machine. It should be obvious how dangerous it would be if the Machine functioned as a global parasite, for it has no consciousness or conscience. It has no soul.

MachineThink

At their most sophisticated level, some machines are capable of a basic mechanical logic when they are controlled by computers. Computers, of course, are machines too. Some computerized machines can be created to operate autonomously and do wondrous things like vacuum our living rooms or explore Mars.

Other computerized machines can be launched from a submarine 1,000 miles away and autonomously propel and navigate themselves at low altitude over uneven terrain to ring your doorbell just before they blow you up. Perhaps what is most fascinating – and frightening – about computerized machines is they must reduce everything they do to a series of billions of decisions choosing between one or zero. That's what digital logic is all about: ones and zeroes. On-off. Either-or. It's what I call "MachineThink."

If a machine makes the "wrong" choice (in terms of doing things that benefit human beings), it ends up behaving as if it has a sociopathic personality disorder. Obviously, in the wrong hands and lacking wise guidance, The Machine can suck humanity of its energy, feelings, and life. This is when it is clearly a local expression of the global parasite. The problems machines create for us is that so many of them are being operated without wise guidance.

Good Machines Gone Bad

We all have machines we know and love. For instance, I love my family structure, my community, my profession, and I even love my laptop computer on which I am writing these words.

When loving human spirit guides the use of machines, we can derive great happiness and magnificent benefits from our interaction with them. A jetliner can take a mother to a joyful reunion with a child she has not seen for five years. But that same plane, if it does not have a loving human at the controls, can crash into a New York skyscraper, killing and injuring thousands of innocent people. The plane does not know or care.

Taken to a corporate level, just the negligent use of The Machine can wreak havoc. On December 3, 1984, 8,000 people in Bhopal, India, were gassed to death after a catastrophic chemical leak at a Union Carbide pesticide plant. The accident-related death toll has since risen to 20,000. More than 100,000 people were left severely disabled in the world's worst-ever industrial disaster. None of the six safety systems at the plant were functional at the time, and Union Carbide's own documents prove the company cut corners on safety and maintenance to save money.

Today, 20 years after, toxins still contaminate the Bhopal water supply, contributing to an epidemic of cancers, birth defects, and other afflictions. According to the victims and Greenpeace, full restitution and medical relief to the victims and survivors have not been made. And no one has been held accountable on criminal charges of negligent homicide.

Bottom-line MachineThink: It's cheaper to pay millions to an army of lawyers than to clean up the poison, assist the survivors, or hold anyone accountable for mass murder.

Kill or maim one person and go to jail. Kill or maim thousands and get invited to the White House to receive a medal of honor. The parasite has infected our values.

Wise Guidance, Human Guidance

Wise guidance requires the use of a mode of thinking that values human beings over inanimate things like rocks, dollars, ideas, and goals. When we fail to provide ongoing human guidance for a corporate Machine, it's like having a brain without a prefrontal cortex. Without consciousness and conscientiousness, the corporate Machine is not likely to make the choices consistent with our most desired future. The goal of a corporation is to make money, regardless of the collateral damage to humanity and the environment.

Individual human beings must discover how to create and

manifest a compelling image of the future they want for themselves if they are to achieve health and success. So, too, must corporations, governments, religions, and other entities if we are to have a healthy world. These Machines must develop an image that represents optimal health of the populations (e.g., stockholders or religious followers) they serve, as well as for humanity and the planet as a whole, or we will have big trouble.

Planning for an optimal, high-quality future requires a different mode of thinking than digital MachineThink. Only human beings are able to make decisions that are wise. Only humans can appreciate, care, love, and have empathy for other living things and the entire ecosystem of Earth. Wise thinking cares about the future of our children, and cherishes relationships and our belonging to something greater than ourselves.

Thinking about Thinking

A Machine without wise guidance, caring, and love, defaults to MachineThink – a very polar and dualistic either-or operational process. In our culture, MachineThink is often prized and considered "objective, unemotional, scientific." And remember, this kind of thinking is something that both machines and humans can do.

There is, however, another fundamentally different way of thinking that is expressly human. Machines cannot do it, although they can sometimes mimic it, like the computers that write poetry (uniformly uninspired) or use complex formulae, heuristic algorithms, and neural networks to approximate artificial intelligence.

This kind of thinking – call it organic, or analog thinking – always looks to higher orders of systems for guidance. Unlike machines, analog thinkers can grasp both either-or and both-and logic. Moreover, with analog minds, we human beings know right from wrong, and value taking responsibility for our actions.

If Union Carbide had had the wise governance of human spirit, Bhopal might never have happened, and the victims might not still, 20 years later, be trying to receive compensation.

In summation, this parasite functions according to a particular paradigm, or way of approaching problems. It is the use of the kind of logic that machines use, and it is done by mechanical machines as well as by many human institutions. It is characterized by a lack of wise human guidance.

Diagnosis #5 – Addicted to Violence

Can violence be an addiction? You bet. Let's take a look at the meanings of the words "addict" and "addiction," and I think you'll see why. And if the prior diagnoses we have considered have been somewhat abstract and overly metaphorical, this diagnosis is quite literal.

The Current Definition of Addiction

When I was growing up, an addict was portrayed as some kind of filthy, dissipated, underfed heroin user – a needle junkie lying in an alley or in a louse-infested flophouse, living only for his next fix. Or in the case of a "drunken bum" or "wino," his next drink.

Since then, the definition of addict has changed quite a bit. People speak of being addicted to sugar, alcohol, nicotine, computers – even "addicted to love." Essentially, addict and addiction are terms whose definitions

have grown to include anybody who is *dependent on anything (or multiple things) to the detriment of themselves or others.*

In the addiction field, health professionals use the label "addict" for a people who continue the use of drugs (including alcohol and steroids), even though they are causing significant problems in their lives. Significant problems include anything that constitutes a threat to the person's health, happiness, relationships, children, or work performance.

We've even developed the term "co-dependent" to describe a person who is addicted to an addict. A co-dependent is somehow addicted to enabling addicts to continue to maintain their style of life – and to even support – their addictions. Co-dependents let their own lives be destroyed rather than face up to their own addiction of co-dependency. Battered women (and men) are often examples of extreme co-dependency.

Some addicts knowingly behave in ways they don't want to behave, or would rather not behave – but they continue to use their drugs of choice anyway. On the other hand, some addicts are unaware of their addiction. But most addicts are in active denial of their problems. In fact, addiction is often called "a disease of denial."

But whether the addict is aware, unaware, or in denial, is irrelevant – addiction is a form of violence on ourselves and on others.

And it doesn't stop there. Any activity that a person, family, community, corporation, religion, nation, or system (machine) engages in that results in harm to the system as a whole (including the ecosystem) is an addiction.

Our built-in co-dependence is obvious. We watch the addiction tear up people's lives, then wag our fingers and tch-tch, while doing nothing to either intervene or require ourselves to make amends. As Einstein pointed out, those who sit and idly watch as a crime is committed are as guilty as the person committing it. Silence is the voice of complicity.

The Many Faces of Violence

Now that we have a definition for addiction, let's look at what I mean by Violence with a capital "V." When I talk about Violence, I mean not only the most obvious physical kind of violence, but also all the other kinds of violence that are tolerated when we abuse each other or abuse ourselves.

Violence is paraded in front of us on movie and television screens, in the news we watch and the novels we read – and it ranges from the "special effects" kind of physical violence to the nasty little acts of social violence that take place on our sitcoms and soap operas. It happens in live venues too. "Professional" athletes engage in brawls with fans as well as each other, musicians get murdered on stage, and stand-up comedians say things that cut to the bone.

Teasing someone until it hurts, stealing from someone, destroying a person's reputation, emotionally manipulating someone, being a sexual predator, or a financial manipulator – all these involve a kind of violence. Selling people a product that you know will not be what they want, without informing them of that, is Violence.

When we look at our lives, some very interesting answers arise – if we are seriously and honestly willing to look at the abusive things that we say and do. Often we don't respect or acknowledge others. That's an abuse of omission. Clearly, such behaviors constitute only a subtle form of violence, but they qualify as Violence nevertheless.

And then there's the abuse of commission. Why do we call someone names, criticize, blame, attack, ostracize, punitively ignore, or vent our spleen on people? Ultimately, we have to say because it relieves a tension that is in us. Still, although we may feel better for a time after having done it, later we may come to deeply regret it – and yet we'll probably do it again.

These abuses have a horribly negative effect on us, and on the people and the world around us. In other words, it really doesn't make our lives better. It is Violence, and it is an addiction.

The Denial of Violence

We are in denial of the Violence we do. Just as the typical addict is in denial of the true extent of his dysfunction, we don't see the Violence or take responsibility for it. What's more, we don't act to change it, in spite of all the great tools we have.

Look at the world around us! In spite of our extraordinary brains, in spite of the rich and deeply compassionate religious teachings that have been bequeathed to us by such wise ones as Jesus, Mohammed, and the Buddha, we still commit verbal and physical Violence. Especially those of us who have the privilege of living in "the land of the free and the home of the brave," we are doing a terrible job of getting rid of Violence.

Our culture is based on a biphasic, or bipolar cycle of conflict and tension followed by relief. This leads us to a belief that enjoyment and happiness are the result of pain being relieved. The result is a failure to experience the highest forms of joy, the joy of simply being, and leads to our creating more problems, so we can enjoy the relief when we solve them. The collateral damage can be huge.

Even our music is tension and relief (e.g., the tension of a dominant seventh chord resolving to the root chord). The movies set up a conflict, often a brutal killing, and then relief is offered when the villain is righteously hacked to bloody pieces by our hero. As we feel the relief, we come again to believe that winning the conflict is what it's all about – that somehow this brings happiness.

This cycle underlies almost all advertising: You are a loser (tension) because you have dandruff. Buy our product and the girls will flock around you (relief). It is the story underneath all our movies (boy gets girl, boy loses girl, boy gets girl back again). It all panders to the lowest common denominators of our emotions. We are encouraged to feel the self-inflicted violence of embarrassment and shame, and then the false relief obtained by buying the product. What a pity that we don't understand the principles of Greek theater, which had, as an intentional goal, to help us overcome our baser instincts. The Classical hero models an error we must be careful never to make. Shakespeare understood these principles. Macbeth, Hamlet, King Lear, and Othello are classic examples of heroes gone wrong because of their inability to understand and modulate the intrinsic polarity of their emotions. We are hard put to find such wisdom in the top selling movies and TV shows of our time.

Unfortunately, most of us just don't get it. Instead, our tools of communication, the so-called media, actually get us to participate in the Violence. Now that the conditioning is set up, we can respond violently, as a nation, by supporting decisions that do untold Violence to the planet (pollution) and its inhabitants (war). Thousands of young men and women die fighting, hundreds of thousands of innocent people get killed, the psyches of our surviving soldiers are permanently traumatized – while we cheer them on.

The underlying message in our media – movies, television, news, and books, too – is never to make the mistake of not having superior firepower. We must never hesitate to shoot first and ask questions later. This goes for war, police work, business, and personal relationships. "Go ahead, make my day," "Bring 'em on," are the words our presidents say, echoing the macho heroes of our films.

The (Nearly) Invisible Violence

There are about 30 civil wars actively being fought, when last I checked. Tens of thousands of children are being starved to death for political ends in Sudan. But we're all so doggoned busy trying to make ends meet, we don't have time to even keep up with the kind of global tragedies that we (as a race of human beings) are responsible for. Instead, we are enthralled with the sordid little details of the latest child abduction, brutal rape or scandal du jour. Legions of Paparazzi swarm around every well-known figure, eager to slake our insatiable appetite for celebrity gossip.

And then there's the Violence being done to the ecosystem. The statistics are dreadfully dramatic in terms of the number of species being lost, depletion of natural resources, and global climatic changes, among other things.

We Americans are especially greedy and wasteful. We use 25 percent of the world's energy resources although we only have 4 percent of the population. Moreover, we're producing 35 percent of the pollution that's affecting everyone. And on top of that, we are the world's biggest arms dealer – we sell the weapons that allow people to wreak Violence on each other in this country and around the world. We've even sold arms to our enemies!

Incredibly, it's all done under the protection of our laws and their loopholes. If this isn't Violence and denial, what is?

Beyond "The Blame Game" – We are not Responsible

By responsible, I mean response-able – having the capacity, authority to respond. Is there anyone who doesn't feel there's too much Violence in the world right now? Is there anyone who doesn't feel personally at risk?

We live in a kind of MAD (mutually assured destruction) environment, not unlike that during the Cold War between the United States and the Soviet Union. Nobody's safe in a world given the democratization of weapons of mass destruction. Most experts predict that it is only a matter of time before Third-World terrorists or rogue nations acquire – and use – First-World NBC (nuclear, biological, and chemical) weapons of mass destruction. And our response? Why, sifting through straws in search of a needle, of course!

Violence as Fun

Let's face it: Violence can be fun. Violence is the core of most video games, for instance. Sometimes, it just feels so good to get angry. I mean, to get really furious! Just let it all out! "Tear that jerk a new one." You may feel better afterwards, but the objects of your Violence don't.

We perpetrate Violence on other social classes, on other families, on other races, on other people in our household, and on ourselves. And there is really never any justification for doing it. It never solves the problem, it just makes us feel better at the moment. And it nearly always makes the problem worse. Yelling at me is highly unlikely to improve our communication, no matter how correct your words are.

Perhaps, if you're a more "enlightened" individual, you can get your Violence vicariously through television, for instance. The violence in our action, science fiction and other genres is undeniable. And even in our so-called comedies: from *Friends* to *All in the Family* to *Everybody Loves Raymond*; it's all vicious, cutting sarcasm. It may be funny on TV – but in real life, such verbal Violence ruins lives and destroys families. And you can be sure the put-downs used on TV last night are repeated in high schools and around water coolers nationwide the next morning!

And yet we keep doing it. Because we're addicted to Violence.

So, this relationship we have with Violence constitutes an addiction, because all addictions are diseases of denial. That's basically it. The behavior that you're doing is just the tool that you're using to make you feel good while you ignore the truth that's staring you in the face. You need something to keep you doped up so that you don't look at the truth. Why do I keep thinking of George Orwell?

Little Violences, Big Consequences

One of the most common reasons given by high school kids who go on a shooting rampage is that they were teased and felt disrespected. The Violence children do to each other is incredibly common. The everyday teasing, bullying, lying, stealing, gunfire, gangs, and other social and physical Violence make the lives of some kids a living hell.

As a child, I was always told to "fight your own battles," "stand up for yourself." Living in New York City, it was the "law of the jungle on the streets," "kill or be killed." And my suspicion is that, although it may not be as visible as it was in my circumstances, a similar kind of child-on-child Violence goes on wherever you might be.

For some reason, we tolerate this kind of thing in children, this interpersonal Violence. The excuses adults often give for allowing this kind of Violence are, "It teaches kids to function in the 'real' world," or "Boys will be boys."

By saying these things, we are implicitly sanctioning the behavior we say we are trying to prevent. We may suppose ourselves to be attempting to deal with it by catching and punishing (often violently) some of the little perpetrators, but what we are actually doing is training a new generation of Violence addicts. Children are genetically programmed to imitate the views of their parents and culture. "Do what I say, not what I do" just doesn't cut it.

Managing by Doing Nothing

Clearly, we have a problem, and if we can address it wisely, we have the capacity – theoretically – to do something about it. Yet we do not. Each of us somehow justifies what we're doing – whether it's open warfare, torture of prisoners, racial or religious intolerance, or even a defensive linebacker taking a cheap shot at the opposing quarterback in a football game. And the list just goes on and on.

We say we're doing something for peace by giving a little money to this or that organization, "signing" an Internet petition, or investing in powerful weapons and high-tech defensive systems to try to prevent "evildoers" from carrying out more terrorist attacks. Indeed, some of us may spend many hours a week intensively working to do something about stopping the Violence. But some of us have hardly any time left over to work for peace because we are working so hard to afford our gas-guzzling SUVs, our luxurious homes, nannies and private school for our kids, the latest fashions, 60-inch plasma screens, and other stuff we've been taught to believe we absolutely need to be happy and "successful."

Often we're satisfied to let our elected officials do the work for us. As a counter to the sarcastic, "We have the best government money can buy," there is a problem: politicians can be bought, but good government can't.

Corporate Violence

It is shamefully easy to come up with a "laundry list" of the behaviors of CEOs, corporations and self-serving special interest groups that have resulted in the destruction of the fortunes and lives of individuals, communities, nations, and the ecosphere as a whole. Not necessarily on purpose, or even with awareness – it's just collateral damage, "externalizing costs" in corporate speak. The recent parade of greedy, dishonest, financial fat cats and corporate criminals is testimony to the degree to which this has become a way of life. In addition, evidence suggests that this is just the tip of the iceberg. And yet we still let them pour huge amounts of money into the election campaigns of our public officials – "bought and paid for" politicians dare not bite the hands that feed them. Thus, they govern and legislate to the benefit of the big money special interests. These special interest groups and corporations all too often are just machines lacking wise guidance. And so, our government perpetuates and supports the Violence done by these corporate machines on our behalf. The United States committed unspeakable genocidal attacks on Native Americans because we wanted their land. We wanted their land so we could import African slaves to work on plantations, helping to strip a continent of its youth and heritage, from which it has still not recovered. Big business supported these atrocities – and business was good [2].

Likewise, throughout its history, the U.S. has covertly and overtly engineered the violent overthrow of foreign governments – and supported the regimes of vicious dictatorships – because underneath all the politics and rhetoric, Violence is good for business. War, it has been said, is how Americans learn Geography.

And are we not complicit in this Violence every time we buy cheap bananas from a U.S.-backed dictatorship, purchase a running shoe made by virtual slave labor and 10-year-old children, or fill up our cars with gasoline made from oil from a country we've bribed – or invaded?

Perhaps President Calvin Coolidge said it best:

The business of government is business.

---

[2]   see *The Corporation* (2004).

116

The Power of the People

The addict commonly sees himself as a victim – what he does, he explains, is only a reaction to the wrong being done him by some external agent over which he imagines he has no control (denial). The victim mentality is endemic these days. We feel victimized by governmental agencies (the IRS comes to mind), faceless corporations, hate groups, religious fanatics, the news media, and of course, those old standbys, used car salesmen and women. Unless and until we give up the victim mentality, we will continue to be helpless victims.

The truth is we don't realize (or maybe, it's remember) how much power we really do have. When's the last time you read the Declaration of Independence or the Constitution of the United States of America? There is another way, as demonstrated by the movement championed by Martin Luther King Jr. – the determined, unrelenting, nonviolent protests and marches of millions of Americans resulted in the breakthrough Civil Rights Act of 1964. Similarly, massive peace marches and sit-ins – again by millions of Americans – helped to end the Vietnam War.

> *All that is necessary for the triumph of evil is for*
> *good men and women to do nothing.*
> – Albert Einstein

Think about it: We stopped a war!

We did it before, and we can do it again. There was a brief time when peace and love – not shock and awe – existed in our collective consciousness. We could choose to remember that time, and bring those values and nonviolent strategies back to our world. *We could if we really wanted to.*

The ultimate goal of this book is to inspire you to believe in your own power – and to help you inspire everyone you touch – to come together as we never have before. We must build a network

117

of trust and action. We must make people aware of the true meaning of Violence and how it harms us individually, collectively, and globally. We will come back to a further consideration of violence and modern ways we might deal with it in a later chapter.

Diagnosis #6 – Spiritual Starvation / Malnutrition

Could we be dealing with a nutritional disorder? Lets consider that our present illness might possibly be the result of a kind of spiritual starvation.

To a remarkable degree, most of us are failing in the all-important task of seeing what is good in ourselves, in our communities, and in our world – and nurturing it. On the other hand, we are also failing to determine those things that are truly dangerous to our health or survival, and effectively neutralize them.

These two failures seem to arise as a result of spiritual abuse so many people have experienced in childhood. At all times, the competent parent, teacher, or caregiver should see the beauty and goodness the child is attempting to express – and to communicate love, understanding, compassion, respect, and reverence for this emerging spirit, even when disciplining.

To fail to treat a child with love and respect is as much an abuse as it is to place a young plant in a darkened room. We would be denying this young spirit the light it needs to reach its potential in the same way.

Today's world suffers from a certain blindness. We fail to see that every person has a spiritual system that guides and determines their experiences, their behaviors, their beliefs, and their lives. Because of this blindness, we are denied the opportunity to nurture them – to help them realize their deepest selves, and to create true personal excellence, success, satisfaction, fulfillment in their lives.

At the level of our families, we fail to honor the family spirit and ancestors, with the result that we often end up disrespecting each other. We spend too little time with our children and pay too little attention to factors that tend to produce violence. We discontinue breastfeeding prematurely, and neglect our responsibility to protect our kids from violent movies and those with sexist content, as well as other negative inputs.

> *The best thing to spend on your children is your time.*
> – Louise Hart

At the planetary level/environmental level, we are not nurturing our forests and diverse biological species. We are not learning from experience and eliminating those ways of treating the environment that are producing such problems as pollution, global warming, and depletion of the ozone layer.

In our planetary culture, we are stretched between the poles of amoral atheism and intolerant fundamentalism. In the name of Jesus and Mohammed, two men thoroughly committed to peace, we declare holy war. Oblivious to the contradiction in our own behavior, we are all too ready to condemn others for the same sin.

One of the most common factors in all spiritual teachings is their focus on the importance of love. Our lack (or disregard) of spiritual guidance may be seen, therefore, as a lack of love. Perhaps it would be more accurate to refer to this diagnosis as a "love deficiency."

> *In the last 1,000 years, Christianity, Judaism and Islam ... have been choosing sides and each has fostered the view that there are two worlds, one good – which is us – and one less good – which is everyone else.*
> – Craig Barnes

Questions to Ponder

1. Which diagnosis, in your opinion, seems to come closest to describing the overall problem with our world, as you see it?

2. Can you think of other Diagnoses that should be added to the list?

Notes to Self

Diagnosis : Take Home Messages

• Stress responses can cause individuals — and governments — to act in ways that merely relieve the symptoms, ways that may relieve the immediate pain, but cause serious backlash later.

• Dysfunctional families, abusive relationships, anger, and violence are destroying the fabric of our lives like auto-immune disorders in which antibodies are formed against the cells of one's own body.

• Corporations, governments, and organizations have become selfish, aggressive, energy-sapping cancer-like growths.

• Many human institutions operate like machines, lacking wise, compassionate guidance consistent with our most desired future.

• Human beings and their institutions must discover how to create and manifest a compelling image of the future they want for themselves to achieve health — individual and global.

• Despite our extraordinary brains and the rich and deeply compassionate religious teachings of such wise men as Jesus, Mohammed, Moses, and the Buddha, we remain addicted to violence.

• We've become blind to the spiritual dimension not only of individuals and families, but of the environment and of the planet itself.

CHAPTER 8

DISCUSSION OF CASE AND THE SYSTEMIC NATURE OF THE DISEASE

What we are doing to the forests of the world is but a mirror reflection of what we are doing to ourselves and to one another.
– Mohandas Gandhi (1869-1948)

By way of review: even a cursory examination reveals many symptoms of severe imbalance in the functioning of the culture of our planet, all the way from the 170 million people killed in wars in the last century to the current epidemic of stress and tension in our personal lives and the so-called "War On Terror." There are, however, discernable patterns that I have presented as "diagnoses." Diagnoses are, in a sense, formulas that help us to track the core issues at the source of the fundamental imbalance. Each diagnosis is a kind of lens that may help us better comprehend these deeper facets of the systemic issues at work here. Our challenge is to reach towards this deeper level in search of that which is the source of these symptoms and syndromes.

Deeper Diagnosis – The Bleeding Man

Consider the man who came to the emergency room bleeding from the mouth. Stopping bleeding is obviously a good idea, but only a fool would try to do this by attempting to pack the mouth with gauze to stem the flow.

In fact, as the doctor on call quickly noted, the blood was quite black in color, so its source was probably the stomach. So the symptom of bleeding led the doctor to wisely get an X-ray of the stomach. An ulcer was discovered, it was called the "disease," and the patient was prescribed acid-reducing medications and evaluated for possible ulcer surgery. This is the end of the search for many mainstream medical practitioners.

In this case, however, a few more questions were asked, leading to the discovery that this particular gentleman had been drinking large quantities of whiskey and treating the resultant hangovers with large doses of aspirin – behavior that would cause ulcer in just about anyone. So stopping the bleeding with antacids and surgery will actually be treating only the symptoms, for he will soon be drinking and taking more aspirin.

In this case, however, he received a deeper (and somewhat more appropriate) diagnosis of "Behavioral Disorder, Alcohol Abuse with secondary Gastric Ulcer."

Our physician, however, was not satisfied with even this, and he inquired even more deeply. He wanted to know more about the motivations that lay beneath this drinking behavior. He discovered that the drinking problem had ensued after his wife had discovered that he had been unfaithful and left him, taking the children with her. The pain of that loss was more than he could have imagined, and multiplied by the intense guilt he felt for causing his wife's deep despair was too much for him to handle. His only solace was the bottle.

The proper treatment, then, was to provide him with the tools he needs to relieve his acute stress, help him understand the deeper causes of his behavior, and provide him with a way to grow from his experience and become a wiser, better person. The freedom from alcohol and the improved emotional balance would then decrease the stress on the gastric mucosa, facilitate a healing of the ulcer, and prevent the formation of new ulcers – at a fraction of the cost of medications and surgery, and far suffering!

A Deeper Diagnosis for the Planet

Similarly, our job now is not merely to select among the various diagnoses, but to determine if there might be a deeper source of all of them. In looking at these diagnoses, we see some common factors; there's a certain mindset, a certain attitude that can be recognized in every case.

Consider, for example, how otherwise caring Americans sat idly by and allowed slavery at home and the Holocaust in Europe. Or the prevalence of sexism, religious intolerance, child and spousal abuse, greed and fraud in business – examples of abuses we see every day - where the lack of sensitivity and caring expressed in our relationships is obvious.

Sure, we have tried to fix things, but when we look at what our attempts have involved, we see a pattern that is frighteningly common – a tendency to react rather than to respond. We see this in the field of medicine, in our government's approach to foreign policy and poverty, in the criminal justice system, and at most other levels of our culture.

What I think we can see is that there is a certain way of framing the problem that, while providing only temporary symptomatic relief, actually creates problems that are often worse than the one we set out to deal with.

The Vicious Circle – Making an Intelligent Decision

To understand this problem and how it may be corrected, let's take a look at how human beings go about making decisions, and how this may be improved upon.

Once the evidence has been gathered, a response must be decided upon – a response that will be based upon beliefs and values. Our goal is to examine that particular framing, attitude, and resulting mode of choosing that leads us to create more problems than we resolve, at every level, from the personal to the planetary.

It is difficult to see the picture when you are inside the frame.
– Folk Wisdom

An excellent example is the proverbial welfare conundrum. Around the middle of the last century, our reaction to poverty was to provide welfare assistance. The rules were that if you got a job, you got no more assistance. The problem was that the kind of entry-level jobs open to these people often paid less than they were receiving in welfare payments – and the jobs were usually unpleasant to boot. So people stayed home, and had babies that grew up thinking the welfare lifestyle was normal. The framers of the law did not understand how to take a systems approach.

A "health insurance" plan I know of was willing to provide $3,000 for a diabetic to have his toe amputated, but not $150 for an appointment with a podiatrist to prevent the deterioration of a mild infection to the point that the amputation would be needed.

Another example is provided by the "Security and Prison-building Industry," one of the fastest growing segments of our economy. The increasing income now available to this industry provides money to buy legislators who are "tough on crime" (e.g., sending a casual marijuana smoker to jail for many years). But, since prisons are prime breeding grounds for criminality, the result of this is that minor offenders have years to learn to become hardened criminals, and to make underworld contacts. Result: we get more crooks and more prisons – more money for the industry and more crime for us.

126

Once again, the problem here is the failure to address the system as a whole, and huge profits for those whose business is the warehousing of "criminals," especially African-Americans[1].

Why haven't otherwise intelligent people realized the inadvisability of this approach before? I believe it is primarily due to the fragmentation of the system, and the lack of tools to make it obvious how inappropriate such "symptomatic solutions" are. And why are we able to see it more clearly now? Because we are now living in a new world, one of much greater availability of information, and of tools to analyze it. As a result, the many pieces of the puzzle are coming together: we have the knowledge, technology, connectivity, wisdom teachings, and information of all cultures at our fingertips. At last, we can see the whole.

The splitting of the atom has changed everything,
save our mode of thinking, and thus we drift
towards unparalleled catastrophe.
– Albert Einstein

Many things have changed. Together they add up to an extraordinary opportunity to reconceptualize our culture and our world, and reverse the trend noted by Einstein. Only 40 years ago, to find info on yoga or Tibetan yoga, or history of Qatar, or a biography on Lincoln's vice president was very difficult or impossible. Now it is as close as the computer. Thus, facts and ancient wisdom can now come together in a way that we can clearly see relationships and commonalities that were not visible.

Consider – we have:

• Tools of examination from science, and methods of analyzing (e.g., cognitive and behavioral psychology).

---

[1] An approach to this problem can be found in the "Freedom From Within" program: www.ShopDrMiller.com

127

• More developed tools for changing minds, advertising, and psychological interventions.

• The technology to spread new perspectives to large numbers of people.

• New ways of thinking and framing the issues we confront, new paradigms and new ways to communicate.

• New ways to organize social systems, facilitated by the Internet.

Paradigm Shift: Seeing With New Eyes

*The deeper we penetrate and
the more extensive and
embracing our theories become,
the less empirical
knowledge is needed to
determine those theories.*
– Albert Einstein

"Paradigm Shift" is a notion developed by Thomas Kuhn[2] to describe how science has developed through time – not in a smooth way, but by protracted plateaus and sudden upward surges. In my writings I have referred to the kind of thinking that permits such shifts as "transformational thinking." It's a way of framing and reframing the information with which you are presented intentionally, and deciding what modes of logic and reasoning you will use in examining it.

---

[2] T. S. Kuhn, *The Structure of Scientific Revolutions* (University of Chicago Press, 1962).

Kittens and Chinese Children: Invisible Truths

*Perhaps all the dragons of our lives are
princesses who are only waiting to see us once beautiful and brave.*
– Rainer Maria Rilke

Little Chinese children don't know they're speaking Chinese. They don't know that the cultural behaviors they are learning are specific to the Chinese culture. What's more, in addition to these there is an entire set of attitudes, beliefs, and ways of dealing with the world they are learning. And all this happens without any awareness that their minds are being shaped in a specific way.

Having no idea she is speaking Chinese, the child knows only that she is asking for milk. And just as she is likely to continue to speak and think in Chinese for the rest of her life, she will also tend to continue to behave in the way her culture has trained her.

Another striking example is offered by the scientific experiments in which kittens are intentionally raised in domes painted with horizontal stripes, and never exposed to any vertical lines or objects. When, a year later, as adults, they are placed in a normal environment, they are totally unable, to see objects like the legs of tables and chairs. They walk directly into them, much to their consternation, over and over again. The vertical shapes are invisible to them, because the nervous connections needed to perceive vertical lines have not been made – they have not grown "an eye to see" them.

Similarly, there's a way of framing and reacting to our world that we have learned. There are certain things that have been

129

virtually eliminated from our learning environments, resulting in our making the same mistakes repeatedly. Our brains, however, unlike those of the grown kittens, are capable of learning to frame and respond in a new way.

It is almost as if we need to evolve a new organ, a new tool – in other words, new eyes.

> *When the pickpocket meets the saint,*
> *all he can see are his pockets.*
> – Old Adage

Polar Thinking and Organic Thinking

The mode of thinking native to our culture reflects the Newtonian-Cartesian Paradigm for conceptualizing the universe. It envisions the universe and everything in it as composed of little spheroids of various unique substances (tiny globs of iron, wood, or water). These spheroids are thought to bump into each other like billiard balls, according to Newton's three laws of motion.

This model of the universe works fine in most simplistic, everyday situations, but it breaks down when we reach the dimensions of outer space, or at molecular and atomic levels. It's good as far as it goes, but it is incapable, for instance, of understanding the phenomena of electrons and protons, radioactivity, nuclear explosions, or black holes. To understand these, a different paradigm had to be developed, following which we gained the ability to create fantastic new developments.

In our exploration I will be focusing on two particular modes of thinking. The first I will refer to in various ways: as black and white, bipolar, digital, dispersive, or digital thinking. The other kind of thinking conceptualizes the world as being made up not of opposites, but of wholes. It sees a continuum of grey between the extremes of black and white. I call this paradigm, variously, as: organic, unitive, wholeness-enhancing, analog, or whole systems thinking.

130

Polar thinking brings to mind the kind of chemical bonds that predominate in the world of inorganic chemistry. The chlorine atom takes an electron from the sodium atom, thus becoming a negatively charged ion and developing a strong attraction to the now positively charged sodium ion. Bound together as a crystal of salt, they nevertheless rapidly separate (ionize) when dissolved in water.

Systems thinking, on the other hand, recalls the world of organic chemistry, the essence of all known life on this planet. Based on the unique properties of the carbon atom, bonding does not require that one atom gains while the other loses. Instead they share electrons. Carbon is a very balanced chemical, with four electrons in its outer shell. To reach the desired eight, it simply shares, for instance, the electrons of a nearby carbon atom or two oxygen atoms.

Seeing Beyond Opposites and Opposition

All truth passes through three stages. First, it is ridiculed, second, it is violently opposed, third, it is accepted as being self-evident.
– Arthur Schopenhauer

In our culture, we have a tendency, partly due to the subject-object structure of our language and our Newtonian-Cartesian history, to frame situations in terms of "opposites," as black or white. This is the root of the issue.

Ultimately this is related to a certain specific way of approaching the dualistic nature of life. Our culture sees black and white as opposites, as opposing forces, or opposing ideas. The conflict is fundamental to how we think about things, down even to the separation of subject and object that occurs in the infrastructure of our very language. We thus are led to view difference as opposing, from the teasing that starts in kindergarten, to the loss of self-esteem that young women experience in junior high, to the conflicts in high school, right on into the business, political, and social conflicts that each person faces.

Instead of seeing black and white, male and female, active and passive, fast and slow, stressed and relaxed, me and you, as opposing (opposite) pairs, they can be seen as simply two manifestations of a whole. Not either-or, but both-and. When situations are seen in this light, people begin to look for common ground, sincerely, not in the phony way, for instance, that American Indians were lured into treaties that no white man ever really expected to keep. After all, developing friendships and seeking to find common ground is incompatible with slavery, corruption, and so many of the other global dysfunctions.

In addition to seeing the complementary nature of these pairs, we can visualize them as representing ends of a continuum. Thus, instead of black and white, we see shades of grey, or better still, a spectrum.

Sometimes we can understand a situation by focusing on the difference between the extreme ends of the continuum. This is useful when understanding those forces commonly associated with dispersion of matter and energy, just as an enzyme can break down a substrate or a glass can shatter when dropped on the marble floor. There are certain things, like wars, earthquakes, smallpox infections that can be said, from any human perspective – to be very dispersive — even violence.

By contrast, there are times when we understand better when we utilize the paradigm that directs us to focus on *relationships* between items, and on wholes. It is immediately clear that we find wholes being created when we examine the patterns of living things. The cell must remain whole by repairing tears in its cell membrane. The multi-cellular animal must hold its cells together. Higher animals need the unitive force of the maternal instinct and love to feed helpless pups or infants for months or years before they stand any possible chance of surviving on their own. The need for this drive towards wholeness is perhaps most obvious in the selfless dedication of parents in raising human infants, who are completely helpless and are totally dependent upon a strong and caring bond for years and years before being able to function as independent adults. It is clear that much higher levels of health and performance tend to result from having a family that functions smoothly as a whole, compared to a dysfunctional family or broken home.

At one end of this continuum is a condition of unity, of wholeness and togetherness. For example, a family that gathers joyfully and lovingly many times a year more than likely has a greater level of wholeness (unity) than a family that meets rarely, and whose members don't like or trust each other. In this family we'd be seeing a predominance of forces that separate.

Here's another example: Most mothers love their children deeply, and would sacrifice themselves to save their offspring. Mothers are very protective and do without many things that they enjoy, so that their kids might enjoy a better life. A mother scrubs floors on her hands and knees for years to save up enough money so that her daughter might go to college. And this kind of love often gives rise to extraordinary gratitude on the part of those children who really appreciate what they're getting from their mother.

How to facilitate wholeness of a family is important, and leads to the additional question, "How do we hold together a community, a state, a nation, or for that matter, a planet?"

Going with the Flow

Clearly, then, when one is about to address a significant issue, success or failure, gain or loss will often be determined by whether we choose the correct paradigm, the unitive or the dispersive. At the personal level, for example, in psychotherapy, people who are angry

with themselves or others, who carry around excessive fear, or who feel an extraordinary need to control their environment are over-responding to polarities in life. Instead of resolving those polarities, they're actually increasing the polarities (and their illnesses) by the approach they use.

I am reminded of the Chinese finger trap, or being stuck in quicksand. Fighting the forces that trap you will only make things worse. Often, counter-intuitively, the solution requires going with the energy flows and movements of the forces in your environment in order to achieve control over them.

In working with individuals, the process of deep relaxation is most valuable. It enables people to quiet the emotional, mental, and physical levels of system. We build trust and take the risk of building fragile futures that we breathe life into through creating visions of wholeness. We take people from being polarized to thinking in terms of unities — whether it is the wholeness of their life, of themselves and their boundaries, of their family or their work, or their performance.

What's in a Name?

> *"To see is to forget the name of the thing one sees."*
> – Paul Vallery

The terms Unitive and Dispersive are good descriptions of the two ends of the spectrum; they do a good job of reflecting the underlying processes towards which they point. There are other pairs that come to mind too. Each seems to accentuate a particular manifestation of the fundamental concept I am aiming towards here. They include:

Accommodation and Assimilation
Every organism, when it encounters something in its internal or external environment, has to make a choice – to eat it, avoid it, or ignore it. In other words, should it be accommodated or assimilated?

Anabolism and Catabolism

When we look at the living structure of bones in our bodies, we see two main types of cells that are responsible for building and maintaining bone. These are osteoblasts and osteoclasts. Both are needed.

Blasts without clasts produce oversized, misshapen bones that are heavy and unwieldy. Too many clasts relative to blasts leads to a kind of osteoporosis in which the bones break easily and are unable to support the weight of the body. As in every case, health depends upon striking the appropriate balance.

Bonding and Differentiation

In the growth of every individual there are phases of bonding, such as the mother-infant bond and the bonding of mating couples. There are also times of differentiation – such as when the toddler walks away from mother and enters the "terrible twos," or when the college student lives away from home for the first time.

Eustress and Distress

Our understanding of the phenomenon of stress is pertinent here too. Distress, or harmful stress, occurs when there is a demand (a stressor) made on an organism without balance, resulting in physical, mental, and emotional disturbance and disease. If that same stressor is balanced with the proper amount of relaxation and relief, the result can be growth and pleasure[3].

Please keep in mind that what we are trying to focus on is that which is shared among all these pairs – what are the common factors in all these pairs? On one hand we have catabolism, accommodation, differentiation, stress, dispersion, imbalance, disease, and war. On the other there is anabolism, assimilation, bonding, eustress, unity, balance, wellness, and peaceful prosperity. A student

---

[3]   See excerpt: *Deep Relaxation, The Master Skill*
http://www.drmiller.com/news_library/book.*html#deeprelaxation*

of the Tao might call these Yang and Yin, and learn that they are not "opposite," but two essential aspects of a whole, neither being able to exist without the other. Sometimes I find it useful to think of this fundamental pair as "Violence" and "Love."

Love and Violence

Love is the pursuit of the whole.
– Plato

Although "love" is an excruciatingly overused and abused word, there is a common factor involved whenever it is used. In every case, the active principle has something to do with togetherness, attraction, unity, and unification, a joining together in some way – be it physical, emotional, philosophical, esthetic, or others.

This unification is obvious in the example of sexual loving, or in the case of the love between the mother and the infant, or the love of a worshipper for God. And in sports, (or war) we see the same phenomenon of unity that permits one team to win against all odds – and athletes will often speak of the love they feel for their teammates. Whenever a certain quality of wholeness is maintained – whether it's of a body, a relationship, or a racecar – it tends to

give rise to enormous power, performance, pleasure, and survival potential.

When, in psychological experiments, subliminal flashes of phrases are flashed in front of students, some will produce improved performance on subsequent tests. Fascinatingly, researchers find that the most effective phrase is "Mommy and I are one." In other words, the experience of wholeness and connectedness enables the subconscious mind to perform better.

Sometimes, as mentioned, I like to refer to those energies of the unitive, wholeness-producing type as Love. I use the capital L intentionally, to go beyond the more superficial differences among the different expressions of love (philatelists love stamps, Tommy loves Mary), to try to reach towards the essence of the concept that is at the core of all wholeness and togetherness – and that under-lies the efficient operation of all systems, whether single cells or galaxies. This is what I am calling Love.

The other end of the spectrum I've chosen to call Violence. Here I use a capital "V" to denote I'm speaking of something on a much more fundamental level than in the usual sense of *violence*.

To some, it might seem like somewhat of a stretch to define as Violence such a seemingly minor irritant as, for example, teas-ing someone about their new haircut. On the other hand, there is an important reason to consider it as such! Many people have been permanently traumatized in their early years by several such con-frontations, or even a single confrontation with teasing kids, or the town bully. True, some may not be harmed by minor Violence such as this, but some will be!

Obviously, no one can live a real life without experiencing, and perpetuating some Violence, either on a minor or major scale. It is clearly a necessary ingredient in life, and it would be naïve and silly to attempt to eliminate it altogether. My goal is not to eliminate it, but to understand it, and learn how to restore bal-ance whenever it has gen-erated an unhealthy imbal-ance. This balance can be restored, of course, by examining the current situ-ation using the paradigm that seeks wholes, peace, and resolution.

Guilty Innocence: Ginger

When I saw Ginger, she had an enormous amount of shame and fear. She avoided social situations and often felt wrongly accused. She was fragile, shaky, nervous, tentative, and phobic.

The crucial event in her life came about when she was in the third grade. Someone had scratched "bad" words on the mirrors in the girls' bathroom. Everyone who had been given a hall pass during the time this occurred was called into the gymnasium, and as all the girls and teachers stood in a circle, the principal had demanded to know who had done it. The emotion in the air was so tense you could cut it with a knife. Ginger was horrified that someone had done such a thing, and, since no one was speaking up, she suddenly became afraid someone would think it was she. That thought was so frightening to her that she began to perspire and blush. The principal spotted this and whirled toward her. "Aha, it was you... and I thought you were such a good girl." Ginger was too stunned to speak. Her knees felt like they were going to go out from underneath her. She was having her very first anxiety attack, feeling the fight or flight response and was, naturally, speechless. Enormous shame was heaped upon her and her protestations of innocence were ignored. "Her body had given her away, after all," they said.

So Ginger has suffered for the rest of her life because of the way the situation was approached. This is a clear example of how an approach can be designed with far more attention to dispersive procedures, rather those procedures that produce wholeness, unity, love, and health.

A New Paradigm

But the proles, if only they could somehow become conscious of their own strength, would have no reason to conspire. They needed only to rise up and shake themselves, like a horse shaking off flies. If they chose, they could blow the party to pieces tomorrow morning. Surely, sooner or later, it must occur to them to do it? And yet...
– George Orwell, 1984

It is very instructive to examine how real-life situations are handled, from the perspective of whether the approach reflects the paradigm of Love (unitive) or that of Violence (dispersive). When dealing with a challenge, whether from the perspective of the over-all activity or of the individual steps taken to deal with it, we can ask, what paradigm is informing our choices? My experience and belief is that a person (or a nation) will tend to make a better (wiser) decision if all aspects of a current issue, especially potential re-sponses, are evaluated with respect to how much the act is advanc-ing Love relative to how much Violence.

In addition, I have found that in most of the troubled areas of our lives, the dispersive factors (Violence, unkindness, polar as-pects) ultimately far outweigh the unitive and loving aspects of the situation. Bringing these factors more into balance, which generally involves a certain kind of transformational thinking, will generally produce the kind of change we want most. Doing this may involve our going to another level, as it were, to discover the balance point. This is sometimes called Second Order Thinking.

Even a cursory inspection will reveal that one factor common to all the diagnoses we generated is that the Violent, dispersive ele-ments are far more dominant than those reflecting Love and whole-ness. Their proportions are far from ideal. Just as the recipe for a delicious entrée may call for both salt and water, if the cook is too generous with either, the result might be tasteless, or even inedible.

Just as we see Violence and imbalance at the community and global level, we sometimes find ourselves engaging in nega-tive, conflictual, disso-nant, violent behaviors towards ourselves as individuals, as any therapist or physician will confirm. We may do Violence to ourselves at many levels: at the inter-nal level of body, mind, or emotion (e.g., the

diseases and dysfunctions of stress), or at the level of our behavior (addictions, dependencies, and spousal/child abuse). The Violence we do to ourselves, whether in such ways as guilt, resentment, or addiction, can also lead us to do Violence to others for our own profit, comfort, or sense of empowerment.

The Global Imbalance

> *Wholeness incorporating diversity is the transcendent*
> *goal of our time, the task for our generation worldwide.*
> – Ralph Gardiner

We live in a world in which Violence can be seen to be at work being destructive at every level of system. The irritation at family members, other drivers, co-workers, and our local environment, teasing in schools and prejudicial behavior; but the more obviously violent acts we see in terrorism, war, on the streets and in physically abusive homes. Like white cells that have become programmed to sabotage the body by attacking the cells of the brain, spinal cord, or bone marrow, each of us is angrily attacking others, those we should be bonded with and work together with for the common good.

The essence of this problem seems to be that the attitude of aggression and Violence and the science of Violence have become so well-developed and so permeate the culture that, in effect, we are destroying ourselves. This has in far too many ways replaced respect, empathy, compassion, teamwork, and love as motivating forces.

Wholeness, from the holistic, systems perspective is needed. What if we were to learn, on a massive scale, how to respect, honor, nurture, love, protect, and steward those people, institutions, beings, and things that truly deserve it. Likewise, we need to learn the proper use of violence, how to protect ourselves and neutralize those truly noxious entities, and how to temper this violence so that we do as little destruction as possible, with as little collateral damage, consistent with restoring balance and health (just as when we are medically treating an individual or family).

> *Where there is love, there is life.*
> – Mohandas Gandhi

Necessary Love

Life, itself, is that aspect of what's going on that has to do with wholeness, like attracted to like, groups of cells recognizing how they can form an organism, groups of organisms, discovering how they can form a tribe for survival.

At each level, individual cells or organisms gave up some of their uniqueness, independence, and autonomy so that the whole might be served. They didn't all do this, but those that didn't do it have mostly vanished, because there are so many dangerous things out in the world. A group has a much better chance of surviving, and if you don't survive, your genes don't get passed on.

Necessary Violence

Both anabolic and catabolic processes are needed – both Love and Violence. So sometimes it is necessary to employ Violence at one level in order to serve Love's need to balance at a higher level. It's certainly true that sometimes one must leave an abusive relationship. This is cer

tainly doing violence to the shared home, etc., but it is in service of wholeness at another level.

On one side there's a loving, organizing principle of wholeness, but in order to survive it became necessary to fight, do violence, protect oneself by attacking, etc. Removing a cancer with surgery is a Violent act, but it may save your life. When the United States entered the Second World War, this represented a series of violent actions that ultimately protected us and those we loved. It would not have been good to wait until the Nazi war machine had figured out how to attack us across the ocean.

The most important human endeavor is the striving for morality in our actions. Our inner balance and even our very existence depend upon it. Only morality in our actions can give beauty and dignity to life.

– Albert Einstein

Sometimes It Takes an "Act of God" To Get Our Attention

Both the Al-Qaeda "jihad" against the U.S. and the U.S.-led crusade against the Iraqi regime are extreme and unmistakable examples of attempts to use Violence to solve problems, in spite of enormous suffering on the part of innocents caught in the crossfire.

Compare this to the global response of unconditional Love that flowed out to the victims of the tsunami catastrophe in Southeast Asia. This was, in many ways, humanity operating at its highest expression of wise guidance. Although the disaster was localized, the response was globalized. From individual people to good corporate citizens to entire nations, we saw the tremendous power of Love in action – an affirmation that we are all in this together. What can we say of our response to the damage of Hurricane Katrina? A response of Love would have been responsive to those trapped by the floods. To delay sending support would have been, in effect, abandoning them to Violence.

And now we have the economic upheaval that surfaced in 2008. The coming months and years will be extremely telling. We can split into camps that blame and attack each other, which will be easier, now that we are all in a weakened state. Or we can see that what unites us is far more important than that which seems to divide, that what we have in common is worth settling our differences for. Will Love or Violence prevail? The opportunities abound for both. Could it be that you and I might actually have a role in answering this question? Can you imagine that?

Questions to Ponder

1. I have referred to the same paradigmatic difference as "Old Paradigm/New Paradigm, Either-Or/Both-And, Dispersive/Unitive, and Violence/Love. Realizing that no set of terms can completely describe the situation, what terms do you feel best describe the situation we are exploring here? You may want to choose a set of terms different from those I have suggested.

2. Does my choice of Violence and Love seem too extreme, or far-fetched to you? Why, or why not?

Notes to Self

Discussion: Take Home Messages

• Internet technology is bringing ancient wisdom and current information together in a way that enables us to see relationships and commonalities more clearly, to see the whole picture.

• Our culture, even the structure of our language, leads us to frame situations in terms of opposites: black or white, us or them.

• Seeing opposites as essential aspects of the same whole allows us to find common ground incompatible to corruption and other dysfunctions.

• The violence we do to ourselves with guilt, resentment, or addiction can lead us to do violence to others for our own profit, comfort, or sense of empowerment.

• The global response of unconditional love, as demonstrated during times of disaster (such as 9/11 and the 2003 tsunami in Southeast Asia) is an example of humanity operating at its highest expression of wise guidance.

CHAPTER 9
PROGNOSIS: WHAT CAN WE EXPECT?

*All conditions and all circumstances in our lives are a result
of a certain level of thinking. If we want to change the
conditions and circumstances, we have to change the level
of thinking that is responsible for it.*
– Albert Einstein

*A significant portion of the earth's population will soon recognize,
if they haven't already done so, that humanity is now
faced with a stark choice: Evolve or die.*
— Eckhart Tolle

Prognosis and Paradigm

In arriving at a *prognosis*, the doctor is called upon to be a fortuneteller. He or she looks into a metaphorical crystal ball, guided by evidence and diagnoses and informed by personal ex

perience, skill, wisdom, and intuition, and tries to predict the future. What he or she sees obviously depends not only on information available, but also upon how the looking is being done. We must always be aware that whatever we end up perceiving has already been interpreted and modified by the *myth* [1], or *paradigm* that we are using. "One man's terrorist is another man's freedom fighter," as the saying goes.

The perspective with which we have approached our patient is based on a particular scope and scale – we have attempted to examine all levels of the system, the entire collection of internested Russian dolls, extending from the individual up through the family, the community, and the culture. Now we must imagine what is most likely if we do *nothing*, and allow ourselves to continue to approach our challenges in the traditional way – versus what might happen if we, as individuals and as a civilization, undertake to engage our world in a new way. This is not the easiest of tasks.

Any predictions we make about the future must, of necessity, be based upon beliefs we have – beliefs generated by our particular paradigm (myth). This is easily observed in the reasoning, attitudes,

---

[1] A myth is a narrative that is accepted by certain groups of people. It contributes to and expresses systems of thought and values. The use of this term by scholars implies neither the truth nor the falseness of the narrative. To those who accept its validity, however, a myth is "true" by definition, since it embodies beliefs, concepts, and ways of questioning and making sense of the world.

and expectations of individuals. When confronted with identical situations, the racist, the radical fundamentalist, or the sexist behaves quite differently from someone who is of a more liberal persuasion. In a similar manner, we can observe how cultures, too, are constrained by their myths.

The Boston Red Sox were afflicted with the myth of "The Curse of the Bambino," and, it has been argued, their beliefs about themselves definitely predicted their future – they were unable to win a World Series. "Deutschland Über Alles," the myth of German superiority, fueled the German Army to enormous productivity and zeal, and unparalleled depths of depravity. Radical Islamic extremists, guided by the belief that it is a mortal sin to draw a picture of Mohammed, issued a death sentence fatwa against cartoonists who had depicted the prophet in their cartoons. Others detonated explosives, destroying centuries-old statues that certain Buddhists might have given their lives to protect.

Indeed, the United States of America grew out of the myth that "...to secure these rights, Governments are instituted among Men, deriving their just powers from the consent of the governed, – That whenever any Form of Government becomes destructive of these ends, it is the Right of the People to alter or to abolish it, and to institute new Government..." The Declaration of Independence.

When Myths Collide

The purpose of a myth is to give structure and meaning to a set of events and to reveal the nature of their connections, so as to enable us to have a feeling of understanding what is going on in the world around us. "The volcano erupted because man sinned against the gods." "HIV AIDS is God's punishment of homosexuals." "God created the world in six days."

Our culture has often encoded its repeated experience in the myths represented by the aphorisms: "You can't fight City Hall," "You don't need road manners if you are an 18-wheeler," "We are fighting them over there so we don't have to fight them over here," or "African-Americans are inferior to White Americans."

I can remember, early in my life, marveling at how the things people told me were absolutely true often contradicted other "absolute" truths. "Always look before you leap," they admonished me when I seemed too impulsive. Then a couple of days later they told me, "He who hesitates is lost." Well, how can I stop to look without hesitating? I'm sure you can find many contradictions you have run into in your own experience.

Similarly, cultural myths clash with each other. The Christian Right sees the Muslims as agents of Satan and vice versa. And so it goes with myths – every one of them seems to be right to a certain extent, but, as I learned regarding the aphorisms of my childhood, it is essential to remain highly cognizant of the context. As the Zen Master said, "Today's enlightenment is tomorrow's delusion."

Nasrudin as Judge

Nasrudin[2] was appointed judge, and the first case before him involved a dispute over a cow. "He said he wanted to purchase the cow from me, I gave it to him but he never gave me the money," exclaimed the first man.

Solemnly, Nasrudin said, "You are right."

"But," interrupted the bailiff, "you can't decide yet, you haven't heard the other man's story."

"Ok, what is it?" replied Nasrudin.

"He said he would sell me a cow, I gave him the money but he never gave me a cow," began the second man. "You are right!" Nasrudin solemnly intoned.

"But," complained the exasperated bailiff, "their stories are completely contradictory, they cannot both be right!"

Nasrudin stroked his beard and pondered the situation for a few moments, and then turned to the bailiff and said, "You are right."

Hydra, and the Myth of Conquering Nature

In Greek myth, the slaying of the Hydra represented the second labor of Hercules. Hydra was a monster with nine fearsome, attacking heads. Moreover, whenever Hercules knocked off one of these heads with his club, two would grow back to take its place. Thus his attacks simply brought forth more horrors.

This myth has been interpreted through the centuries as the struggle against the forces of nature. Nature was indeed fearsome to early cultures, which had minimal or no defense against the weather, predators, natural disasters, or disease. Our superficial attempts often created even more problems; if you have tried to eliminate the weeds in your garden by cutting their stems, you know how much more vigorously they return, since cutting the stems actually causes the roots to deepen! The myth of the Hydra is a good way of understanding Nature, at a certain level.

Our Modern Hydras

Like an unwise Hercules, factory owners beat and killed obstreperous workers, the British decided to punish the 13 colonies for resisting their taxes, and the U.S. naively invaded Vietnam. These strategies, like Hercules's first attempts[3], often led to unwanted consequences.

---

[2]   Nasrudin (a Persian word meaning "Victory of Faith") was a satirical Sufi figure who lived in the 13th century.

151

The Crusaders slaughtered every man, woman, and child in the (Arab) towns they invaded, thinking they could accomplish genocide in this way (in the name of Jesus, of course). Similarly, the Europeans who settled in the New World set about systematically trying to exterminate the Native Americans by driving them off productive lands, forcibly taking their children to be indoctrinated in missionary schools, and giving them smallpox-inoculated blankets. And numerous lynchings of blacks in the South took place well within the memory of many of us.

southern lynching of "nigras"

http://matthewyglesias.theatlantic.com/lynching.jpg

Hitler's "Final Solution," the nuclear bombing of civilians in Hiroshima, and the napalming and agent oranging of the Vietnamese all reflect this same metaphor, the "Kill the Hydra" philosophy[4]. The "Shock And Awe" campaign of the Iraq war is an even more recent example.

Successful Violence?

It should be clear that all these attempts at problem solving are based on a belief in the Black-White Paradigm of differentiation,

---

[3]   Hercules was clever, and he learned from his experience. His brilliant solution, as you may remember, was to have his son stand by with a hot iron, ready to cauterize each neck immediately after he had lopped off the head. Finally, the last remaining head, the central, immortal one, he placed beneath a large rock.

[4]   For a more complete elucidation of this theme, see:
      Derrick Jensen, *The Culture of Make Believe*

polarity, conflict, and Violence. The goal is to try to destroy what we perceive as the "Other."

But is this approach ever successful? By certain measures some people (depending on their paradigm) might judge at least some violent approaches as having been effective. The growth of the United States would certainly have taken a different trajectory if we had allowed the Indians to continue to chase buffalo, instead of running the "savages" off and converting their lands to ranches, farms, mines, and oil wells. The agricultural history of the South would certainly have been different if we did not use slave labor on the plantations. The argument could be made that the destruction and enslavement of these people helped propel our nation to the rank of sole global superpower.

The Slash and Burn approach has also allowed us to eliminate tuberculosis, smallpox, and polio as threats to the civilized world. Yet, as I have discussed at length elsewhere now that we have effectively rescued ourselves from those diseases caused primarily by external agents, and because of the ever-upward-ratcheting levels of stress and insecurity (which are the byproducts of external competition), more and more of our human ills turn out to be the result of how we approach life, how we see ourselves, our beliefs, attitudes and reactions to our physical, social, and cultural environment[5].

Likewise, it may well be that many of the other apparent "successes" are, in fact, bearing bitter fruit. The resentment at the Crusades, for example, seethes beneath the anger of Islam, and the legacy of racism at home continues to exact an enormous

[5]   Emmett Miller, *Deep Healing* (Hay House, 1997). www.ShopDrMiller.com

Bodies of American-Indians at Wounded Knee
http://www.nebraskahistory.org/images/publish/1381.jpg

toll. And although Albert Einstein's invention, the Atomic Bomb, brought a rapid end to World War II, he had grave misgivings about creating it, since he knew that our culture was not wise enough to control it, and that he had unleashed a great evil into the world.

The splitting of the atom has changed everything save our mode of thinking, and thus we drift towards unparalleled catastrophe.
– Albert Einstein

The Scope of Our Prognosis

Just to set the scope of our prognosis, I offer the following highlights – not at all intended to be an exhaustive list, just food for thought. No matter what level of system we address – the single individual, the family, or the larger social structure – it should be clear that, in many cases, attempts to attack and eliminate the source of a self-generated problem will weaken and perhaps lead to the destruction of the system itself – the "cutting off your nose to spite your face" phenomenon.

At the individual level, the result of our using attack strategies has created the situation in which we produce potentially fatal physical diseases (e.g., heart disease) as a result of the unremitting stress of anxiety, anger, or depression. Self-flagellation, unremitting guilt, withering shame, self-loathing, embarrassment — all are attempts by the individual's system to punish something inside us, something the unconscious is blaming for the perceived problems in our lives. Problems like obesity, withdrawal, rage, and drug and alcohol abuse that often ensue only exacerbate the problem. Mostly, all these behaviors serve to weaken and damage the whole. Our attempts to cauterize are destroying the life spark within us.

Relationship/Family Level

At the level of family and other relationships, it is not unusual to see the anger, manipulation, and outright physical abuse that disrupt so many lives and relationships. In our "spare the rod, spoil the child" way of raising children — our attempts to "beat the devil out of them" have simply produced frightened, angry, confused adults. Studies show that physical punishment, for example, correlates strongly with the likelihood of being incarcerated, compared with the incarceration rates for those for whom the rod was spared. Divorce continues to be commonplace, and fewer people even want to take the risk to be married. Disrespect is rife, at home and at work. Families have been split apart by industrialization, and family ties have been weakened.

At the next level, communities are divided along racial and religious lines, street gangs fight turf wars, and police abuse the citizens they are supposed to serve and protect. Walmart competes with "Mom and Pop shops," physicians and dentists compete with each other, and nearly everybody cheats whenever they can get away with it. Co-workers sabotage each other, and friends practice character assassination. "Where's the love?" as the popular expression goes.

At the national level, we see the relentless expansion of inner city ghettos – such lawless places of the dispossessed that even the police will not enter them after dark. Early solutions were to try to keep them "on the other side of the tracks," but in time this proved inadequate. The new approach is for the wealthy to build gated communities — gated communities that, with higher and higher fences and more security guards, begin to remind me very much of the forts built on Indian land to protect settlers. And we have become the excluded Native American riffraff! What goes around, comes around.

Every year sees more and more of the wealth of our country (and of the world as a whole) being concentrated into the hands of a tiny percentage of our population, the "super-rich." Political parties battle it out, yet somehow nothing ever seems to change, especially if it means going against the wishes of the corporations who finance the elections of our "representatives."

Much of our reality is created not by interaction with trusted, wise guides and colleagues, but by the "media," who don't give us the truth, but instead present us with the interpretation their advertisers want them to present, that will make them money. Likewise, politicians manipulate the press to stifle the voice of independent investigative journalism. Truth is "on the town."

At the international level, the use of force against the "Others" worked pretty well until rather recently. We were able to identify specific states and the localized groups of people who were the troublemakers, round them up into concentration camps, and destroy them. Once upon a time the criminals could be simply exiled to Australia, America, or some other out of the way place! The world was much bigger back then.

The situation, however, is changing, with the attack on the World Trade Center, and the economic crisis of 2008 as the "poster events." Now, added to our long history of state-sponsored terrorism, is a new kind of terrorism. This non-state sponsored terrorism, whose techniques of murder and intimidation are currently being perfected in the Middle East, are proving to be devastatingly effective against much stronger and better financed opponents, and are certain to grow in popularity in coming years – to the detriment of us all. And the greed that lies beneath unregulated growth of economic globalization has already shown us its destructive potential.

Given all this, we now need to come up with a prognosis. This prognosis will be presented in two parts – the first: if we continue as before, the second: what might happen if we change our approach.

Prognosis Scenario 1: If the Current Paradigm Continues, What Will Happen?

One scenario predicts that with the continued growth of the worldwide consumer economy and the "MacDonaldization" of a homogenized global culture, capital will continue to accumulate in the hands of a small group of people that will be relatively insulated from the global economic cataclysms that will continue to occur. We can also expect repeated violent backlash arising from disenfranchised groups of peoples who do not want their unique local customs, foods, religious beliefs, and cultures to be assimilated.

... The centralized mass culture specifies for most people most of the time, in any politically relevant sense, what's real and what's not (existence), what's important and what is not (priorities), what's good and bad, what's right and wrong (values), what's related to what else and how (relations). In this way the mass media synthesize the reality – the centralized mass culture – in which and to which our collective behavior is the only possible response.
– General Omar Youngblood

Extreme Islamic radicals have become the most obvious symptom and symbol of this backlash. Not only have we physically invaded the Muslim nations of Afghanistan and Iraq, but we have also begun to impose our cultural and political values. Nowhere is this extreme polarity more obvious than when we compare the veiled women they see by day with pornography brought to them at night via the Internet. Many still recall the racist, religious, and imperialistic violence they have suffered at the hands of Western

http://aftermathnews.wordpress.com/2008/08/11/
bush-china-must-end-detentions
-ensure-freedoms/

157

nations. They don't like being called "sand niggers" or "towel heads" either!

The "War on Terror" seems to be creating more terrorists than it is killing. Terrorist cells are now operating worldwide. And remember, Muslim extremists would be virtually powerless if they did not have a strong backing of more moderate Muslims around the globe, including some in the U.S. The combative behavior of our government continues to make more enemies of both moderate and extreme types in this part of the world, leading to ever more recruits eager for martyrdom, and more contributions for bombs and WMDs.

Problems with the Hydra Myth

Terrorists are not localized groups of people. We cannot napalm them. Further, as we are seeing in Iraq, our attacks are simply creating more and more suicide-bomb volunteers, and more and more "live fire" training grounds for terrorists and guerillas.

The government seems all too ready to tell us that it totally expects another terrorist attack, probably one much worse than 9/11. But it is not clear that the government has considered the possibility that, with this approach, we may actually be our own worst enemies. Violence only begets more violence. (On the other hand, it can be used to get yourself elected!)

Moreover, the next terrorist attack might not even be from Muslim fundamentalists. Arab Muslims are not the only disaffected group that feels as if its way of life is being gravely threatened by globalization, capitalism – and the economic movement of the world toward a two-class society of the very (few) rich and the very (many) poor.

As we concentrate on protecting our borders from foreign terrorists, we might be ignoring the gradual rise of homegrown revolutionaries who feel cheated, robbed, and abused by the overall system that mindlessly commits, perpetrates, and tolerates regular, ongoing violence at home. We are already seeing the emergence of local separatist groups that are becoming more powerful and revolutionary than ever. White separatists and the far-Right Christian extremists are already arming themselves with assault weapons and explosives, and no one is sure what the "Black Muslims" are planning. Our country is running the risk of splitting into violent radical groups with plenty of support, as are radical Islamic terrorists, from moderate sympathizers.

We do see some positive responses here and there. One set of bellwether groups are the Earth First-like organizations. The Sierra Club, for instance, concentrates on peaceful change through the process of law, lobbying, and legislation. Greenpeace, for the most part, is following a proactive agenda of protest and nonviolent disruption of groups and companies they feel are harming the Earth.

The shadowy Earth Liberation Front, on the other hand, has already gone underground as violent eco-terrorists. So far, the E.L.F. violence has focused on property destruction ranging from putting spikes in redwood trees and burning car lots full of Hummers, to torching construction sites being built on environmentally sensitive wetlands. To date, E.L.F. attacks have amounted to little more than random acts of vandalism – but that could change if the government continues to roll back, as it has in recent years, environmental regulations so as to permit commercial incursions – like logging and oil-drilling – on protected forests and wildlife refuges. The list of examples goes on and on – and if you want more current examples, I'm sure you can find plenty in last week's newspaper. Given these few data points, I think you can construct for yourself the endpoint, and it is not pretty. Indeed, if we do not change our direction we really are very likely to end up where we're headed.

Every kingdom divided against itself is brought to desolation;
and every city or house divided against itself shall not stand.
– Jesus, Holy Bible, Matthew 12:25

Prognosis, Scenario 2:
With a Shift to Organic Thinking

The application of the Organic paradigm leads us to entertain the following postulates:

• All living systems have a strong drive toward wholeness (healing).
• There is a wisdom within systems that can be utilized to restore balance.
• The wise person or group focuses on discovering how to look within for this wisdom and how to apply their wisdom outwardly to create wholeness and balance.

There are indications that, if this wisdom is accepted by communities, a very different outcome can occur. We might envision this to be a world that works for everyone, where we realize that we are all connected in so many ways. After all, we know that if we quell the violence within an individual, balance, healing, and improved performance ensue. Similarly, when peace and love come to the members of a family or community, equivalent changes occur.

In the individual, we can see this at work in those who practice meditative disciplines, loving kindness, and prayer. One of the most rapid and most effective ways to awaken inner wisdom is through the use of deep relaxation and imagery[6]. The number of people bringing healing change into their lives is increasing daily. The challenge we face now is to develop ways to apply this at the family, community, national, and global levels of system.

---

[6] See *Awakening The Leader Within* for more about this www.ShopDrMiller.com

The world is my country,
all mankind are
my brethren, and to do
good is my religion.
–Thomas Paine

The next step, then, is to choose to see the possibility that, just as an individual can heal themselves by applying these principles, other levels, from the community and national to the planetary level can expand to become a worldwide, collective wisdom that transcends language, nations, religions, and other local myths.

A Positive Vision of the Future

There is a powerful, but often overlooked (or concealed) fact of life – that when enough people really care enough to want something to happen, it happens! The good news is that millions have, in recent years, begun to realize that the world is rapidly approaching a tipping point. Many are also awakening to the fact that while "Armageddon" is certainly one potential outcome, an equally dramatic, but positive future is now possible. Many people believe that if enough of us really want that future, we can have it. That future could include the following:[7]

Species-wide Self-respect and Self-Esteem: Compassion and authentic respect for the uniqueness, preciousness, spiritual es

[7] The vision articulated here is that of LIGHT, the Leadership Institute for Global Healing and Transformation http://www.drmiller.com/light/index.html

sence, and intrinsic value of each human being. The true meaning of healthy self-esteem has been realized and is reflected in the respect and dignity for every human being that has become the norm.

Transformed Healthcare: All human beings have access to holistic healing tools, (those that address mind, body, emotion, behavior, and spirit) and skilled practitioners. A human approach to health care that includes the use of modern scientific and technical advances is universal. The collective resources of the world's healing wisdom and knowledge are available to every human through purposeful use of modern communication technologies. People are to employ the self-care and wellness approaches that prevent 80% of the illnesses we now see.

Humanity-Centered Wedding of Technology and Art: Technology and Art have been brought together to create powerful models, inspired guidance, and rich imagery for Deep Healing, personal development, and collective evolution, at all levels of system, in dramatically effective ways.

Unity in Diversity: Humanity has awakened to a planet-wide awareness of the intrinsic beauty of all living beings; hierarchical social models of control and dominance have been superseded by distributed leadership models that are based on justice, equality, respect, love, and community. Our cultures have turned away from a focus on acquisitiveness and things – and toward honesty and integrity in authentic relationships. We have realized that what we share is so much more than what divides us.

Love: We have discovered Love as the positive attractive force of affiliation that brings people and things together in harmonious ways. We have achieved understanding of the experience of Love as an intentional state (not something that people fall in). Our notion of Love goes beyond the pseudo-love of neediness, dependence, dominance, and abuse and embraces the qualities of sharing, mutual respect, affection, and appreciation of our common essence.

Communication is compassionate and caring, sensitive to others' feelings and needs, supportive and nurturing of the positive and good in others.

Nonviolence: Disagreements are handled in ways that begin with respect for each other's rights, beliefs, and traditions, and end with the application of nonviolent approaches that allow second order change, transformation, transcendence, and subsequent resolution. Armed conflict is no longer an option. Violence in all its forms – child abuse, sweatshops, human trafficking, economic imperialism, corporate abuse of workers and the environment, and crime, are rapidly disappearing. Unconditional positive regard and respect have become the norm in all human interactions, including individual, family, workplace, community, and government.

Community Values: We have recognized the value and potential of our communities, of the collective. Families, education, nutrition, housing, recreation, wise land use, freedom of information, respect for earth systems, spirituality, and sustainability are widely supported with appropriate and effective action.

Perhaps all these changes will not, perhaps cannot, occur in any of our lifetimes. But why not get as close to this ideal as we can? Besides, who could have predicted Jesus, or Muhammad, or Moses, or Gandhi?

You may say I'm a dreamer,
But I'm not the only one.
I hope some day you'll join us,
And the world will live as one.
– John Lennon

The "Serenity Prayer," made famous by Alcoholics Anonymous provides some guidance, "God, give us the grace to accept with serenity the things that cannot be changed, the courage to change the things that should be changed, and the wisdom to distinguish the one from the other." Clearly, what is needed most these days is wisdom. Our treatment, then, must be designed to awaken the wisdom we need.

Ah, but a man's reach should exceed his grasp,
or what's a heaven for?
– Robert Browning

Questions to Ponder

1. What cultural myths do you see that are causing imbalance, at the personal, family, community, or international level?

2. What do harmful myths all have in common?

3. What else would you add to the "positive vision of the future?"

Notes to Self

Prognosis: Take Home Messages

• More and more of our human ills are the result of how we approach life: our attitudes, beliefs, and reactions to our physical, social, and cultural environments.

• The ongoing growth of the consumer economy will continue to make a small group of people wealthy and immune to the economic cataclysms that will continue to occur.

• If we quell the violence within an individual, balance and healing ensue; similar changes occur when peace and love come to members of a family, community, or nation.

CHAPTER 10
DEVELOPING A
TREATMENT PLAN

A good plan today is better than a perfect plan tomorrow.
– General George S. Patton

Once we have examined the possible diagnoses we reached after careful consideration of the signs, symptoms, history, physical and lab findings, we need to evaluate the possible strategies for applying all available resources that can best facilitate the healing process. We devise a healing plan.

Then, we institute the treatment we have chosen, and continue it long enough to get some feedback on how it is working. Diagnosis and a treatment plan represent simply the *beginning* of a therapeutic interaction, so we put our healing strategy into action, wait a while, then reevaluate and modify on the basis of that feedback.

The treatment consists of suggestions, advice, and sometimes strong urging ("doctor's orders"). The skillful doctor is a skillful guide – he or she must interact with the patient in a manner which both empowers and inspires them to see the wisdom of behaving in a certain way. This may include changes in diet or lifestyle, the administration of medication, surgery, and so forth.

Now it is time for us to devise a treatment for the current situation. And, much as in the case of the medical doctor's treatment plan, we will need to suggest a set of specific interventions to be used on a trial basis. But first, let us look at the notion of *treatment* itself.

One of the great tragedies of the Western system of medicine is that it has tended to focus only on disease and dysfunction. It defined "health" as being merely the state of being free of signs and symptoms of disease – instead of acknowledging the wider range of experience that would include disease prevention, and the concepts of wellness and peak performance[1]. The amount of human suffering and wasted resources that have resulted from this shortsightedness is incalculable. So we want to be careful to not make a similar mistake as we address our current global dysfunction.

The Spectrum of Health and Wellness

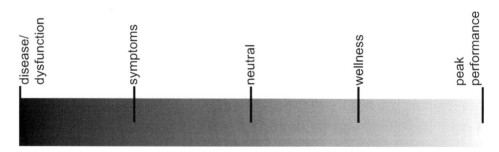

Let us consider the spectrum from disease to Peak Performance:

Clearly, it is desirable to choose behaviors and interventions that cause us to move from the left to the right on this scale, no

---

[1] Adapted from Jack Travis, *Wellness Workbook* (Celestial Arts, 2004).

matter from which point we begin. At the individual level, physical stamina and strength represent optimal measures of physical health, wellness, and performance. Mental acuity, logical thinking, and creativity are signs of higher performance at the cognitive level. Emotional awareness, balance, richness, and expression represent optimal performance at that level.

In addition, it should be obvious that a corresponding spectrum exists at each other level of system:

In other words, we can choose behaviors that lead away from illness and dysfunction and towards health, wellness, and peak performance in our family or nation as well as in our personal lives. Here, of course, healing is the creation of wholeness, congruence, sustainability, and Love.

"Healer, Heal Thyself."

Our first responsibility is, of course, to our individual health and wellness. "Know Thyself," said the Oracle at Delphi. And when you see imbalance, dysfunction, conflict, and Violence within, wisdom dictates that

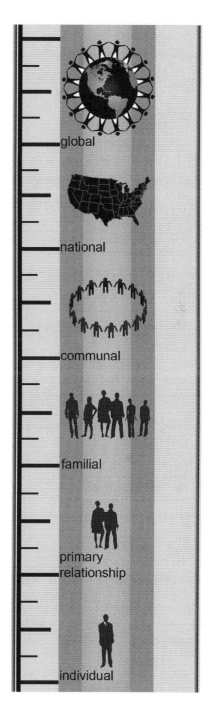

global

national

communal

familial

primary relationship

individual

169

you make it one of your priorities to apply the healing principles, techniques, and interventions to your personal health – first, whenever possible. Then, as you are becoming personally more healthy, balanced, and productive, you can also discover how to direct an appropriate proportion of your energy in applying them at other levels of system, such as family and community.

Try this thought experiment: Imagine thinking of each individual person as being, in many ways, like a single cell of a complex organism. Each has a boundary – skin or a cell membrane – an inside and an outside. Each has to take in food, process it, and excrete waste, balance internal processes, and maintain a certain kind of relationship with the external environment.

In addition, each must function (well or poorly) as part of a community of similar others. We call this community an organ in the case of the cell. We may call it a family, team, or society in the human case. And, just as the cell has the responsibility to maintain its health and wellness if it is to perform well in concert with the rest of the community, each person has a similar responsibility.

The value of Self-knowing is clear here, since the highest levels of health, wellness, and performance can be achieved only if you understand your true value and purpose, and play your unique, appropriate role in your family, team, or community. Just as you want the cells of your liver and brain to do a good job of serving their function, instead of dying, or becoming cancerous, you cannot truly be happy or whole until you are intentionally on the path to discovering your deepest values and personal purpose. This is why greed, envy, gluttony, narcissism, and selfishness can never lead to deep and lasting satisfaction, any more than Twinkies can provide the vitamins and minerals your body needs, no matter how many you eat.

Higher Orders of Wholeness

In other words, being a good citizen, a contributing member

of the group, is more than just a good way to assure sustainability, it is actually a *prerequisite* for achieving the feelings of fulfillment that are the ultimate goal of every one of us. So, once we have begun to attend to our inner needs, we *must* begin to intentionally channel the appropriate amount of creative energy to our fellow cells, or humans, to create higher-level wholes (holons).

In many ways, ontogeny does seem to recapitulate phylogeny. In much the same manner as evolutionary theory suggests that more complex species developed, we see an evolution that can occur in the personal lives of each of us. Just as each of the first single-celled amoebas thought only about themselves for a long time, until they began to realize the extraordinary benefits of staying together and forming a multicelled creature. This was a "shift of paradigm" for them. Instead of focusing on differences, contrasts, and conflict with their environment, with a sole focus of individual survival and "thrival," they began to sacrifice and contribute their energy and functions to the efforts of the whole.

The tools we will soon be exploring are systemic healing interventions, so they can be applied immediately at the personal level, and as they are learned, they will prove to be just as useful at other levels of system. So we will start with the development of inner wholeness of mind, emotion, body, and spirit (many aspects of which you may already be attending to in your life). Following this, we will explore means for intentionally participating in the creation of wholeness at other levels of system, from family through community and nation, and globally as well.

At the individual level, there are two important functions I would like to mention at this point, for they are central to all healing (recalling that true healing means wellness and high levels of performance as well):

- **Identity**: knowing yourself, having a center, and boundaries.
- **Homeostasis**: creating balance in a way that protects and nurtures self.

For further details on the process of individual healing, I would suggest Deep Healing[2].

171

Healing and Peak Performance: Family/Community Level

Healing, that is, moving from dysfunction towards wellness and performance, at the next level of the hierarchy, means applying the New Paradigm at the level of family, team, or community. The crucial functions of healing here are:

1. Creating and maintaining *healthy* personal boundaries
2. Reducing polarity, dispersion, and violence, and
3. Forming healthy, generative relationships with others, thus creating a whole at the next level.

These functions have been particularly difficult for us in the U.S. We have been so steeped in the philosophies of racism, nationalism, individuality, and competition that we tend to view it as a potential loss to our individual selves to consider making a sacrifice for the whole, any whole, be it family, team, country, or humanity as a whole. Of course there are exceptions, but on the whole, sacrifice at such a level tends to seem like the exception, not the rule.

It has often been said that "war is how Americans learn geography." The American culture has been insular and narcissistic, because it had so many natural resources and was located so far from the rich warrior nations of the world that we could virtually ignore that the rest of the world exists. The downside of this is that we have not learned the value of being good neighbors. We were spared the wartime devastation that so many other countries have known; war was something that happened "over there." So, in a sense, it is no surprise that we are in denial about the real results of violence.

Actually, up until very recently, violence has paid off for us. The world has changed, but like the rat who had been trained to expect a cheese reward in at a specific spot in the maze, we keep going down "tunnel number 9," even though we are not getting the

---

[2] Emmett Miller, *Deep Healing* (Hay House, 1997). www.ShopDrMiller.com

successful payoff that always used to be there. For many in our culture, it is quite a leap from enjoying the best lifestyle and consuming more than our share, to considering fairness, equality, compassion, and integrity – and then acting on it.

Domestically, we are at the end of raw capitalism. In foreign policy we are at the end of raw militarism. Philosophically, we are at the end of simplistic dualism. The old myths that have supported these three pillars of American faith, capitalism, militarism, and dualism, are now diluted, weak, and unpersuasive. A revolution in thought will be required to adjust to new realities.
– Craig Barnes

The challenge we face is to discover how incredibly important it is, at every level of system, to honestly consider approaches to our problems beyond the familiar ones of Violence and conflict, from our wars to our daily relationships: to go beyond nonviolence to Love, and to discover the many ways we can allow our lives to express Love, on a moment to moment basis.

How we can accomplish this process by awakening the leader within, and sharing leadership in ever-higher levels of social system, will be addressed in the next chapter. Clearly, we will need powerful tools, indeed, to make this change, so far astray have we gone.

Tools for Change: Positive and Negative Tools for Violence

The technological advances of the human race have turbocharged our primitive drives for money, sex, and power. Greed, as we are beginning to realize, is never satisfied, "more" is never enough; greed becomes amplified, as the tools it has available grow stronger. Greed attempts to satisfy itself by wreaking Violence (active and passive) on others and the environment, and it has produced powerfully destructive tools for doing Violence. We can see how so many of our commonly used tools for personal interaction create abuse because they're fundamentally weapons for doing Violence. Just look at the lies, trickery, manipulativeness, extortion, emotional blackmail, and abuse (verbal, emotional, physical, etc.) that take place within and around each of us – every day.

The inner damage we do to our own souls with such abusive implements as guilt and shame is obvious. Then, consider, in addition, the brutal weapons we use in our relationships – the disrespect and prejudice, the rejection and resentment, the name-calling, threats, and betrayals. How enormous are the dispersive (Violent) forces that are released when we compete with each other, at home, at work, and socially. And then there's the ubiquitous false advertising, widespread corruption in government, politics, business — all protected by a media that succeeds in creating so much confusion (by focusing on fundamentally inconsequential polarities) that the true issues are poorly addressed, if at all.

These are all weapons, just as are the assault rifle and "Saturday Night Special" handguns that keep the U.S. the most violent industrialized nation in the world. How unfortunate it is that most of us are unconscious of how we are daily being fed (literally and figuratively) by it.

With a little reflection, we can easily see that one of the most effective tools for violence has been the modern corporation – most recently demonstrated by the massive damage wrought by financial sector corporations. The economic disaster of 2008 and the role that multinational corporations are playing in the process of economic globalization indicates how major a force corporations are in the shaping of our lives and our planet. So let us take a little diversion to focus briefly on the corporate phenomenon.

It might come as a surprise to many to learn that humanity has not always had corporations; they had to be invented, just as we needed to invent the cotton gin, the internal combustion engine, and the computer. We may find it illuminating to approach the corporation, metaphorically, as a machine.

The printing press, a machine, was able to advance human culture and knowledge to an unparalleled degree, yet, on the other hand, it has produced much slavery, suffering, war, and death as a result of printed lies, propaganda, and false advertising. The Internet has increased our connectivity immeasurably, and facilitated many positive things, but it too has contributed to much human suffering. It has led many young people into sexually abusive situations with predatory perverts, and has enabled terrorists to post publically instructions on how to create weapons of terror, for example. The machine that we call the corporation has a similarly checkered history.

The Immortal Corporation Machine

A corporation is treated, under the law, as a person – it has rights under the law, many of the same rights as a flesh-and-blood person. Yet it is most assuredly not a person -– it cannot breathe, it cannot bleed, it cannot love. A corporation is a machine, a legal fiction, created by another machine: the legal system.

Be clear on this, for it is the root of many problems: Corporations – nonliving, mechanical, essentially immortal entities (once, corporate charters were for a limited period of time) – have been given the rights of living, feeling, mortal human beings. These mechanical entities, some with enormous power, have been set loose on humanity without adequate governing mechanisms. In recent years corporations have even been given the right to patent life forms. There is no requirement that corporations exhibit socially acceptable behavior in the way that individuals are required to. There were attempts to pass laws that would have required them to be good citizens, but they were defeated.

Conventional wisdom was that corporations would behave themselves for their own self-interest – that they would not saw off the branch they are sitting on. A little observation of corporate behavior in the recent past suggests otherwise.

Those of us who have looked to the self-interest of
lending institutions to protect shareholder's equity
– myself especially – are in a state of shocked disbelief.
– Alan Greenspan, former chairman of the Federal Reserve

In many ways some corporations behave like parasites, with no moral code, creating untold permanent damage, without being held to account. Nor are those operating them held responsible, except for the most heinous crimes. Executives receive obscene bonuses and golden parachutes as their companies lay off tens of thousands of employees and slide into bankruptcy, robbing both stockholders and employees of their investments and retirement funds. But the corporation is a machine, and does not care.

Obviously crime pays, or
there'd be no crime.
– G. Gordon Liddy

It gets to do business, be protected by the police and the armed forces, to take on various identities through "Public Relations" (PR), and to influence the government through contributions and lobbyists. The problem is that an individual cares about his/her life, about family and social relationships, about reputation. But a corporation does not. It cannot, because it cannot care. It has no feelings, no soul, no spirit. The bottom line is, what will make the most money.

Not long ago we experienced a disturbing example of how corporations can behave in inhuman ways. One after another batch of toys we had imported from China was found to contain unhealthy levels of lead in their colorful paint. Then we discovered that a discarded plastic byproduct, melamine, was being put in the pet food we were buying throughout the country. Thousands of pets died of kidney failure. As dozens of American companies go bankrupt, their CEOs walk away with multimillion-dollar salaries and bonuses, and the boards of directors make out pretty well also. Why bother caring, if you don't get caught, you get rich, if you do, you declare the company bankrupt, and start another company.

Good Corporations?
An Oxymoron?

To be fair, we should keep in mind the commendable behaviors of some corporations in the past; truly generous, altruistic and heartfelt gifts have been given, and social causes supported. Yet we must remember that these were the result of the choices of the directors, it was their compassion that we must appreciate, for the corporate behavior was their choice. Particular individuals with high moral and ethical principles may hold a position of power for a period of time within a given corporation, but they are no more the corporation than the conductor on a train is the train. At any moment the kind, wise CEO may be replaced by a power hungry tyrant. Moreover, while humans live a lifespan and die, corporations can be immortal[3].

In other words, a corporation may exhibit behavior that makes it appear that it cares, but only because the current directorate cares, and not because it is intrinsic to the definition of a corporation. If the board or the CEO changes, or if another company purchases the company, it could immediately become sociopathic. It is important to keep in mind that corporations are not intrinsically evil, but they will behave in ways that hurt humans if they are not guided with a compassionate hand. Without such guidance, they will do harm, because, as the scorpion explained to the frog he had just stung, "It's in my nature."

---

[3] Curiously, this immortality reminds us of cancer cells, which also have no fixed lifespan – Henrietta Lacks died in 1951, for instance, but the cells of her cancer still live and multiply in laboratories throughout the world.

The Sociopathic Corporation

The behavior of the corporation has been compared to the behavior of a sociopath. Here's where the sociopathology comes in: Imagine that a caring CEO makes a compassionate decision to not fire a group of workers who had dedicated their lives to the company, and even people who worked without pay to help it through hard times. If the stockholders can show in court that firing those workers would have resulted in a higher profit, they can actually force the CEO to pay them that extra amount they would have earned, out of his/her own pocket! Crazy man crazy. The same disastrous fate would befall the board of directors of a mining company who spent money to clean up the environmental disaster it had caused, rather than cleverly leaving the job to the local taxpayers (the reason states like Montana now have a trillion dollar cleanup on their hands)[4].

Why refer to them as sociopathic? Consider the following checklist of the traits of the sociopathic person:

1. The sociopath is irresponsible, as is the corporation, which, to satisfy its goals is willing to put all others at risk, including its employees and the environment.
2. Sociopaths lack a sense of guilt or remorse for any harm they may have caused others, instead, rationalizing the behavior, blaming someone else, or denying it outright. The responsibility for this falls to the corporation's attorneys.
3. Sociopaths also lack empathy towards others in general, and often have a superficial charm about them. Their low level of self-consciousness permits them to make any self-serving statement, without concern for accuracy or truth. Pathological liars, they are willing to con and manipulate others for personal gain or amusement.

---

[4] Jared Diamond, *Collapse: How Societies Choose to Fail or Succeed* (Viking Adult, 2004).

4. Sociopaths are also careless in the way they treat themselves. They frequently fail to alter their behavior in a way that would prevent them from enduring future discomfort.
5. Like the sociopath, the corporation is willing to manipulate everything to its sole benefit, including public opinion.
6. Grandiosity ("I am the best") is a quality corporations share with the sociopathic human being, as is its tendency to be singularly self-interested in creating wealth for its shareholders.
7. Neither has compassion nor feels remorse; both live out make-believe version of themselves, like the image produced by a public relations consultant[5].

This sociopathic condition expresses itself through greed; greed is the very basis of the corporation – a corporation can serve as a particularly virulent way that greed can express itself. In this way a corporation can be like a renegade cancer.

"Pro-industry" politicians, sweatshops and child labor, abusive bosses, lax environmental laws, revolving door prisons and the like are all very nurturing to corporations. Consider one very important tenet of the corporations of the last century – always strive to "externalize costs." A real-world example of this is the situation in which the company can save $100,000 by dumping toxic wastes, even though it produces pollution that society will eventually have to pay $1,000,000 to clean up. The corporation makes this choice, with little thought of the consequences, calling it a "shrewd business decision." In fact, if the CEO were to not make this choice, he would be vulnerable to a suit from the shareholders for not meeting his "fiduciary responsibility" to them!

The corporation is comfortable making its decisions based on quarterly profits; the individual has a stake in the future, for he and his children must live there. But if he tries too hard to maintain the quality of the future (e.g., the environment, the character of the community) he may be fired from the corporation for getting in its way. No wonder there is so much stress in our companies.

---

[5]   See *The Corporation*, a film by Mark Achbar,
    Jennifer Abbott, and Joe Bakan.

Meanwhile, the corporation does not mind dying, if those who are in charge can "make a killing" in the process.

An individual human being, or a family, is interested in "profiting," but also there is empathy, compassion, love, meaning, and spirituality. We have the inner desire to support our community in functioning lovingly and smoothly in its caring for all its members. The corporation has none of these – it generates money until it dies, by ultimately overgrowing its food supply – and as is the case with human parasitosis, often the host dies too. Parasite-like. Cancer-like.

The MacDonaldization of the World

The corporate mentality wants a homogenization of the world – the ideal situation would be that everybody could be convinced to want the same thing, something that is cheap and easy to produce, but that could be sold at a premium due to a monopoly. In this way it acts in a way that is fundamentally opposed to culture.

Culture, quite to the contrary, is highly specific and local; it is as different as a Southern drawl and a Scottish brogue. It is personal, unique to our family and community, and it produces a feeling of comfort and belonging in people. Such uniqueness and diversity of choices makes the corporation's job of making a profit more difficult. Thus one of the jobs of the corporation is to eliminate these local "personalities," and convince everyone, through advertising to

think they want the same thing. One size fits all is a corporate dream – no competition, mass production of a single item.

Licensed to Kill?

Earlier, we talked about the frequently cited story of the catastrophic chemical link in Bhopal, India in 1984, where it has been reported that 20,000 people died, and 150,000 were left severely disabled. More than 20 years after the Bhopal disaster, those who survived the gas remain sick, and the chemicals that Union Carbide left behind in Bhopal are believed to have poisoned the water supply and contributed to an epidemic of cancers, birth defects, and other afflictions. It is widely believed that, since its purchase of Carbide in 2001, Dow-Carbide has refused to clean up the site, and has refused to stand trial in Bhopal, where the Union Carbide Corporation faces criminal charges of culpable homicide (manslaughter), and has fled these charges for the past 12 years.

I do not know whether these corporations are as guilty of these violations as has been reported; the trial has not even begun. What I do know is that it is 100% true, that it can happen in just this way, and that in countless cases corporations have been guilty of similar crimes against the communities in which they exist and operate. And what I do know is that we still have inadequate safeguards against such abuses. And if we do catch the corporation, it just goes bankrupt.

One of the more amazing outcomes of the way our system operates is that corporations have a 007 license – in effect, they are licensed to kill! If a poor man pushes over the grocery store clerk while he is running out with a stolen loaf of bread, he will be tried for murder if the clerk dies, and may spend 20 years to life in jail if he survives.

Meanwhile, a large corporation, like Union Carbide, can perpetrate a disaster such as that in Bhopal and no one is punished, no one serves jail time. And more generally, although some corporations, such as Enron, have been exposed recently, I suspect we have seen but the tip of the iceberg.

... The watchdogs are asleep, and it isn't just the FBI and the CIA. It's the Red Cross, it's the Catholic Church, it's the Wall Street investment people who are supposed to be giving you objective advice to help you in your investments, and it's the auditing firms that are supposed to protect the public against the cheating. So the aftermath of Enron is (that the culprit is) not just a rogue company; it's the watchdogs of the system . . . The watchdogs have become lapdogs . . . interested in their own doggy pursuits, interested in the interests of the insiders, in the interests of the institution, rather than in the people the institutions are supposed to serve . . . Conflict of interest? — the term has been meaningless the last couple of years in Wall Street and other places. It's as if the concept didn't even exist, hardly paid lip service to.
– Daniel Yankelovich
(founding father of public opinion research)

Again, the corporation is not evil by nature, it is simply a limited liability fiction that behaves like a machine, doing whatever it is designed to do. And just as an automobile can either be used as an ambulance to take sick children to the emergency room, or a truck bomb to blow up a busload of school children, the corporation will be what we let it. It doesn't have to be this way, but the truth is that the vast majority of corporations are focused on gaining advantage over competitors and favoring one group (stockholders, directors) over another. The potential to lead us toward greater dispersion and away from the essential awareness of our fundamental connectedness is obvious.

Regarding the Connectedness of All Things

To see the universe in a grain of sand
And a heaven in a wildflower
Hold infinity in the palm of your hand and eternity in an hour.
– William Blake

It has become fashionable, of late, to refer to how we're all connected. As John Muir reminds us, "When one tugs at a single thing in nature, he finds it attached to the rest of the world." Those sentiments were echoed by "Man belongs to the earth. This we know. All things are connected – whatever befalls the earth, befalls the sons of the earth. Man did not weave the web of life; he is merely a strand in it. Whatever he does to the web, he does to himself," (mis)attributed to Chief Seattle.

We all pay at least lip service to the notion that the various religions and belief systems that abound on our planet need to learn how to find common ground. Still, most of us find it much easier to criticize others for their lack of integrity than to take a fearless "moral inventory" of ourselves, to see the subtle ways that we manage to support violence done to others while remaining unconscious of it. This excerpt from Derrick Jensen's profoundly disturbing book, *The Culture of Make Believe*[6], makes the point in a most dramatic way:

In 1918, the husband of Mary Turner, a black woman from Valdosta, Georgia, was killed by a mob of white men, not for any offense he had committed, but rather because another black man had killed a white farmer. I do not know precisely how Turner's husband died. I do not even know his name. I know only that in retaliation for the killing of the white farmer, many citizens of Valdosta lynched

---

[6] Derrick Jensen, *The Culture of Make Believe* (Chelsea Green, 2004).

eleven black men – who were simply in the wrong place at the wrong time with the wrong color skin – before they shot and killed the man they were after.

In the wake of her husband's murder, Mary, who was eight months pregnant, vowed to avenge those who killed her husband. An Associated Press article later commented on her "unwise remarks," noting that "the people, in their indignant mood, took exception to her remarks, as well as her attitude." If you dig beneath the delicate language, it is easy to see what was coming. A mob of several hundred white men and women determined they would "teach her a lesson," or, perhaps more precisely, they would teach a lesson to those others who might be tempted to act as she did. They tied her ankles together and hung her upside down from a tree. Then they doused her clothes with gasoline and burned them off of her. They used a hog-splitting knife to open her belly. Her infant fell to the ground, and cried briefly, until someone crushed its head with his heel. The mob then shot her, not once or twice, but hundreds of times.

Now, let's remove ourselves from the emotionally safe dustbin of history to another death that happened in 2001. This person who died – I do not know her name, or very much about her except that she was seventeen years old – was one of about forty people killed over Easter weekend in Alto Naya, in Columbia. Her killers were what these days we call a death squad. I do not know what the members of the death squad said to her or the other people from her village, before they killed her, any more than I know what the members of the mob said to the husband of Mary Turner. I do not know what they were thinking, or feeling, nor do I know the set of their faces. I do not know whether they laughed, or spat, or whether they were simply doing what they felt needed to be done. I know only that when her body was later exhumed, it was discovered that members of the death squad had cut off her hands with a chainsaw, and used that also to open her belly and throat.

It is easy as it is unwise to simply throw up our hands in the face of these acts, declare them incomprehensible or, just as safely, having nothing whatsoever to do with any of us. I've never stuck anyone with a knife, nor even aimed a chainsaw at a human being. I just don't understand how someone could do this. Maybe they're just evil.

But are the actions really so difficult to understand, and do they really have nothing to do with us? What do we make of the fact that in the aftermath of the killing of Mary Turner and the others, 500 black people quietly and quickly left Valdosta for greener (or, at least, safer, pastures) leaving plenty of fine farmland ripe for new tenants, including those who never held a rope, gun, or knife? Similarly, it is significant that in Columbia, U.S. oil companies – including a company for which former president George W. Bush was a board member before becoming president of the United States – operate in the regions where these death squads kill, routinely?

Now, of course you are probably not one of those who moved into one of the houses left behind by a retreating black family, but this story is only a metaphor to help us see what we are doing. Not to put too fine a point on it, in a sense, you and I are well fed, and living very well on land taken from Indians, whose children are starving in poverty in the concentration camps known as "reservations." How, like corporations, individuals can be when they benefit from the suffering of others, and feel no responsibility for it.

If you are neutral in situations of injustice, you have chosen the side of the oppressor. If an elephant has its foot on the tail of a mouse and you say that you are neutral, the mouse will not appreciate your neutrality.
– Bishop Desmond Tutu

Self-Assessment

1. How important is integrity to you in designing your life?
2. How scrupulously honest are you in your business dealings? (Is it OK, for instance, to sell a car whose transmission you know is about to fail, without informing the prospective buyer?)
3. When you make a mistake, do you try to make it look as though it was someone else's fault?
4. Do you use your size, your loud voice, or clever treats to manipulate others to get what you want?
5. How much do you criticize, tease, browbeat, or use guilt or anger in your dealings with others?
6. In an argument, or in a heated discussion, how important is the truth of the matter versus your being right?
7. Silence is the voice of complicity. Do you speak up and take action against injustice when you see it?

> *The evil in this world is not done only by those*
> *who commit it, but by those who stand back*
> *and watch it happening.*
> – Albert Einstein

8. Are you enjoying the fruits of sweatshop labor, or diamonds mined by slaves?
9. Are you doing your honest share, actively working towards social justice?
10. Are you honest about what you feel in your relationships?
11. To what degree have you learned to truly forgive others (or yourself)?
12. How often do you examine your reactions and responses to the world to discover whether they are productive of Love and togetherness?
13. Do you really want to answer these questions honestly? Do you really want to know the answers? For many this represents TMI – "Too much information, way too much information". How about you? Ignorance is bliss, but in today's world, ignorance can prove fatal.

All that is necessary for evil to succeed
is for good men to do nothing.
– Albert Einstein

Tools for Love

But just as mankind has developed such well-publicized tools for wreaking violence, we have developed other powerful tools that function very well to enhance Love within a system. Used properly they can steadily create ever-deeper levels of healing within an individual, create family/community among individuals, and potentially bring about a new direction for our nation and our planet.

We are most likely to discover these nonviolent, Love-promoting tools being utilized in very individual, personal contexts (e.g. the monastic life, renunciation, meditation, volunteer pursuits, and intimate relationships). These tools are very effective in enabling people to know themselves better and to relate to in ways that create more wholeness and healing in the collective sphere. The knowledge of how to apply, teach, and promote these tools has, until recently, been limited to a relatively small number of people. Further, even in those contexts in which people are striving to learn as use them, they are usually described in jargon, by groups that see themselves as "the chosen ones." Overwhelmingly, those who are not of the "flock," (and that is the vast majority) are made to feel excluded, as "outsiders," and often become resentful. Then, whatever truth may have been gained is often discarded along with the bathwater.

My life's mission has been to support this movement towards critical mass by:

187

- Identifying these tools
- Expressing them in clear, nonsectarian, attractive, entertaining ways
- Making them available to as many people as possible at minimal cost and maximal enjoyment. In this way we have the best chance of reaching critical mass.

Tools For Transformation

So, what is the nature of these tools? We have determined that the planet is in serious shape, and that a mere rearranging of the deck chairs on the Titanic is not going to be enough this time. We need a real transformation, a metamorphosis. The metamorphosis of a butterfly is an apt analogy, for we too must undergo a shift in consciousness not much different from the shift in physical form that the caterpillar undergoes. Just as the new being needs to fly, not just crawl around and consume, we need to soar in our thinking and our spirits.

So these tools are designed to support our shifting to a new paradigm. They will help enable us to see more clearly what is, and to come out of Denial so that we can see the seriousness of the situation. And even more importantly, coming out of denial allows us to become aware of our true potential.

All of scientific thinking changed after scientists had shifted from the Newtonian to the Einsteinian way of looking at the universe. The paradigmatic shift I am suggesting is parallel to this shift, and once we understand the transformation that can occur, as a result of the new paradigm, we can begin to create what we want in a way that was unthinkable before.

The Grains of Wheat

Once upon a time, a man bravely stepped forward and took an arrow to save the life of the king. So grateful was the king that he told the man he could have anything he wanted. The man produced a checkerboard.

"I would like one grain of wheat for the first square on the checkerboard, two grains of wheat for the second, three for the third, and so on, across all sixty-four squares."

"Easily done," said the king, "Granted!" not realizing his grave error. Indeed, the number of grains of wheat needed for the last square of the checkerboard would be $2^{64} - 1 = 18,446,744,073,709,551,615$ grains of wheat. At about 5,000,000 grains per bushel this would add up to about 4,000 billion bushels of wheat – more than all the grains of wheat in his kingdom and all the kingdoms of the world put together.

Critical Mass and the Chain Reaction Effect

This parable is an excellent example of how powerful and surprising a transformational principle can be. Here the king is lulled into thinking arithmetically (1,2,3,4,...), while the wheat is accumulating exponentially (2,4,8,16,...).

A transformational paradigm shift must take place in our everyday thinking to comprehend what happens to produce the nuclear chain reaction that occurs after critical mass is reached. In a Newtonian world, if you roll a pool ball across the table and it strikes another, the other moves off with about the same momentum, while the first stops. If you strike two pool balls with it, both are impelled to move, each with about half the energy the first one possessed.

But a nuclear chain reaction is different. Here, a decomposing atomic nucleus ejects two neutrons. When each of these neutrons encounters another radioactive atom, it causes that atom to disintegrate, releasing energy, gamma rays, and two more neutrons. Each of these neutrons, in turn, when they hit a nearby nucleus, repeats the process. Because the energy released at each level of these collisions is $E=mc^2$, where c is the speed of light, a massive build-up of heat results in a huge fireball.

This process could never have been predicted by a Newtonian way of thinking. Newton could never have dreamed that a handful of radioactive material could release enough energy to create a hole in the ground miles wide. His paradigm could not see it or explain it.

The Principles of Organic Thinking

When we shift to an organic way of thinking, we find we have access to energy we could not have discovered in the other paradigm. My thesis is that a simple set of principles, each of which is easily seen to be true, which, when consistently applied, serves to transform the lives of those who practice them, and, not surprisingly a transformation in the world around them tends to occur as well. This transformation, of the people in their family and community in addition to their physical environment, can be called healing, for it is supportive of holons (wholes) at every level of system, and is based on the principle of balance.

These principles have been denied to most people, and distorted in their presentation to others, usually because those in power feared the freedom "the masses" might obtain if they knew the truth. Think Adolph Hitler. Think Stalin. It should also not be surprising that those who are considered great healers – Jesus, Muhammed, Moses, Gandhi, Mandela, and Oprah, for example – tend to espouse something very similar to this set of principles.

One central principle has to do with how we relate with others, what is the best way for parts of the system to relate to others.

Consider the following statements:

- Love they neighbor as thyself. Do unto others as you would have others do unto you. (Bible: Golden Rule)
- This is the sum of duty; do naught unto others which would cause you pain if done to you. (Hinduism: Mahabharata: 5, 151)
- Hurt not others in ways that you yourself would find hurtful. (Buddhism: The Udana - Varga: 5,18)
- Surely it is the maxim of loving-kindness: Do not unto others that you would not have them do unto you. (Confucianism, Analects: 15,23)
- No one of you is a believer until he desires for his brother that which he desires for himself. (Islam, The Sunnah, the Sayings of Muhammed)
- What is hateful to you, do not to your fellowmen. That is the entire Law; all the rest is commentary. (Judaism, Talmud: Shabbat, 31a)

What is being expressed here is a fundamental Systemic Healing Principle. Essentially every religion teaches this "Golden Rule," regardless of their differing rituals and imagery. Perhaps this is because only those spiritual movements that understand how fundamental this principle is to survival of the group manage to endure the insistently divisive pressure of such human passions, fear, anger, lust, greed, envy, pride, and all the rest.

Notice the statement, "Love thy enemies . . ." Our enlightened teachers tell us that we need to love our enemies as well as our friends, that they are part of us as well. Often they represent part of us that we fear, that we don't like about ourselves. Perhaps it is a part that we refuse to accept in ourselves, that we don't want anyone to know about . . . including ourselves [7].

They tell us that if we don't like what we see in others, what we need to do is to take a good hard look at ourselves. Mirrors don't lie.

The startling truth is that when we accept ourselves[8] the way we are, we will allow others more freedom to be the way they are.

When we use Denial to avoid seeing aspects of ourselves that we do not like, we automatically constrain ourselves to see those same aspects in others (Projection) – and will continue to see those "evil qualities" until they are resolved in us. In this way, fundamentally good people do incalculable damage.

This "Golden Rule" implies a paradigm of wholeness; it is the essence of organic thinking, sharing, integrative, unitive thinking characteristic of Love. Notice, the "opposite" paradigm, the one so prevalent at every level of culture and society these days, has a distinctly different paradigm for dealing with enemies, one that translates roughly to, "Go ahead, make my day . . . It's a smackdown, and the enemy is going down!"

The magic comes as you discover how to allow other people to be who they are: you realize that you are a primary "cause" of how you see them, and how you relate to them. Almost immediately you are no longer frustrated, angry, depressed, or anxious about the fact that people are exactly the way they are, and at this

---

[7]   At the individual level, a therapist would call this behavior Denial. I would call it Denial at other levels of system also. For instance, many people believe that leaders knew that the Vietnam War was unwinnable, yet did not draw our forces out until some 2000 more young men and women in our armed forces, and an untold number of Vietnamese fighters and their families were killed. The reason? The party in power was, apparently, unwilling to look bad by seeming to back down, and thus, lose the next election. If this is true it would represent Denial.

[8]   For a further elucidation and experience of Self-Acceptance, see the Audio CD, *I Am: Awakening Self-Acceptance* www.ShopDrMiller.com

moment this is the only way they can be. And at this moment, you begin to be able to communicate with them, because conversation[9] becomes possible.

Each of the principles shares a quality with this Golden Rule principle. It is necessary to know it, to embody it, and to express it in behavior, in order for it to have the desired benefit. When not understood and expressed, a kind of slavery results, a slavery that was much desired by those in control through the centuries. And so it was that many religious movements co-opted them. In the name of whatever god, goddess, or other deity they choose to worship, religious leaders (perhaps not always intentionally) have manipulated the faithful to do certain unconscionable things by distorting the truth. As Shakespeare noted, even "the devil can cite scripture for his own purpose." Indeed, the Holy Bible was quoted to justify slavery and witch burning, and the Holy Koran to validate terrorism!

Perhaps the greatest sacrilege of all is going to war "in the name of God." Abraham Lincoln once wisely observed that we must stop claiming that God is on our side and be more concerned about whether we are on God's side.

If God were on our side, he'd stop the next war.
– Bob Dylan

The second part of my thesis is that we now posses powerful tools to alter how we think – such tools as meditation, suggestion, guided imagery, and powerful media capabilities. Although these tools are usually used to manipulate and control people – this is how they are used in advertising and propaganda – they can also be used to sell people on their own true beauty, power, and potential. The third part is that current technology (TV, DVD, CD, Internet) gives us the ability to effectively teach these principles, stripped of parochial trappings. Other technology (Internet, e-mail) permits us to spread this information in a chain reaction manner. The outcome might prove to be a world of much more Love and much less

---

[9] Conversation: Communication in which both (or all) the parties are changed by the experience.

Violence.

My belief is that if there are enough of us who understand the possibilities now at hand, we can create a transformation individually and as a culture, that will rival the invention of the wheel and the industrial revolution.

Evolving a Global Consciousness

Now that we have a diagnostic impression and a putative etiology for our illness, that fits the observed phenomena, we can start to develop a way to treat the patient. I will outline here a tentative approach designed primarily to serve as an illustration – to give us a starting point and a platform that we can continuously build upon as we gain experience, feedback – and wisdom. How do we shift to a paradigm that enables us to make wiser choices?

We want a treatment plan that takes into account all levels of the system, from the microscopic (the individual cells of the body) to the macroscopic (the planet) – and of course, everything in between (individuals, families, communities, nations, cultures). In the life of an individual, the physical, behavioral, social, and emotional symptoms often come down to a certain counterproductive way of looking at the world. In turn, this negative point of view gives rise to stress reactions which, in turn, make matters worse.

A course of education or therapy that leads to a **new way of thinking** about oneself and one's relationships is often curative of multiple symptoms all along the line. On the other hand, traditional, repeated, symptomatic treatment seldom suffices to cure the real problem. As I've shown, symptom-only treatment can often make the situation worse (e.g., alcoholism, denial, anger). And in extreme cases, like the diabetes example I offered earlier, treating only the symptoms could kill the patient.

The same is true when a relationship is out of balance. As every mental health practitioner knows (or should know), the presenting problem of a patient is rarely the real problem. Moreover, when treating either the presenting problem or the real problem, asking for mere behavioral change often doesn't work.

There is a school of thought that believes behavioral change will lead to emotional and cognitive change. There is even a little ditty about it:

If I change the things I say and do,
I will change my feelings too.

Sometimes that works, but it is a simplistic theory at best. For instance, you may be able to get an alcoholic who wants to save a relationship to stop drinking, but that does not address the deep-seated reasons he or she was drinking. Furthermore, the alcoholic will frequently simply choose another substance to abuse – and the relationship problem is not cured.

It's not that some people have willpower and some don't. It's that
some people are ready to change and others are not.
– James Gordon, M.D.

Our challenge is to fundamentally change the way we think and perceive the world to truly overcome the negative and coun- terproductive stress reactions we have within ourselves and in our relationships. The basic principles offered in the coming pages ap- pear to work at every level of system. At the individual level, we can transform our personal thoughts, behaviors, and self-statements, and in this way alter the functioning of the cells of our bodies (e.g., our immune systems). We can then share our enlightened way of thinking and interacting with our families, friends, co-workers, and all our other social relationships, sometimes even total strangers. These same principles can be applied at the macro (social) level. We can transform our communities, our local and national govern- ments, corporations and institutions, schools, and religions, and yes, even our local and global ecosystems.

It sounds good on paper, but the order of magnitude of change I'm talking about cannot be manifested if we restrict our- selves to the old familiar way of unbalanced polar thinking. We must first balance ourselves along the Polar/Organic continuum. Only then will we be ready to learn and apply the multidimensional spectrum of organic thinking to ourselves, and everybody and everything around us. So let's start at the beginning, the etiology.

Etiology: Personal and Global Stress

An excess of inappropriately applied Polar (dispersive) thinking is the root of the imbalance; it represents Violence. What we need is a New Paradigm, one that includes Organic and Second Order (transformative) thinking. This requires that we put a greater focus on the hallmarks of love which are balance, homeostasis, unitive thinking, holistic health, oneness.

> *There is nothing either good or bad,*
> *but thinking makes it so.*
> – William Shakespeare

Although there is a natural tendency for people to perceive stress as coming from the external world, what we have discovered is that the true origin of stress is within ourselves. Stress is a mental, physical, and emotional expression of unresolved polarity and conflict in the mind/nervous system. When an important flight is cancelled, when we're suddenly laid off, when we begin to suspect our spouse is having an affair . . . we experience this internal conflict as stress. And, since stress is a prime factor in most illnesses, a vicious circle is created, stress gives rise to illness, illness, in turn, gives rise to more stress, leading towards ever greater dysfunction. In a sense, stress is internal friction that abrades and disrupts the system when it is chronically unresolved.

We have been looking at both personal/individual stress and at global stress — postulating many of our global problems are the result of stress and conflict. Personal stress is the result of our personal feelings of helplessness resulting from unbalanced stress triggered by how we experience our environment. Global stress is the result of conflict between groups within the culture, and those conflicts themselves are the result of stresses within individuals. Ultimately, continual stress produces an increasing sense of help-lessness or rage (a disguised form of helplessness), which can lead to overt violence and war. This helplessness ranges from the personal ("I'm trapped!") to the cultural ("You can't fight city hall") to the global ("It's too late, we will never convince our governments to cut carbon emissions.").

Helpless but Not Hopeless

Psychologist Martin Seligman, Ph.D., postulated the theory of "Learned Helplessness" in the 1970s. He began by studying the effects of inescapable shock on active avoidance learning in dogs, where he made some remarkable discoveries that had a major influence on research into human depression.

Seligman restrained dogs in a Pavlovian harness and ad-ministered shocks to their feet. Once they had been conditioned to unavoidable shock, the dogs were placed in a shuttle-box where they could avoid shocks on one side of the box by jumping over a short fence. Whereas, dogs who had not received this "helpless-ness conditioning" would instantly jump over the fence the moment they received the shock, Seligman's failed to do so; they just stood there and allowed the painful shocks.

Seligman reasoned that prior exposure to inescapable shock interfered with the ability to learn adaptive behavior in a situation where avoidance or escape was possible. Seligman used the term "learned helplessness" to describe this phenomenon, and went on to demonstrate it with human subjects in many experiments.

The central idea in the Learned Helplessness theory is the notion that all animals (including humans) can be conditioned to become helpless (and hopeless). You can probably verify this within your own experience: even when circumstances change, most people are very slow to alter their thinking and behavior to respond to this change. In fact, many will actively resist adaptive change! We really don't realize how much power we have. The victim mentality is very widespread. We end up being the victims of scam artists, politicians, demagogues, corporations, and religious zealots – all of whom would lose their power over us if we overcome this helplessness and start thinking for ourselves. So they use powerful tools, such as the media, advertising, and threats of one or another God's punishment.

We have the power to change what is wrong, but most people stubbornly cling to the status quo out of fear and/or ignorance. They don't realize or believe they have the power to change themselves, let alone the world.

Unitive Behavior and Responsibility

At this point in history we actually have the possibility of tapping into the roots of what has made human culture and survival-possible. The challenge is to envision it on a new plane, to discover a new level of systemic thinking.

Families, tribes, and societies seem to function best when each individual member possesses:

• A sense of belonging to the whole group, and
• A feeling of responsibility to the whole group.

Such human communities tend to be self-sustaining because everyone is inculcated with a unitive ethic. The success of this kind of thinking is demonstrated by the survival success of the human species – helpless as individuals, dominant as groups.

Today, at the macroscopic level, the multicultural level, however, this all-for-one-and-one-for-all way of thinking does not exist – at least not yet in enough minds. Instead we have the "Us vs. Them" mentality that has, throughout history, led to competition and conflict. In this way, an otherwise very loving and cooperative community can become xenophobic and violent when it encounters another group of people – even if this other group practices the same kind of love and communal support of its own members. Each group dehumanizes and demonizes the other to justify robbing, raping, and killing, which benefits the perpetrator at the expense of the other, and seriously degrades the whole. Usually the resulting war is sanctioned by the god each group worships, it is considered god's work to kill those who are seen as infidels. Even when the two groups seem to worship the same god, they manage to find a way to nitpick their way to war. Consider the Catholic and Protestant Christians killing each other in Ireland in the name of Jesus, or the Sunni Muslims and the Shiite Muslims doing the same in Iraq.

I believe that our stunning success as a species is partly the result of the fact that primitive societies did not have the weapons to do serious damage to each other. Often, they would leave the field of battle with fewer than 10 percent casualties. Sometimes, only symbolic losses needed to take place (as in the Native American practice of counting coup) in order to define and maintain boundaries.

As weapons grew more sophisticated, however, so did the kill ratio. First the club, then the spear appeared. Then in rapid succession, came the gun, the bomb, and soon nuclear bomb-equipped, multiple re-entry vehicle missiles that evade radar. Wars were once fought between armies; now wars are aimed at the destruction of civilians. The result of this has been that when cultures clash, the casualties of the vulnerable culture are often catastrophic (the Holocaust, Hiroshima, Rwanda, Darfur).

Today's rapid technological pace has taken things to a new order of magnitude. Now, one disaffected sociopath or vengeance-seeking terrorist with an Internet connection can discover ways to kill hundreds or thousands with technology's coup de grace, the backpack sized weapon of mass destruction (chemical, biological, nuclear): polarity thinking writ large.

How can it be that, with all our technological progress, with the massive explosion of information that is our environment, we are less safe than ever? Why is it that with our enormous under-standing of psychology, we do not address and resolve those de-stabilizing conditions that threaten us all? Why do those who are in power not lead us to make the obvious changes that are needed?

Perhaps it is because the technology we use to operate our minds is in great need of attention. The prime necessity of human life, the sense of belonging, of feeling related to the whole, is get-ting more and more scarce. And we cringe (or strut) helplessly along, wondering why so many things are going wrong, and whom we can blame for it, who we can punish for it. We live emotionally encapsulated lives, as individuals as well as groups. We look for differences, and attack, rather than look for similarities, and em-brace. It is time to upgrade our software, our operating system.

But will we? Our future may well rest on this single answer.

Questions to Ponder

1. Answer the Self-Assessment questions on page 186.

2. What changes in your thinking seem desirable to you?

3. In what ways would you like to see changes in the way governments approach challenges?

Notes to Self

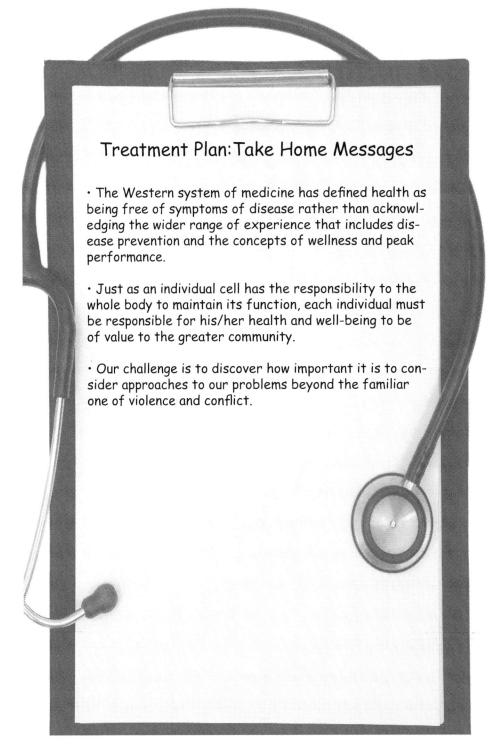

Treatment Plan: Take Home Messages

• The Western system of medicine has defined health as being free of symptoms of disease rather than acknowledging the wider range of experience that includes disease prevention and the concepts of wellness and peak performance.

• Just as an individual cell has the responsibility to the whole body to maintain its function, each individual must be responsible for his/her health and well-being to be of value to the greater community.

• Our challenge is to discover how important it is to consider approaches to our problems beyond the familiar one of violence and conflict.

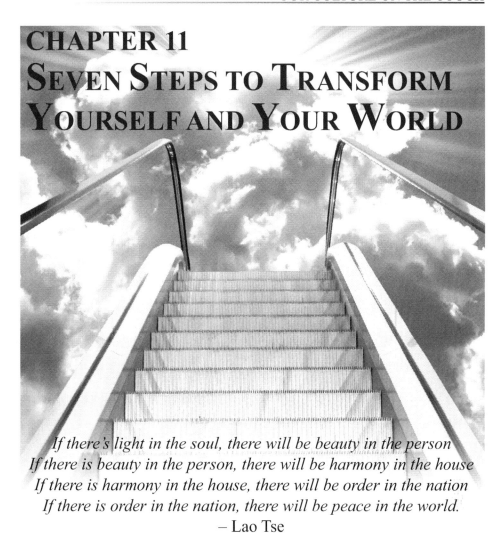

CHAPTER 11
SEVEN STEPS TO TRANSFORM YOURSELF AND YOUR WORLD

If there's light in the soul, there will be beauty in the person
If there is beauty in the person, there will be harmony in the house
If there is harmony in the house, there will be order in the nation
If there is order in the nation, there will be peace in the world.
— Lao Tse

The Seven Steps of Systemic Healing

Over the years, in my study of science, healing, transformation, and wisdom, certain key skills have emerged as central, regardless of which level of system is being addressed. Whether your focus is healing of body, mind, emotions, or spirit in your own personal life or in your family, community, country, or globally, these

203

steps comprise a valuable guide to success. There is no particular magic about the number of steps; I could have easily added in a few more, but chose to go with what I feel are the most basic, and crucial, in the interest of simplicity. What's more, the order is not sacrosanct, but is generally the most logical one. A slightly different order may work for you or some steps may merge with each other. Personalize this program to fit your individual needs and the needs of the system you are addressing.

Survival of the Wisest

Always bear in mind that the tools we are working with are systemic healing tools. Because they are integral to the deeper structure of the system, they enable us to go beyond superficial fixes, beyond merely symptomatic relief. We need to let go of the attraction to gizmos and gadgets, fashions and fads, fake leaders and false prophets. We need to understand what it means to attempt to go beyond what the Buddhists call samsara (suffering) and maya (illusion) – to see that there is one unifying theme running through all of perceivable creation. We might call it "survival of the wisest," to use Jonas Salk's phrase. Whether we are talking about paramecia or people, about cabals or countries, those who allow their behavior to be guided by the principles of wisdom tend to emerge from the fray least damaged and more empowered by it.

Ideally, we want to have the presence of mind and quiet centeredness to accept the world as it is and let go of dysfunctional emotional attachments. In addition, we want to have the courage to act decisively, guided by our deeper convictions, to change what needs to be changed. Wisdom gives us the ability to choose to respond to any particular challenge with either acceptance or action based upon the deeper needs of the system, rather than superficial, prejudicial, emotional reactions that derive from post traumatic stress. All of us – as individuals, communities, and cultures – have been traumatized by an angry, frightened world, each in its own way. Until we free ourselves from the emotional effects of that trauma, our perceptions will be distorted, preventing us from making decisions that are truly wise.

For thirty years, at least, we have been guided by myths that greed is good, strength comes from guns, and the world is divided between good and evil. These metaphors are not dead, but at the end of 2008 they are gasping, writhing on the ground.
– Craig Barnes

The fundamental processes we will explore are essentially the same, whether you want to examine and change yourself, your family, friends, community, nation, or the world as a whole. The same principles will apply. The difference is that if you are aiming primarily to improve yourself personally, you will apply these approaches simply within your private life, whereas, if you are working to improve your marriage or your workplace or the world, it is best to participate in the process together with certain others.

Some people will find some of the steps more challenging than others; the step of "Letting Go" is an excellent example, since it often involves releasing addictive behaviors, emotions such as anger and fear, and familiar (if harmful) ways of thinking (e.g., prejudice, guilt, blame, shame).

On the other hand, you may find some of the steps familiar, and rather easy. If you have been meditating for years, for example, the step of "Presence" may be almost second nature to you. Similarly, those who have experience in recovery programs will recognize some of these steps; feel free to employ the tools and techniques you have already learned as you follow this guide.

Experiential Learning: When Knowing Isn't Enough

Because some of what you read here may be somewhat familiar to you, you may be tempted to "speed read" through it. In today's world, we often think we "know" something when we recog nize the idea, or are able to parrot it back from rote memory. True healing and transformation, however, requires that you proceed slowly enough to really *experience* every phenomenon presented in each of the steps, even if you know that you have already experienced it in the past. It is best to consider this a kind of training. Take the time to *experience* each of these steps into the present moment, *feel the associated feelings*, and appreciate their relevance in your life.

> *There's an old Chinese tale about a certain monk who, after having spent many years in the monastery in deep study with the master, went out in the world to perfect his wisdom. After many years, he returned, eager to share his discoveries with his master. "Ah," said the master, "you have returned. And what have you learned?" "I have learned," said the monk, "that when the clouds no longer hide the mountaintop, the rays of the moon pierce the clear waters of the lake." "I can't believe it," responded the master with a shake of his head. "You are an old man with hardly any teeth, and yet you still do not understand the essence of wisdom." "Please, then, master," begged the monk, falling to his knees, "What is the essence of wisdom?" "It is that," the master began, "when the clouds no longer hide the mountaintop, the rays of the moon pierce the clear waters of the lake."*

Merely knowing the words is not enough – the goal is to embody them, to feel them so deeply that you know that you know. I will describe each of the seven steps first in terms of its application at the individual level, and then offer some suggestions for application at the family, community, and global level. No matter at what level of system you ultimately wish to apply these ideas, it is best to begin by applying them to the personal (inner) level. For instance, attempting to transform your city council without having applied these principles within yourself would expose you to accusations of hypocrisy, since your lack of integrity is likely to soon be noticed, and your power to influence the group would decline rapidly. Unintentional discrepancies in integrity lie beneath many failures. In later chapters, we will explore more specific ideas for application at other levels of system.

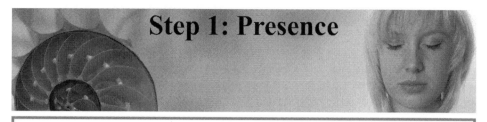

Step 1: Presence

> • **Truth:** *The root of all suffering is wanting things to be different from how they are at this moment in time.*
> • **Goals:** *To free the mind and nervous system from distraction, constrain thoughts and feelings to the "here and now," so as to create clarity of mind, freedom from emotional or cognitive distortion, and a relaxed, centered perspective.*
> • **Process:** *Centering, quieting, releasing.*

. . . Begin by letting your body rest in a comfortable position, in a place where you will be free of interruption . . . and choose a point in the distance to focus on. Keep your eyes fixed steadily on that point, and notice how that point is the only one that is clear, everything else fades into a blur . . . and that's OK, because, right now, you don't need to attend to anything else around you. Let yourself be aware . . . that, for the next few minutes . . . you are choosing to take charge of your mind . . . Awaken the wisdom deep in the core of your being . . . the leader within . . . and intentionally guide your emotions and your body, for the next few minutes.
– Awakening the Leader Within [1]

Regardless of your final goals, it is best to begin with the development of the ability to create a centered, focused, balanced state of mind. This provides us a stable base from which to begin to interact with the environment. The qualities that create health and wellness, when applied within, also produce peace and productivity when applied to families, teams, communities, and the like.

---

[1]   www.ShopDrMiller.com

Aldous Huxley described the perfect human paradise, a beautiful tropical island filled with delicious food, entertainment, and healthy friends. The trees would, he cautioned, need to be filled with Minot birds chanting over and over, "Here and now . . . here and now." Without them, he reasoned, we would most likely fail to notice the perfection around us; so pervasive is our cultural tendency to live in the struggles of the immutable past and the fantasized future.

Presence, then, involves:
- Letting go of Illusions (Denial, maya, samsara)
- Acceptance of Self and the World
- Coming into the Here-and-Now
- Imposing Internal Honesty.

Although usually experienced in a solitary setting, in a safe, private place, Presence can also be facilitated with two or a small number of motivated individuals.

The benefits of Presence include:
- Markedly increased ability to be aware of truth and wisdom
- Increased number of options for how to perceive the current situation
- Enhanced creativity and honesty
- Access to deeper levels of power, including access to (normally involuntary and unconscious) physiological processes
- Greater ability to attune with others and engage in meaningful conversation.

. . . This moment is the only moment that exists, and in this moment, you know it is safe to relax completely. The past does not exist . . . not even one second of the past can ever happen again . . . so you can let it go . . . There is no past . . . just some stories written in books in a library in your mind . . . no need for those stories at this moment . . . closing the door of the library . . . and as the air breathes you . . . become aware that the future does not exist either,

209

and it never even has . . . That the future is not some place you are going, it is a place you are creating in this moment . . . and in this moment, you can choose . . . to lead your mind to become aware of what is really most important, and to engage in the kind of thinking that will create the future that you desire at the deepest level of your being . . . and fulfill your deepest purpose and mission . . .
                                    – Awakening the Leader Within

Being relaxed and present gives rise to a peaceful demeanor, thus keeping open the door to the possibility of a peaceful, non-Violent solution, and a Loving resolution. This is why preparing for any potentially conflictual interpersonal contact should include this step of being present. Tools such as meditation, deep relaxation[2], self-hypnosis, or the kind of prayer that takes one into a receptive state of Presence are of enormous benefit. (That sort of prayer that consists of requesting favors of God, such as winning the football game on Sunday, generally do not facilitate the state we are aiming towards here.) Certain pieces of music or an appropriate movie or video can also produce a relaxed state, although it is best to have a portable means of entering the state of calm presence.

We need to find God, and he cannot be found in noise and restless-ness. God is the friend of silence. To see how nature – trees, flowers, grass – grows in silence; see the stars, the moon and the sun, how they move in silence ... We need silence to be able to touch souls.
                                    – Mother Teresa

The process of becoming and being more present is an ongoing one, and as you explore each of the succeeding steps, you should find yourself coming more and more into the moment, and more and more able to free yourself from distractions.

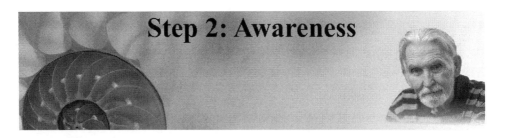

Step 2: Awareness

• **Truth:** *The truth is always the strongest argument. Your philosophy is not best expressed in words, but in action, in the choices you make. Those choices are ultimately your responsibility.*
• **Goals:** *To be clearly aware of the truth of who you truly are, appreciate the truth of the world around you and its imbalances, and choose those imbalances you wish to address.*
• **Process:** *Relaxation, Observation (knowledge comes from study, wisdom from observation), Honesty*

. . . And here . . . and now . . . allowing yourself to know that . . . within you is a wise guide . . . a wise essence . . . that knows how to breathe you . . . how to circulate oxygen and energy through your body . . . to balance the functioning of every cell in your body . . . to sense the presence of this wisdom . . . and allow your wise guide to join you . . . here in your special place . . .
– Awakening the Leader Within

Realizing the Truth of the Current Situation

Before we can establish control over a situation, we must:

• Realize that we are currently out of control.
• Realize that if this dire situation is to be remedied, it is we who must do it.

We are the leaders we have been waiting for.

211

In the shared myths from our cultural past, the boss, the master, the father figure was visualized as either being knowledgeable, wise, or fully in control of the situation (omniscient and/or omnipotent). Often he (usually the subject of these myths was male) was visualized as arriving heroically, often at the last moment, and saving the day (like Batman). The function of the masses was to simply do their leaders' bidding, spread their word, and persecute those who did not believe as they did.

*It is the customary fate of new truths to
begin as heresies and to end as superstitions.*
– T.H. Huxley

It is easy to identify at least two significantly different categories of leaders. On one hand, there is the group represented by Julius Caesar, Saddam Hussein, Adolph Hitler, and Joseph Stalin. The other group is exemplified by such as Moses, Jesus, Mohammed, Lao Tse, and Confucius. The prime difference we can see between these two types of leaders is in their intention; did they strive to spread the truth, or did they construct lies; were they in it for all of us (Love), or just as a way to enrich themselves (Violence)?

*The broad masses of a nation are always more easily corrupted in
the deeper strata of their emotional nature than at the conscious
or intentional. In the primitive simplicity of their minds, they more
readily fall victim to the big lie than the small lie, since they themselves often tell small lies in little matters, but would be ashamed to
resort to large-scale falsehoods. They cannot imagine colossal lies,
and they cannot believe that others could have the impudence to
distort the truth so disgracefully. Even though the facts proving that
they are lying are brought clearly to their minds, they
will still doubt and waver and continue to think
that there must be some other explanation.*
–Adolph Hitler, Mein Kampf, Murphy Translation

212

Compare this perspective to:

"And you will know the truth. The truth will make you free."
— The Holy Bible John 8:32

And:

Each of you, make yourself an island, make yourself your refuge; there is no other refuge. Make truth your island, make truth your refuge; there is no other refuge."
— The Buddha

In one case, the paradigm involves a "top-down," pyramidal structure of dominance of the many by the few. And, in certain circumstances, such as commanding an army or aircraft carrier, such a command-and-control structure is essential. We can't have every soldier or sailor meet for consensus gathering as to whether or not to return fire, for example. So, some of the time, using this kind of paradigm (or myth) is very appropriate. It is, of course, important that *wisdom*, rather than habit or denial and resistance, help us define these times.

Clearly, however, on many other occasions the paradigm of dominance and control will lead to certain disaster, whereas a different paradigm, one that results in leadership that sees and acknowledges the value of each individual, will be dramatically more successful. Globally and locally, we find ourselves in just such a situation now – one in which this old, top-down, command-and-control model, with its implied stifling of the individual, has outlived its usefulness as a primary paradigm for government. Though it *may* have brought about some positive changes in the past, it is becoming painfully obvious that in recent times this approach has led us perilously close to self-destruction. Far too often, those who have called the tune to which the people of our world are dancing have been dominating, demanding, and self-centered.

Far too often our elected "representatives" have not actually represented our interests (though they earnestly strive to appear to do so). They are out of touch with those they were elected to rep

213

resent (think Abramoff scandal), but they are very much in touch with the financial interests (lobbyists) that provide them the funds to win in the next election. What these financial interests are promoting, however, are often inimical to the population as a whole. The interests of the few are being served instead of the interests of the many. This is the system that has been leading us over the cliff.

It should be clear by now to even the casual observer that we have been misled by a system that has fed us lies in order to manipulate us, and we have been the denying victims. Although the enormity of the big lies is staring us in the face, many people still seem to be incapable of imagining the monumental size of the treachery, and how important it is to act now.

Playing "Follow the Leader" is dangerous when the leader does not have our best interests at heart. The kind of leadership we now need is the kind that starts in the depths of each heart, where the inner leader lies sleeping. Now is the time to awaken this inner potential.

Emerging from Denial

To awaken the inner leader means coming out of Denial. Just as it is necessary in individual therapy to come out of denial, coming out of cultural denial is essential to solving global issues as well. We need the willingness to look at reliable information concerning the phenomenon of globalization, how it is being managed, and the manifold local problems that will ensue[3]. I believe globalization is inevitable. The only question is: Will it be globalized economic collapse, poverty, and conflict? Or will we bring about globalized health, wellness, sustainability, and peak performance?

The evidence is quite convincing that the majority of our population is in denial about the true situation in the world today, from the behind-the-scenes machinations of our governments and

---

[3]   For an excellent example of how a community can respond to globalization, see the work done by Sustainable Connections in Bellingham, Washington http://www.sconnect.org/

institutions to the dangers of global warming, overpopulation, and environmental destruction. "Man-in-the-street" interviews concerning knowledge of current events and the state of the world yield farcical results. Living in this fairytale world of ignorance-born bliss is exposing us to unparalleled catastrophe. If we are to survive – and there is no guarantee that we will – it would be the very essence of wisdom to see clearly the truth in our personal lives, our relationships, our communities, our nation, and our planet. And we must start by looking honestly at ourselves.

When we look closely at any level of system, we often discover that the underlying cause of our problems is that paradigm that leads us to focus on differences, duality, and polarizing issues. It is only when we allow ourselves to risk seeing how blind we may have been that we can begin to see the world as it really is at this very moment. And only then we can become aware of the truth of the current situation with a deep willingness to accept what is, to accept what has gone before – and accept what must be done. We must be willing to discover painful negatives … and to accept them – for only then will the ego let us see the truth.

We might discover that we have been insensitive, abusive, and even cruel in our behavior toward others. If we are fortunate – and brave – we will discover this in ourselves, and at all the other levels of system.

Allow me to use a personal experience as an illustrative example. Christopher Columbus "discovered" America. As a child, I was taught to admire Columbus, and I even played the part of Columbus in a school play. It was only many years later that I discovered that Columbus was so interested in gold that he captured local Indians, forced them into slavery in the mines, and then chopped off the hands of any of them who failed to bring up a minimum amount of gold every day. My hero, Columbus, a butcher?!

Strange times are these in which we live when old and young are taught falsehoods in school. And the one man that dares to tell the truth is called at once a lunatic and fool.
– Plato

Another experience of being misled and betrayed in my life concerned this bit of writing from Thomas Jefferson, the architect of the Declaration of Independence. Here was a man whom I had also been taught to admire; yet he wrote, concerning "Negroes":

Comparing them by their faculties of memory, reason, and imagination, it appears to me, that in memory they are equal to the whites; in reason much inferior, as I think one [black] could scarcely be found capable of tracing and comprehending the investigations of Euclid; and that in imagination they are dull, tasteless, and anomalous. . . But never yet could I find that a black had uttered a thought above the level of plain narration; never see even an elementary trait of painting or sculpture . . . Among the blacks is misery enough, God knows, but no poetry.
– Thomas Jefferson

What about the "created equal" bit? And where does that leave Jefferson's slave mistress Sally Hemings and family?

And more: How shocking it was to discover that the stories, pictures, movies, and cultural attitudes that were fed to us in our youth had led us to objectify women, rather than treat women as human beings. After all, our mothers are women!

We cheered as the cavalry rode in and killed off the savage Indians on the movie screens of our childhood. How can we now stomach the truth of the genocide basic to this country's birth, the despicable and inhuman ways it was perpetrated, and the perfidious ways it was sold to the American public? And then there are all the other really reprehensible things that have been perpetrated and covered up by our government.

Hard to stomach all this, yes – but we must! The past cannot be changed. We do not have to live in it, but we can learn from it. *But only if we fully accept it* can we truly be open to the truth. And if we are not guided by an accurate reading of the truth, we are in big trouble, indeed.

History is a vast early warning system.
– Norman Cousins

Self-Identification

It is essential to realize that the negative statements we have been taught to believe about ourselves must be regarded as lies; they are part of the Black-White Paradigm. By far, the most effective belief to have about yourself is that you are truly beautiful inside. But to make this shift in paradigm, the key is to discover the truth about who you truly are. Beyond your race, religion, and name, beyond your role as a parent or employee, *who are you?*

Our deepest fear is not that we are inadequate. Our deepest fear is that we are powerful beyond measure. It is our light, not our darkness, that most frightens us. We ask ourselves, who am I to be brilliant, gorgeous, talented, and fabulous? Actually, who are you not to be? You are a child of God. Your playing small doesn't serve the world. There is nothing enlightened about shrinking so that other people won't feel insecure around you. We are born to make manifest the Glory of God that is within us. It's not just in some of us, it's in everyone, and as we let our own light shine, we consciously give other people permission to do the same. As we are liberated from our own fear, our presence automatically liberates others.
– Nelson Mandela, in his inaugural speech,
quoting Marianne Williamson

Can you imagine that this just might be true? If it sounds "airy fairy," remember, it was spoken by the black man who spent 27 years in a South African prison for his fight against apartheid. It might be of immense value to your own health and performance, as well as the health of all those social groups of which you are a part, if you would choose to believe it. As usual, if particular words (like God) make this difficult, substitute other words (Spirit, Love, Es-

217

sence, Truth, Self, etc.) that better reflect your worldview, and see how it feels.

This Self-identification is an important part of the systemic healing process. We must ask ourselves: what can I learn about this Self that I want to nurture? When do I feel most fulfilled and whole? What is a healthy relationship with my family or community? What is my deepest essence, what is my center, what is my circumference?

. . . And aware of your gifts, talents and resources . . . and with your deepest values . . . and where you can be in touch with your heart's desire . . . that place deep within you that knows there's something important you must accomplish, something you really care about . . . something you really want to do. And as you continue to breathe out all distractions . . .

– Awakening the Leader Within

Many elements of our society work day and night to distract us from knowing who we really are and focusing on what will make us truly happy. If we discover real fulfillment, it would thwart the plans of that economic system whose chief desire is to control us, to make us buy as it wishes, vote as it wishes, and believe its spin on the news. Aware that It is often painful to let go of comfortable fantasies and false leaders, the system controls us by offering numbing medicines, fairy tales, false promises, alcohol, and palliative relief for the symptoms we experience as a result of the inner conflict between our essence and the lies we tell ourselves. So we follow the anesthetic path and develop addictions and attachments in an attempt to relieve our inner suffering.

Operating in parallel with denial to shield us from reality is the process psychologists call "projection." From our schoolyard days through adulthood, our social environment has encouraged us to participate in criticizing, blaming, attacking, and demonizing other individuals and groups, as instructed. Soon we really begin to believe that, "All the football players from Northside High are weenies and that Southside will win the game Saturday." Nor do we alter our opinion when we lose; we blame it on the referees.

We have also been led to behave in this way in our attitudes toward, and our treatment of, other races, religions, and countries – and, voila, we sow the seeds that will grow into the conditions needed for the next war. And with the war, we suffer a massive shift of wealth from one set of pockets (ours) to the pockets of those who build bombs and tanks and planes and other weapons of wholesale destruction[4]. Probably every one of us can recall how we were induced to cheer for this or that team, tribe, god, or country. The challenge for us all, as we are belated becoming aware, is to discover the enormous amount we have in common and to develop a vision that includes everyone. There are important choices to be made, personally and collectively, and the time has come to look deeper than our material wealth, looks, social standing, or physical strength. The time has come to go deeper within and find the Self, the soul, the spirit – for this is the only reliable fulcrum from which to proceed in creating balance (homeostasis).

Who Are You?

> *There's no feeling quite like the one you get when*
> *you get to the truth: you are the captain of the ship called*
> *YOU. You are setting the course, the speed, and you are*
> *out there on the bridge, steering.*
> – Karl Frederick

At any given moment you may not be able to answer "Who am I?" with a totally satisfactory answer, but, if you ask this sincerely, and seek always the answer you most resonate with, you can get the best sense of yourself as possible at the moment. In turn, this can enable you to continuously develop a deeper and deeper

---

[4]   For an excellent review of how war redistributes wealth can be found in: Kevin Phillips, *Wealth and Democracy: A Political History of the American Rich* (Broadway, 2003).

219

sense of your true nature.

For many people, the search for their true selves takes them into the area of spirituality. For those with a specific religious or spiritual path, their deeper values, especially those dealing with their spiritual life, turn out to be highly congruent with the values of those they consider to be their spiritual leaders. Paying attention to those spiritual teachings that have touched you most deeply provides ongoing insight into who you are, and who you are becoming[5].

God is absolute truth. I am a human; I only understand relative truths. So my understanding of truths can change from day to day. And my commitment must be to truth rather than consistency.
– Mohandas Gandhi

"Self"-Awareness at Higher Levels of System

Just as we can inquire, "Who am I?", we can also ask, "Who are we?" If we want to make choices that are wise, that will bring us fulfillment and satisfaction in the future, we need to know who we are. We need to decide if "we" refers just to my family and friends, just to those whose religious beliefs are the same as mine, or to a larger group. Likewise, we need to examine how we relate with others, both those who we see often, and those who are at a distance from us.

Relationships that consciously and consistently address themselves to the fundamental principles of honesty, integrity, au-

---

[5] The CD *I Am: Awakening Self-Acceptance*, explores this. www.ShopDrMiller.com

thenticity, loving kindness, open-heartedness, mutuality, harmony, and Right Action – whether they are comprised of two, 20, 2,000 or 200 million members – tend to serve a higher purpose. We may righteously ask of our relationships, "What is that whole we all serve (Identity)?" What do we want it to be (visioning)[6]?

The strength of the team, or nine, or crew, is not the strength of the star. It is what the body together can do that carries the victory far. So you shall give your might to the rest, to bring the whole team through – and then, at the time of your single test, they will give their strength to you.
–Author Unknown

For many people it has been quite difficult to confront the many challenges that lie ahead. Yet it is clearly time to go beyond denial and projection. We need to deal honestly with the situation, even though we will have to deal with the anxiety and despair that will arise as we look at the truth.

By entering the state of mind developed in the Presence exercises of Step 1, presence, we obtain the ability to free our creative energy from those many neural networks that are working so hard to avoid seeing what is. We open the door to the acceptance of the suchness of the moment, and enter the Here and Now, where we can see the potential resolutions of our conflicts and get the guidance we need. Presence allows us to free up the internal processing power that will permit us to transform from the old paradigm to the new, and to see what was invisible before.

The result of allowing ourselves to truly see what is happening all around and within ourselves (our inner potential), while in a clear and present state of mind, is quite stunning. We begin to feel the quickening of a sense of empowerment, for we realize there are things we can do to significantly contribute to the healing process

---

[6]　The *Personal Excellence* program teaches the process of visioning based upon deeper values and personal mission. www.ShopDrMiller.com

that is needed at this moment. And, perhaps quite unexpectedly, we may discover a sense of duty to something deep within us. These discoveries give us the ability, the power, to be able to choose to make a change, the choice that activates action.

Making the Choice to Heal/Change

. . . Aware that there is a conscious, intelligent wise part of you that has made wise decisions in the past and can choose wisely – now allow that inner wisdom to guide your awareness to the important is-sue in your life that will benefit from your wise leadership. It may be a very individual, personal issue, like self-healing . . . or it may have to do with your work, or a creative endeavor . . . or perhaps it is a relationship or family issue . . . or even something of significance in the larger social sphere of community, or the situation that concerns you may be global in its scope . . . Whatever the issue is that you choose, let yourself remain relaxed and calm . . .
– Awakening the Leader Within

What are your priorities at this point in your life? If you step out of your daily trance and become aware of *whom you really are,* you become aware that there are values you really care about. They are deep values, beyond the superficial ones programmed in through fear and ignorance. You discover val-ues you feel so deeply about that you realize that you have a duty to the deepest part of yourself to heal the imbalances within your life. Some may refer to this realiza-tion as *dharma.* You know that you have the choice to ignore this duty, like a child going out to play without doing homework or emptying the garbage.

222

Once you have allowed yourself to see the truth with clear eyes, you will gradually (or sometimes suddenly) begin to see that you have a choice – whether or not you will choose to address those aspects of your life that is out of balance.

Balance (homeostasis) is the second of the fundamental aspects of the systemic healing process (having a clear idea of your identity is the first). The process of bringing things into proper balance and keeping them there is the essence of healing.

The Tao Te Ching, one of the chief texts of the Taoist point of view, addresses this directly, alluding to the systemic nature of the process:

> *When a country obtains great power,*
> *it becomes like the sea:*
> *all streams run downward into it.*
> *The more powerful it grows,*
> *the greater the need for humility.*
> *Humility means trusting the Tao,*
> *thus never needing to be defensive.*
> *A great nation is like a great man:*
> *When he makes a mistake, he realizes it.*
> *Having realized it, he admits it.*
> *Having admitted it, he corrects it.*
> *He considers those who point out his faults*
> *as his most benevolent teachers.*
> *He thinks of his enemy*
> *as the shadow that he himself casts.*
> *If a nation is centered in the Tao,*
> *if it nourishes its own people*
> *and doesn't meddle in the affairs of others,*
> *it will be a light to all nations in the world.*
> – Tao Te Ching

Seeing what is out of balance is a prerequisite for creating homeostatic change. The principle of Presence shows us that to use all our abilities we must free ourselves from the limitations of the past, and recognize the power of the present moment[7]. Your life changes profoundly the moment you truly understand that this moment is the only moment that really exists. This gives us the freedom to make full use of our wisdom – and if the decisions we make at this moment are truly wise, they will actually create the most desirable future. Free from the excess baggage from the past or anxieties about the future, we can exert our maximum power in the present and move steadily towards the outcomes we most want.

The Need for a Systemic Approach

A point I repeat continually is that, at this point in time in our lives, symptomatic change is not enough. It is time for systemic change. We must choose, intentionally, a deeper form of healing. Anything else is virtual suicide!

What needs to be changed? Some very important things, at both the personal, or individual level, and some at the collective level require our attention urgently.

At the personal level, think of the behaviors you might deal with such as overeating, substance abuse, anger, fear, unwanted habits, anxiety, worry – you know what they are. You know it is time to make a change in the behaviors of your body, mind, or emotions when you have become aware that:

1. These behaviors are not helpful in your life. They do not express your truth, or your true Self – and they are not supportive of your goals and aspirations.
2. The results of these behaviors tend to be unpleasant: pain, frustration, unhappiness, addiction, anger, or hopelessness.

---

[7] A fascinating exploration of this concept can be found in: Eckhart Tolle, *The Power of Now* (New World Library, 1999).

3. You cannot think of a good, logical reason to want to behave in this manner anymore. (Immediate gratification is neither a good nor a logical goal.)

The same is true at other levels of system – if your community or nation has behaviors that satisfy these criteria, it is probably time to look seriously at changing them.

For example, think of a behavior pattern you would like to see change. You might choose a pattern at one of several levels of system, or, if you are really ambitious, think of one at each of the levels – personal, family/friends, community, nation, and global.

1. Can you see that this pattern involves an imbalance, an excess of dispersive forces and Violence compared with wholeness and Love?

2. Knowing this, are you willing to use this opportunity to make a wise choice?

3. Are you willing to consider some other behaviors that would better achieve your life goals, while preventing or avoiding those negative results that Violence tends to bring?

One of the things we understand about a systemic approach is that the choice must not be merely at the cognitive level. How many of us really follow through on our New Year's resolutions, or lose the weight we decided we would lose? What we need is a way for the choice to be made at the emotional, the physical, and the communal level as well. Simply being willing is not enough. When you consider making choices at higher levels of system, ask yourself:

1. Is this change in attunement with your deepest values?

2. Is it important to your personal mission in life?

3. Do you feel a sense of responsibility and duty to make this change?

4. Is it important enough for you to make the required sacrifices?

When you have truly made the choice, you have committed yourself. But these commitments are not like the commitments you make to go to a party, or to return a phone call. It is a deep commitment to your Self. If you are truly aware of your deeper Self, and if you have integrity, then when you make a commitment, it is truly a promise, a sacred vow of the deepest kind.

We must become the change we wish to see in the world.
– Mahatma Gandhi

Young Gandhi

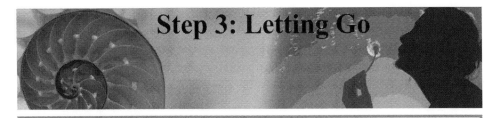

Step 3: Letting Go

• ***Truth:*** *To be successful in any significant endeavor we must use our innate human capacity to choose between different sorts of bondage, bondage to desire and self-esteem, or bondage to the wisdom and Love that lightens all our lives.*

• ***Goals:*** *To master the technique of leading your deeper mind, your nervous system, to release those thoughts, emotions, symptoms, and attachments that you have decided are unnecessary to your current intentions, and that could distract and interfere with that which you do intend.*

• ***Process:*** *The development of the capacity to mentally recognize and eliminate distractions, unnecessary mental and emotional activity, and emotional attachment to issues and concepts that no longer serves the values and purposes of the whole.*

Imagine letting go of whatever you need to free yourself from in order to accomplish your goal . . . And feel the deep fulfillment and satisfaction of participating in life in a way that is wise, congruent with your deepest values, and expressive of the real You . . . Feel it strongly . . . the more powerfully you can feel it, the more you are leading and motivating your body to behave in just this way . . . Breathe into this feeling, breathe strength and power into it . . . as you imagine complete success . . . and breathe it throughout every cell of your body . . . Good . . .

– Awakening the Leader Within

Letting Go: The Releasing Phase

Making a choice always involves giving something up: the option that you did *not* choose. No matter in which direction you face, you will always have your back to someone. To choose to have or do A is to choose to not have or do B. Sometimes that which you must give up is something (or somebody) you may have held onto for a long time. This is one of the most difficult things about choosing, a difficulty that destroys many a well-intentioned plan. This is especially true in today's culture. We have been trained to hang on to things. Getting is good, losing is bad; bigger and more are better. Wrong! At a certain point, we begin to realize that "more" is never enough. We need to train our system to release *what we tell it to let go of.*

> *If you want to become full,*
> *let yourself be empty.*
> *If you want to be reborn,*
> *let yourself die.*
> *If you want to be given everything,*
> *give everything up.*
> – From the Tao Te Ching

Letting go, in any individual case, may involve many different aspects of life. It may refer, in a particular case, to the letting go of accumulated stress, letting go of a physical illness or dysfunction, a relationship, a lifestyle, an addiction, self-doubt, dysfunctional emotions, material attachments, or anything else that hinders your release of lower levels to be guided by higher levels of system. Though the issues I have presented as examples may seem very different from each other, the inner process of letting go is remarkably similar in all these cases.

In some cultures, this part of the process is referred to as "detachment"; others may call it "surrendering," "turning it over," or "placing it in the hands of Jesus." Letting go is a skill taught in many religions and spiritual traditions for very good reasons. Unless you are willing to let go of earthly items, you cannot make room for spiritual ones.

This step involves your using whatever tools you have for letting go (meditation, prayer, self-hypnosis, and so forth), or acquiring some if you have none. You will find that, generally speaking, all these are fully compatible and integral with the tools, techniques, and perspectives we are discussing. If you have one that works for you, go ahead and use it[8].

To be able to make a choice most effectively, you must be willing to take *responsibility* for the results of your choice. If you give up excess fear, for example, you may find unparalleled courage surging through your body. Not infrequently, the kinds of breakthroughs that often accompany these kinds of explorations are nearly overwhelming. Sometimes the shock can even trigger archaic fear and anxiety that we have learned to feel in the past. To cushion these powerful changes, it is invaluable to have a process by which you can reliably create deep relaxation.

In the West, traditionally we have learned very little about letting go, and, though it is part of the more esoteric aspects of most of our religions, many followers of institutionalized religions are really not introduced to it – indeed, they sometimes feel threatened by the thought of it – although it is a common practice for their monks and nuns.

In therapy or in coaching, it is common to utilize meditation, hypnosis, or deep relaxation to release tension from mind, body, and emotions. This makes it possible for us to explore alternate strategies. Fear, anger, grief, and other such urgent emotions block us from seeing and making wise choices, and these are excellent tools for freeing ourselves from those restrictions.

Now, if we follow our systemic approach on up through our family, social, and planetary problems, it should be clear that,

---

[8]   Those who do not have a specific path of this kind may find CDs such as *Letting Go of Stress, Relaxation and Inspiration* and *Accepting Change and Moving On* prove to be helpful. www.ShopDrMiller.com

as groups and nations, we are far more likely to be successful at resolving stresses and conflicts if we can sustain a relaxed, open state of mind, one that will foster healthy ways to approach our challenges, instead of the negative, angry, or frustrated ways that have not served us well in the past. The right kind of leadership guides the group to approach challenges in this way.

Letting Go of Fear and Tension

Fear and its associated physical and emotional tension are part of a defensive response to a *perceived* challenge or threat. When prolonged, this tension, in turn, serves to close the doors of the mind rather than to expand them. This expansion of our awareness and consciousness is needed to perceive patterns that are taking place at higher/deeper levels of system. Unless we open the doors, we can be led astray by our prejudices and the fear of being wrong. The result: short-term gain, long-term pain.

> *No passion so effectually robs the mind of all its*
> *powers of acting and reasoning as fear.*
> – Edmund Burke

> *Power is of two kinds. One is obtained by the fear of punishment and*
> *the other by acts of love. Power based on love is a thousand times*
> *more effective and permanent than the one derived*
> *from fear of punishment.*
> – Mahatma Gandhi

With a little relaxation (or a lot), we can gain access to a higher level of truth. That same relaxation can help us endure the otherwise intensely stress-producing awareness of what you have been blind to.

Through letting go of what is not essentially ourselves, we

become acquainted with the true Self and we can look deeper to the purpose or intention behind our inner fear or anxiety. Thus, we discover our deeper purpose in the current situation. It then becomes easier to release anger and frustration so that they do not surface as violence and abuse of others or self.

Letting Go of Anger

Because anger is an inborn emotion that enables us to do Violence to others and the environment – not to mention ourselves – special care needs to be taken to ensure that harmful aspects of anger are released ... harmlessly.

Anger and frustration, like other emotions, are actually *behaviors*, although we often conveniently ignore this truth. Until we become accustomed to being responsible for our internal behaviors, we may feel as if our emotions are happening to us. In other words, we blame the environment and the people in it ("He made me angry, she hurt my feelings"). Once we honor the presence of these internal behaviors, we have taken the first step towards being able to choose to change those behaviors.

Our anger, frustration, and resentment are simply the feelings that arise when we are not willing to accept that something in the world is not the way we expected it to be, hoped it would be, or wanted it to be – instead of honoring the truth: that things can only be as they are at this moment. Such inappropriate emotional reactions disempower us; we become functionally frozen, and less able to act creatively to address our challenges. The resulting helplessness often simply intensifies the frustration or anger[9].

---

[9] For an excellent approach to using methods other than avoidance, anger, or coercion in dealing with others, consider:
David J. Lieberman, *How to Make Peace with Anyone*
(St. Martin's Griffin, 2003).

The source of all suffering is wanting things to be
different from how they are at this moment in time.
  – The Buddha

Like all emotions, sometimes anger can be of use in certain situations; sometimes it is even a wise choice. More often, however, it gets in the way of a more appropriate solution. Since anger, like all emotions, is a behavior (an internal behavior), we have the ability to change it, just as we can change other behaviors. When we have awakened this ability, we have the ability to choose wisely: whether to let the anger go, or to use it intelligently.

Forgiveness and the Either-Or Paradigm

Forgiveness is an essential element of releasing anger, resentment, and blame of others, and is central in resolving inner feelings of guilt and regret. The lack of forgiveness creates internal conflict as well as polarization in external relationships. Researchers such as Dr. Frederic Luskin, in his studies at Stanford University, have confirmed how forgiveness promotes social relationships and physical health. Forgiveness has been shown to reduce anger, hurt, depression, and stress – and lead to greater feelings of optimism, hope, compassion, and self-confidence[10].

The Polarity Paradigm and Our Culture

The social and cultural environment we live in, amplified by the media, gives us quite a different set of signals. The underlying message is that there is an enemy out there – it may be dandruff, stubborn stains, the head of another country, or the thief that is

---

[10] An excellent resource for addressing forgiveness is Dr. Luskin's website: <http://www.learningtoforgive.com>

waiting to rob your house. The strategy is, at the basic level, to rein-force your feelings of helplessness and impel you to purchase their symptomatic relief.

To be able to strike the balance in our lives at every level, then, we must be able to recognize, and then interrupt the cycle of anger/violence within. Ultimately, what we want to do is to make a wise decision whether to use an anabolic or catabolic response. To make such a wise decision is impossible if we are being driven by anxiety, because the catabolic, defensive, violent response is the only one that feels like it will relieve our anxiety. As a result, we cannot judge impartially from a place of wisdom[11].

Thus, we must first "disconnect" the circuitry that is driving us toward reflex anger and violence. This requires that we use our conscious mind and our wisdom to know – even if we don't feel it – that we are not in immediate physical danger and thus can afford to let go of the defensive posture/attitude. Then we can see the value of entering a state of deep relaxation. Muscle tension, anxiety, anger, racing thoughts, bracing, and the visualization of worst-case scenarios – they all go away. Presence, Awareness, and deep relaxation enable us to let go, and to accept things as they are at this moment. They can be different tomorrow or in five minutes, but we must accept that at the moment, things are as they are, and cannot be different[12].

Application to Groups

In response to wise leadership, groups can let go, physically, emotionally, and in their relationships. They can release anger, fear, and prejudice, and choose to sacrifice in the service of their common belief. The process of deep relaxation, prayer, and

---

[11]   *Abolish Anxiety Now!* presents a healthy set of behaviors to use to balance anxiety www.ShopDrMiller.com

[12]   See *Accepting Change and Moving On* www.ShopDrMiller.com

233

group imagery is in widespread use, with great effectiveness. If the entire group watches a movie or video that is heartwarming, and that touches all present, tension leaves, relaxation, openness, and empathy ensue. Similarly, an inspiring speaker, one who moves the hearts of the audience, can produce the required receptiveness to move on to the next step, as can a DVD or a CD with the right message on it. This works for teams, families, communities, in the workplace – or wherever and whenever optimal performance is desired. Can you allow yourself to believe that our communities, our collective selves, generally have all these values and principles at their core, and we are simply offering an opportunity to reconnect?

Application to the Cultural or Planetary Level

After the tsunami of 2004, and after the attack on the World Trade Center in 2001, there was an enormous outpouring of global sympathy and good will. Strangers smiled at each other on the streets of New York. Many people volunteered to help. People forgot their differences; their shared loss was so much more effective at revealing bonds than the differences and defensiveness they usually displayed. Important events, and the way they are interpreted, can move large numbers of people. (As tragic as such events might be, they might prove to be the most opportune time to effect major, lasting elevations of global consciousness and community.) If so, the Economic Crisis we are experiencing may be the perfect time for people to wake up.

At the level of the community or larger, we may not be able to induce a deep state of relaxation, but using the tools developed by Hollywood and Madison Avenue, we have the capacity to design media that can induce a sufficiently receptive state that people could learn the skill of letting go. For those at higher levels in the leadership hierarchy, meditative and imagery experiences are of special value.

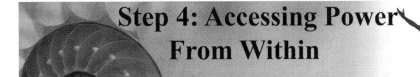

Step 4: Accessing Power From Within

> • **Truth:** *With an eye made quiet by the power of harmony, and nurtured by the deep power of joy, we see into the life of things. Seeing deeply, we choose deeply . . . and commit deeply.*
> • **Goals:** *To be capable of accessing your inner wisdom, awaken the leader within your being, choose the goals and visions that are capable of bringing you fulfillment, and commit yourself to their realization.*
> • **Process:** *Focusing on Truth, Awareness of Personal Potential, Proactive Memory Utilization*

. . . And, for a moment, you might recall one or two times in the past when you have made wise choices . . . times when you were able to overcome distractions and see the whole . . . when your choices reflected your deeper values . . . when you used your intelligence and intuition well, and acted with courage and compassion . . . Or simply be aware that this wisdom has served you in the past . . . and allow yourself to feel gratitude to the Source . . .
– Awakening the Leader Within

Choosing the Right Issues

Thus far, we have discussed coming into the present moment, becoming aware of what we want to focus upon. We next considered the possibility of making the choice, the commitment to heal, and then letting go of what was not going to be of value in this next leg of the journey. Now we are light on our feet, ready for action, and aware of our power.

At this point, we find ourselves like the Zen archer. We stand on a firm spot to take aim. Now we see much more clearly without all that clutter in the way and we're standing on a solid spot, our feet firmly planted.

And like the Zen archer, we are suddenly faced with the real work, what target do we want to shoot at? Everything up until now has just been preparing our instrument, cleansing our tools, preparing our vehicle (body, mind, emotions, intellect) for the journey. The Zen archer goes out with but one arrow, and the focus of the day is on choosing exactly what is to be the target – and hitting it with the first and only arrow.

Allow that inner wisdom to guide your awareness to the important issue in your life that will benefit from your wise leadership. It may be a very individual, personal issue, like self-healing ... or it may have to do with your work, or a creative endeavor ... or perhaps it is a relationship or family issue ... or even something of significance in the larger social sphere of community, or the situation that concerns you may be global in scope .... Whatever the issue is that you choose, let yourself see the facts ... What is happening? ... Where is the imbalance?... What are the challenges? ... Simply observing, from this centered place of balance and wisdom ...
– Awakening the Leader Within

We Have Been Misled

Although we need to be able to be in the present moment, the past is of great value, for it is a master teacher. Indeed, the memories we have of our past (individually and culturally, are excellent guides, if we employ them properly. Without an awareness of the past, it is impossible to intentionally choose any goal, because we can only see the world through our past experiences. The question is, "Which of our past experiences do we want to call upon as guides in choosing our future? Do we want to base the future on our disappointments, our mistakes, our failures, the times we felt frustrated, angry, annoyed, and defeated?

Of course not! We want to be aware of what is truly of most value to us. Life is short, and most of us are tired of the superficial goals. Yet, when we look back, we see that we have often been misled. We have been misled from within by out-of-control passions such as fear, anger, depression, and greed, and by our addictions, our stresses, and our prejudices. Because we have lacked Self-awareness, Self-esteem, and Self-empowerment, we learned that we are too small to matter, that the problems are the fault of other people, those who have power over us. From the crib on, we're told to "behave," to stay in line, to be seen but not heard. Through our training, we learned to believe we are helpless, that we're not enough.

From without, we have been misled by those who have huge financial resources, who control the media, and who are motivated by greed, not by compassion and love, like the wise elders of old. Our future as a people is being determined by 30-second political commercials, corporate lobbyists, media that serve the power elite, and those who manipulate us by fear and mass anxiety.

My experience in working with people seeking to change their lives is that there is a wise leader within each one of us, one who can make the choices that will lead to healing at every level of system. This leader does not strive for superficial goals, but bases future choices on what really has heart and meaning for us. Those healing choices become clearer as you focus on those experiences that moved you at the deepest level, for these are the best ones to serve as models for your deeper mind. The deeper levels of your mind learn best through modeling, and by holding in mind a clear image of what you want. When you motivate and guide the unconscious levels of your mind, you multiply the probability that you will succeed in bringing about the future you most deeply want.

Sometimes we become aware of our true goals rather spontaneously as a consequence of having chosen to release what we don't need anymore. We often have the feeling that the releasing

237

process has served to push aside a kind of veil that had been obscuring our true goals. We realize they've actually been there all the time. At some level, we have always known our true mission, but somehow we always seemed to be distracted from it. Our culture, spearheaded by the media, specializes in casting this veil of distraction.

Some people find, on the contrary, that there is a period of time following the letting go process in which no mission, vision, or life goal appears. If you discover that this is true for you, the best choice is to empty yourself of preconceptions and open yourself to listening – both to the silence within (so long periods of meditation are particularly valuable) as well as to the wisdom of wise guidance from those you trust, and important signals from the environment. Take the time to patiently open to nature's profusion around you, to create authentic opportunities for communication with others in intimate or group settings. Counseling and guided imagery may prove invaluable in helping to reveal and clarify your goals.

Personal Empowerment: Owning Your Tools

Contrary to what you may have been led to believe, it is you who are important, and the inner resources you possess are most valuable. Now is the time to discover your best skills, talents, trainings, and gifts – with special emphasis on those that you love to employ.

In our high-stress, high-distraction world, many of us have forgotten or neglected these important resources and focused primarily on developing only those skills we could get paid for. It is quite startling how many people do not enjoy the activities their jobs require, and how much they wish they had an arena in which they could use talents and skills closer to their hearts.

In addition to becoming aware of your personal resources, you may also discover what led to their taking a backseat in your life. What traumas or social disapproval (e.g., teen peers who teased you for some imagined defect, adult relationships where you experience betrayal) led to negative associations and defense reactions that were designed to protect you then, but now hold you back? It is of immense value to desensitize ourselves to such leftover blocks to inner healing so we can remove them and release trapped energy for right action[13].

The Power of Doing Right

In your heart of hearts, you want to do the right thing, to be a good person. Most, if not all, people want to live up to such principles as fairness, equality, freedom, kindness, and integrity. These are the stated principles of most religions (though they are often honored more in their breach), and living according to them is a goal of the faithful everywhere. Agnostics and atheists, as well, usually accept and value these principles. Yet it is sometimes difficult to see them being played out on a daily basis by the people in our lives. And it's no wonder, given the information overwhelm of our current world, the incessant pressure to betray our deepest consciousness, and the lack of support – most people don't know how to "follow their hearts."

Applications at the Societal / Cultural Level

Sometimes this inability or unwillingness to do the right thing seems to have been the case at the national level in the U.S. as well. Not long ago, the U.S. became the only remaining superpower, and it was faced with the choice of whether or not to be a benign, compassionate, and supportive influence in the world. Many people feel the U.S. did not take the lead in addressing climate change, genocide, pollution, poverty, starvation, and similar global issues.

---

[13] See *Writing Your Own Script* www.ShopDrMiller.com

Instead, it seems the U.S. was quite abusive to the people of this planet – which was, in fact, the actual experience of people around the planet: upon hearing the news that Barack Obama had been elected, people around the world danced and celebrated as vigorously as people did in the U.S.

Like a demanding child, we were too busy playing video games, and to confront problems like global warming, we would have to sacrifice something. Not likely, unless there is a wholesale change in how we, in our culture, value material things, and how we value ourselves (spiritual things). In so many ways, only our greedy self-interest has seemed to motivate us in recent decades.

On the other hand, if we are present and clear, our pure self-interest may lead us to a new set of behaviors that just turn out to be honorable and "right" as well. It would be most illogical to think we could continue to behave, individually, and as a culture, as we have been, without disastrous consequences. The attacks of September 11, 2001 and the economic crisis of 2008 are spreading cracks in that edifice upon which we all depend for civilized life. If we want a world to live in, we need to behave differently.

When we unite for a moral purpose that is manifestly good and true, the spiritual energy unleashed can transform us.
– Al Gore

Is it not clear that you would be irresponsible to think we can continue to ignore at the individual level the higher principles we want our leaders and our society to honor? Is it not a duty of yours to fully embody your deeper principles in your daily behavior, and to demand the same of your leaders? Making choices with heart, meaning, and integrity represents enlightened Self-interest.

Accessing Power from the Past

Your past experiences are the key to discovering what your deeper resources, values, skills, talents, and loves are. What is it

240

that you are good at doing, that you love to do, and that advances the values you want your life to serve? Great power and potential lie within each of us, and within us as a group. What we need is a way to make them manifest.

It is a strange paradox; people in our part of the world, with all we own, tend to feel like victims. Yet every one of those people from Third World countries we see on the news every day, shaking their fists at us, burning our flag, and chanting hate slogans, each feels he is an important part of something meaningful. Indeed, they are willing to die for their beliefs (misguided though they may be). The Kamikaze fighters of World War II demonstrated that a low-tech vehicle filled with primitive explosives, and piloted by a man with a "Give me liberty (or whatever is his goal) or give me death" kind of zeal has the possibility of overwhelming even an enemy with enormous technological superiority.

What if we, too, were motivated by a faith and enthusiasm of similar degree, but inspired by *our* personal beliefs, and aware of the importance of making the right changes in our personal lives? Certainly many of us are so deeply motivated – but obviously not yet enough of us. What if we were as committed to bringing a new kind of thinking and behaving into our lives?

After 9/11, we called the terrorists "cowards." I am not sure that is a fair characterization, or the right message – not if our true desire is to create peace with those who are suspicious of us. What if we all felt as strongly about our most deeply held values as suicide terrorists feel about theirs? We are not going to get through this one if we wait around for someone else to clean up the mess. We need to accept the importance of service. Why is it that we so often reserve our most admirable qualities for times of war.

Having a deeper awareness of your Self is one of the keys to acquiring the needed commitment and strength, as well as the power of true purpose and mission. You can achieve deeper awareness of your Self through focusing selectively on specific experiences from your past. When you skillfully guide awareness to positive and empowering experiences and revivify them, your nervous system secretes the same neuropeptides that were produced at the time of the original event. Through the use of imagery, the unconscious levels of your mind can be motivated to create similar successes in the future. In a similar manner, once a community or society is in touch with its deeper values, it can use this awareness, through its media and communication systems, to produce a social environment more congruent with those values. On September 11, 2001, people treated each other differently; there was a sense of connection and community, of compassion and empathy, that could have been sustained, if only the right minds had been there to lead us. On November 4, 2008, there was once again an obvious outpouring of Love, as millions dreamed together that a new and healthy world might now be achieved. If there is anything to that morphic field theory, then it ought to be much easier to connect others on a more human, trusting level for quite some time.

So, what kinds of experiences can you identify in your past that you would love to repeat? What kind of feeling would you like to experience more often in the future? It is obvious that the future cannot be a carbon copy of the past – nothing ever happens again. But in what way do we want to influence what the future will be?

Once you locate some examples of the kinds of feelings you want to be the tone of your life, the next step is to take some time to relive them in your mind, re-experiencing the *actual physical and emotional feeling* as strongly as possible. The focus is on the emo-

tion, the feeling, the inner qualities, because when you feel strongly, the feeling changes the kinds of chemicals (neurohumors) being secreted by the cells of your brain. These "molecules of emotion" can now be used as a programming (or conditioning) stimulus for the unconscious part of your mind, which can then be encouraged to help you to create new events in the future that are similar – at least in the sense that they will evoke the same inner feelings of joy and satisfaction. The act of feeling these emotions creates a set of neuropeptides whose purpose it is to galvanize and inspire desired behaviors of mind, emotion, and body – much as a coach's halftime pep talk might inspire a football team to victory.

So, become aware of the qualities of experience that are most important to you, and practice entering the relaxed state, recreating the scene in your mind's eye, and feeling the feelings. Peace, fulfillment, love, joy, inspiration, celebration, courage, serenity, and wisdom are a few candidates to consider. You might mentally relive activities like skiing or dancing, being with special people, experiencing success in some endeavor, or even certain epiphanies you've experienced, certain sacred moments in your life[14].

If you have any difficulty getting in touch with the emotions of experiences such as these, one strategy is to share the event with a friend. Describe that special moment, using as much emotion as you can, trying to convey to them the feelings you had at the time. This can help you to feel your emotions in the present. Then close your eyes, visualize the scene, and focus on those feelings. It is a good idea to repeat this imagery experience on a regular basis, until it is easy to stop, any time of the day, and recreate these feelings. They will then serve as a positive guide for your mind and body.

Empowerment Through Awareness of Responsibility

Although some people are often very eager to avoid responsibility, it turns out that responsibility can be the source of great power, inspiration, and commitment. The choices we make reveal to what we are responsible, and ultimately who we will become[15].

---

[14] The following programs are valuable for facilitating these experiences: *Personal Excellence*, is a complete training on 6 CDs. *I Can* and *Optimal Performance* are single CDs that address this issue. *Deep Healing* also presents tools for accomplishing these ends. www.ShopDrMiller.com

As we come out of denial and heal from our learned helplessness, we begin to realize that each of us, individually, has a responsibility, and the power with which to carry out that responsibility.

No man is an island entire of itself; every man is a piece of the Continent, a part of the main . . . Any man's death diminishes me because I am involved in Mankind; and therefore never send to know for whom the bell tolls; it tolls for thee.
– John Donne

First, be aware of how much you are willing to let yourself "believe" that there is an effective way to deal with these issues, at whichever level of system we choose to focus on them. Next, realize that the starting point for this transformation is right here, right now, in the center of your being. Think of all the different ways you have heard wise teachers and spiritual guides say the same thing – that the place true enlightenment starts is within you.

Though we travel the world over to find the beautiful, we must carry it with us or we find it not.
– Ralph Waldo Emerson

This is not a new idea:

And why beholdest thou the mote that is in thy brother's eye but considerest not the beam that is in thine own eye? Thou hypocrite, cast out first the beam out of thine own eye; and then shalt thou see clearly to cast out the mote out of thy brother's eye.
– The Holy Bible: Matthew 7:3

Nor is the concept limited to our Western culture:

[15] An interesting treatment of this issue can be found in the book: *Personal Responsibility: The Power of You*, by Janice Dorn, M.D., Ph.D., <http://personalresponsibilitybook.com/>

I have not the shadow of a doubt that any man or woman can achieve what I have if he or she would make the same effort and cultivate the same hope and faith.
– Mahatma Gandhi

One way you can access your personal power at the individual level is through the techniques I developed in Deep Healing[16]. Other approaches may also be effective for this purpose. The idea is to find out what has traditionally moved and inspired you most deeply, what has given you the feeling of being fully alive. These might be certain activities like skiing or dancing, certain epiphanies you've experienced in the past.

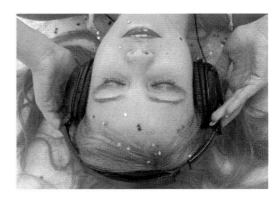

accessing empowering experiences
through mental imagery

In Group Settings

In groups of individuals, the principles and techniques of *Wisdom Circles*[17] allow for expansion of the power of the group, as do the tools of the *World Café*[18]. Ultimately, these groups – with intentions of the highest good – could coalesce on the planetary level. We will return to this topic soon.

---

[16] See *Deep Healing* www.ShopDrMiller.com

[17] www.wisdomcircle.org

[18] www.theworldcafe.com

Application at the Culture-wide or Global Level

I know of no safe depository of the ultimate power of society but the people themselves; and if we think them not enlightened enough to exercise their control with a wholesome direction, the remedy is not to take it from them, but to inform their discretion by education."
– Thomas Jefferson

What resources do we have on this planet that could guide us from our current divisive, unkind, cruel, abusive, immoral behaviors and belief systems to the discovery of a new perspective, one that would enable us to approach the challenges before us in a way that would serve our true deeper values? Could we be kind, fair, democratic, loving, and compassionate as well as strong and resolute? I think so. And I believe that if we empower people to create along this line, we can find an elegant and effective way to do it. Here is just one suggestion:

There are many world opinion leaders – including religious leaders, cultural leaders, political leaders, and scholars – who agree that the imbalance between violence and love is at the core of our problems. The teachings of wise ones from so many times and places tend to converge on the same basic principles. Lao Tse, Jesus, Moses, Buddha, and Mohammed all seem to agree with more recent spiritual and social leaders, such as Gandhi, Mother Teresa, and Martin Luther King, when it comes to these tenets.

Imagine that a meeting were to take place in which the wisest and most beloved teachers and leaders in the world entered into an ongoing conversation, with the goal of exploring questions that matter to us all. Then imagine they were all to agree on what would be the next issue that people worldwide should focus on, and some guidance as to the way people should be guided to behave in a way that increased connection instead of increasing division. If everyone on all their mailing and e-mailing lists were to set their minds to enacting this change, a powerful shift could happen overnight. The coming together of the different cultures and countries would model community behavior and tolerance for differences for people throughout the world.

And what if we were to develop powerful tools, training materials and the like, to awaken the wisdom within people and empower them to change their lives? We have the ability to teach the skills and awarenesses that can enable people to utilize this wisdom. With the blessings of their leaders, many more people would be able to overcome prejudices and participate in creating the change. We know how to produce the self-change technology to create rapid deep change. Digitized audio and video programs have been shown to possess this ability, and better programs could be developed, particularly if elite producers, writers, actors and special effects became available. How could Spielberg, Lucas, Attenborough, Bono, Oprah, Moore, and all the other usual suspects possibly refuse to participate in such a venture?

When to Change

The time to change is NOW. Right now. We don't have a second to lose.

Now comes the threat of climate crisis – a threat that is real, rising, imminent, and universal. Once again, it is the 11th hour. The penalties for ignoring this challenge are immense and growing, and at some near point would be unsustainable and unrecoverable. For now we still have the power to choose our fate, and the remaining question is only this: Have we the will to act vigorously and in time, or will we remain imprisoned by a dangerous illusion?
– Al Gore, in his Nobel Prize acceptance speech, 2007

Making Change Happen

The Internet/World Wide Web exists. It is real. It is alive. And you can't kill it. It can't be turned off. It was designed to be infinitely and efficiently redundant. To take down the Internet, you would have to end civilization as we know it.

Our goal here is not to end civilization as we know it, but to create civilization as we know it could be. And that's where the Web comes in. It can go virtually anywhere in the world to anyone and everyone in the world. Certain groups (mainly religions and governments) are trying to stop it, but it is ubiquitous and it infiltrates everything.

On the other hand, the Web provides an enormous opportunity to bring about the changes we need. I believe we have all the tools we need to make the transformation happen: Just look at the power of YouTube, Google, MySpace and groups like MoveOn.org, Facebook.com, eBay, Wikipedia, Amazon, and Craig's List.

We, the people, now have a global voice, which can become a chorus, to create a future where we cannot only survive but thrive.

When we unite for a moral purpose that is manifestly good and true,
the spiritual energy unleashed can transform us.
– Al Gore

Using the power of Web-enabled media (as well as the other media) consider the impact of An Inconvenient Truth, Fahrenheit 911, or Sicko. These are just some of the examples of the power of the media. Why not dedicate it to distributing the collected wisdom of mankind – principles of liberty, equality, health, education, justice, nutrition, and all good things? Peace, even.

We have all the tools, but we haven't yet had the will to assemble them carefully, in a way that would serve life in the best way. Still, we have the power at our fingertips if we choose to use it. Never before in history has there been an opportunity for so many people, worldwide, to gather together around a shared vision – and to empower it through the interactive nature of the Internet. We have been asleep with compasses in our hands, dreaming that we are lost.

I think what we want may be incredibly near at hand, although we have not yet sufficiently desired or intended to make it a reality. We have bellyached and complained and blamed and shamed, but we have not yet put our collective mind to it. We always tend to blame the other person (e.g., spouse), group (opposing political party), or global adversary (those murdering terrorists); it is they who are refusing to play fair, to share, to really come to the table willing to make peace. It is never we.

In such situations, my finding is that there are usually qualities of one's Self that are not being clearly seen. What our adversaries are saying is true to a certain extent, although our adversaries are blowing it entirely out of proportion, just as we tend to blow their defects out of proportion. The power we gain when we brought on our perspective to include the Hermetic Principles, "As Above So Below" – and understand what Jesus meant when he said about finding the mote in another's eye. Empowerment allows us to be truly responsible.

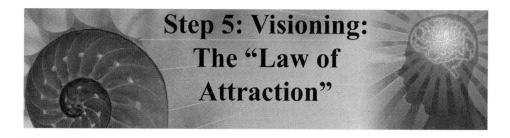

Step 5: Visioning: The "Law of Attraction"

> • **Truth:** *Vision without action is a daydream. Action without vision is a nightmare. Visioning is the art of seeing things invisible.*
> • **Goals:** *To create a compelling vision of the future, and to impress that vision upon your mind and nervous system.*
> • **Process:** *Deep Self-Awareness, Accessing Wisdom, Future Outcome*

. . . Visualize this outcome in your mind's eye, realizing that the future is being created right now, in this moment . . . and imagine it as already being true . . . feeling the inner joy, success, and gratitude . . . feel it at the emotional level within you. The more strongly you can feel it . . . the more powerfully . . . you are now stimulating the creative parts of yourself . . .
– Awakening the Leader Within

By "visioning", I mean choosing, creating, and empowering a compelling mental image – an important, deeply felt goal, outcome or target. By holding this vision in mind, then choosing those behaviors that lead most securely towards it, you facilitate its coming about. As you make progress, you will find yourself joining with kindred spirits to work towards it[19].

---

[19] Examples of how to use the visioning process may be found in *Personal Excellence, Healing Our Planet, and Awakening the Leader Within.* www.ShopDrMiller.com

The "Law of Attraction"

I have often been asked about the "Law of Attraction," as this is a term that has become popular recently. When these principles of visioning are utilized, and especially when our motivation is to allow better expression of our true selves, our spirit, so to speak, then what happens often appears to be quite magical. It sometimes feels as if, rather than ourselves being drawn towards the achievement of this vision, we actually have the experience of the vision being drawn towards us! The vision seems to be attracted to us – as if holding the vision in mind, especially during the state of deep relaxation, somehow "magnetizes" the cells of our bodies, thereby drawing us and the desired outcome closer together.

Many people believe that holding a vision in mind actually has a physical effect on the world; many do not accept this. There is no definitive proof either way – but what is clear is that it feels as if it is happening, and as this perception tends to strengthen faith, courage, and commitment, it is often quite helpful simply to assume the Law of Attraction exists – and works.

Until one commits, there is hesitancy, the chance to draw back – always ineffectiveness. Concerning all acts of initiative, and of creation, there is one elementary truth, the ignorance of which kills countless ideas and splendid plans: The moment one definitely commits oneself, then providence moves too. All sorts of things occur to help one that would never otherwise have occurred. A whole stream of events issues from the decision, raising in one's favor all manner of unforeseen incidents and meetings and material assistance, which no man could have dreamt would have come his way. I have learned a deep respect for one of Goethe's couplets:

Whatever you can do, or dream you can, begin it.
Boldness has genius, power, and magic in it.
– William Hutchinson Murray, mountaineer

Take a few moments to consider these questions. The answers you come up with may give you a clearer sense of what you would like to commit yourself to:

1. What do you deeply desire to do with your time?
2. What are the Goals and Visions that you/we really want to achieve?
3. What are the "must dos?" What are those things that, if you fail to do them, you are likely to look back with deep regret?
4. What are your/our goals as an individual? A family? A culture?
5. Who do you want to be? What is your potential? And what strengths do you have to bring to the struggle of achieving that potential?
6. What moves you – at the deepest level of your soul? What positive, loving, thrilling life experiences float your boat? – What kind of experiences would you absolutely enjoy creating in your world?

Now start to practice creating images that evoke the feelings stored in your mental images of these things.

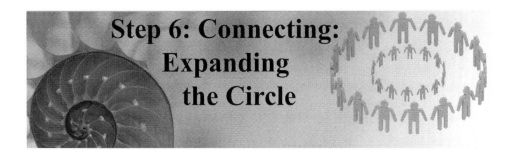

Step 6: Connecting: Expanding the Circle

> • **Truth:** *Coming together is a beginning. Keeping together is progress. Working together is success.*
> • **Goals:** *To multiply personal power by joining forces with others who resonate with your vision, or parts of it.*
> • **Process:** *Beginning to make connections with like-minded others (kin-dred spirits)*

In the century now dawning, spirituality, visionary consciousness, and the ability to build and mend human relationships will be more important for the fate and safety of this nation than our capacity to forcefully subdue an enemy. Creating the world we want is a much more subtle but more powerful mode of operation than destroying the one we don't want.
– Marianne Williamson

The use of Imagery and the state of Deep Relaxation provide powerful ways you can self-program profound changes. Once we have a vision, we can use various approaches, such as those presented here, as well as those offered by such movements as the Millionth Circle [20] to inspire and guide our choices and actions. Regular meetings, in person, or on the phone or Web, are essential to maintaining a shared vision or goal with a group.

---

[20] <www.millionthcircle.org>

Establishing Relationships and Support Systems to Nurture Desired Changes

Whether your goal is to make an inner change or to make a change in your environment (people, places, conditions), it is very helpful to find, or create, a support system that reflects your core values and principles. Take the time to choose carefully, but do not hesitate to actively seek that network that can inspire you, restore confidence when it falters, and give you an opportunity to tap into that new being, that remarkable sense of wholeness, that emerges when two or more devote themselves to that higher order whole. "You" and "Me" become "We."

> *Don't ask, "What's in it for me?" Ask, "What's in it for us?"*
> – William Jefferson Clinton

In coming together with "kindred spirits" around questions that have heart and meaning to you all, you are reflecting the coming together of the single cells to form the first multicellular animal, or the first animals that discovered the value of staying together in a herd, or having the baby stay with the mother for a period after birth.

And just as the many organs of the body developed the central nervous system to guide the whole, we are joining to form a kind of higher order brain, the coming together of the people of the world to serve what we all hold in reverence: Life, the environment, health, healing, Love.

The Hundredth Monkey Effect

At higher levels of system, we see something akin to the so-called "100th monkey effect." This is the popular name given to the metaphor of several islands of monkeys who lived on a certain tuber. A small group of monkeys learned that if they washed the tubers, the sand wouldn't grit in their teeth. Gradually, other monkeys watched them do it, tried it, found they liked the results, and kept doing it. As the story goes, once a certain percentage of monkeys on the island had discovered the technique, suddenly, the next day, all the monkeys were doing it – as though there was a kind of telepathic quantum leap. One is reminded of what happens when a pile of uranium reaches critical mass. It is also reminiscent of how fads catch on in our society. Once there were only a few with cell phones, and no one had even heard of an iPod – now it is hard for many of us to imagine life without them[21]!

The Millionth Monkey

When a critical number of people change how they think and be-have, a new era will begin.
    – Jean Shinoda Bolen

If at first the notion of people coming together in sufficient numbers to reach critical mass sounds far fetched, the reality might surprise you. Paul Hawken[22] is one of those who has been studying

---

[21] Some (apocryphal) versions of the story even have it that monkeys on other islands, those who had never actually seen another monkey demonstrate this new technology, suddenly started washing their potatoes.

[22] Paul Hawken is an entrepreneur and social activist living in California. His latest publication is *Blessed Unrest*, published by Viking Press. <http://www.paulhawken.com>

how people have been joining together to create a healthier planet. He states, "This is the largest social movement in all of history: tens of millions of ordinary and not-so-ordinary people willing to confront despair, power, and incalculable odds in order to restore some semblance of grace, justice, and beauty to this world."

The media, controlled as it is by the powers that be, rarely report on this earth-changing social movement. Those who make up the movement come from both the nonprofit and nongovernmental world, and their interests are in climate change, poverty, deforestation, peace, water, hunger, conservation, health, human rights, and more. Their goal: to safeguard nature and ensure justice.

Mr. Hawken looked at government records, tax census data, and other sources, counting the number of environmental organizations, social justice and indigenous organizations, and finally concluded that there are over one million organizations working toward ecological sustainability and social justice, perhaps as many as two million.

By conventional definition, this is not a movement. Movements have leaders and ideologies. You join movements, study tracts, and identify yourself with a group. You read the biography of the founder(s) or listen to them perorate on tape or in person. Movements have followers, but this movement doesn't work that way. It is dispersed, inchoate, and fiercely independent.
– Paul Hawken

And there is no name for it. It appears to be an organic, even a biologic phenomenon, rather than a movement in the conventional sense. This new kind of social phenomenon can't be divided because it is atomized – small pieces loosely joined. It forms, gathers, and dissipates quickly. Many dismiss it as powerless, but this kind of structure, on a smaller scale, has been known to bring down governments, companies, and corrupt leaders through witnessing, informing, and massing.

This phenomenon has roots in the environmental and social justice movements. At times, it resists globalization (e.g., to prevent

the annihilation of local cultures); at other times it embraces globalization (e.g., worldwide action to stop global warming). This meta-
movement phenomenon arises spontaneously from different economic sectors, cultures, regions, and cohorts, resulting in a global,
classless, diverse, and embedded action, spreading worldwide
within days, if not hours. This is, by far, the largest coming together
of human beings in history.

　　This fluid, ad hoc collective action network is made up of
research institutes, community development agencies, village- and
citizen-based organizations, as well as corporations, networks,
faith-based groups, trusts, foundations, and other NGOs. Their/our
goal is to meet the multi-front challenges of corrupt politics and
climate change, corporate predation and the death of the oceans,
governmental indifference and pandemic poverty, industrial forestry
and factory farming, depletion of soil and water, genocide and disease, oppression, and persecution.

The promise of this unnamed movement is to offer solutions to what
appear to be insoluble dilemmas: poverty, global climate change,
terrorism, ecological degradation, polarization of income, loss of
culture. ... It is not burdened with a syndrome of trying to
save the world; it is trying to remake the world.
　　　　　　　　　– Paul Hawken

　　Watching the developing big picture, I am reminded of
watching a Superbowl football game. The line of scrimmage moves
closer to one goal line, and then back in the other direction. Globalization pushes hard in one direction, powered by those who want
more standardization, regimentation, and suppression of local culture. The other team, the one of which Mr. Hawken writes, resists,
and pushes hard in the other direction.

　　The question remains: Will enough of us decide to join this
team in time to prevent runaway climate change, and the wholesale
global collapse of life support systems, including those that support
human life?

Every day, an estimated 100 plant and animal species are lost to deforestation . . . A conservative estimate of the current extinction rate indicates that about 27,000 species a year are being lost.
– National Wildlife Federation

The question *still* remains: will we reverse the trend of centuries of frenzied self-destruction? Will enough of us decide to become part of the solution instead of part of the problem? As former Vice President Al Gore said in the conclusion of his speech accepting the Nobel Prize: "The future is knocking at our door right now. Make no mistake, the next generation will ask us one of two questions. Either they will ask: 'What were you thinking; why didn't you act?' Or they will ask instead: 'How did you find the moral courage to rise and successfully resolve a crisis that so many said was impossible to solve?'"

Perhaps our growing appreciation of the facts will inspire enough of us to appreciate the wisdom of the prayer of St. Francis:

Lord, make me an instrument of thy peace.
Where there is hatred, let me sow love;
Where there is injury, pardon;
Where there is doubt, faith;
Where there is despair, hope;
Where there is darkness, light;
Where there is sadness, joy.
O divine Master, grant that I may not so much seek
To be consoled as to console,
To be understood as to understand,
To be loved as to love;
For it is in giving that we receive;
It is in pardoning that we are pardoned;
It is in dying to self that we are born to eternal life.

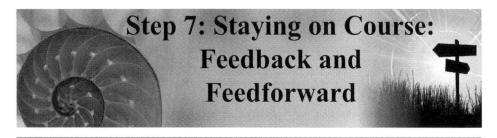

Step 7: Staying on Course: Feedback and Feedforward

• **Truth:** *The road to Hell is paved with good intentions. Genius is the art of making continuous efforts.*
• **Goals:** *Sustainability of the effort, the goals, and the vision through ongoing commitment and proper use of feedback.*
• **Process:** *Continual attention to making sure victories are celebrated, losses are grieved, and that the vision continues to evolve with beauty.*

Many people weaken themselves by feeling guilt, shame, and judgment whenever they have fallen short of their goals. This is foolish. When you have fallen short of your goals, it's very important to appreciate and reward yourself for having tried, then to tap into your wisdom and resources to decide how to avoid making that error again. No need for drama here, just a rational adjustment . . .
– Awakening the Leader Within

As you work with the ideas presented here in these steps, you should soon begin to see successes blooming among the less-than-successes. To stay on course, it is important that you pay sufficient attention to these successes, and that you let your nervous system bask in the positive emotions they evoke. Just as you interest a dog in leaving his romp in the field and come into the house for training by offering a dog a cookie, you keep your system interested by providing rewards for proper behavior.

The road to success can be quite difficult at times, and you may well experience some sore feet and bruises. These are times you need to practice your skills of acceptance – experience the disappointments and frustrations briefly, then let them go. Re-focus your energy: if you have accomplished the objective you had set out to achieve, even partially, or if you have realized another important objective that you discovered along the way, it is essential to reinforce this positive experience. You do this by actually allowing yourself to feel enjoyment as you contemplate your achievement.

The awareness that you have been successful sometimes comes with the presentation of a formal award, a win, a promotion, a Nobel Prize, or the applause of a crowd. On the other hand, you may simply have the experience of a friend letting you know that what you have done has made a difference in his or her life, and that your efforts are appreciated. Sometimes, you may be the only one who knows; learn how to let that be enough!

"SUCCESS" – To laugh often and love much; to win the respect of intelligent people and the affection of children; to earn the appreciation of honest critics and to endure the betrayal of false friends; to appreciate beauty; to find the best in others; to leave the world a little bit better, whether by a healthy child, a redeemed social condition, or a job well done; to know even one other life has breathed easier – because you have lived. This is to have succeeded ...
– Ralph Waldo Emerson

Shifting Your Feedback Paradigm

Gaining power from the awareness of success is difficult for some people, because they have been taught to believe that when they are not perfect, they should punish themselves and treat themselves in such a way that they feel guilty, ashamed, worthless, a failure. And many have been taught that even if they are perfect, that is just merely what is expected and needs no celebration. This is the Inorganic (Either-Or) Paradigm, and is not the one you want to use at this time, since it produces destruction and failure.

It is wise, when such reactions occur, to recall that these

260

ways of thinking and feeling are simply by-products of the bipolar paradigm of thinking with which so many of us were raised. "Behave yourself. Be seen and not heard. Don't talk back. Do what you are told, and you will avoid being punished. Winning isn't everything, it's the only thing."

Most of us have been systematically deprived of the kind of unconditional love that says, "You are valuable, you have a right to your feelings, your thoughts, and your body." You are not here to live up to anyone else's expectations – and not to your own expectations either. Sometimes, your own expectations are leftover demands from an unreasonable or dysfunctional past that are no longer relevant to you now.

It's okay if you mess up. You should give yourself a break.
– Billy Joel

Imagine that the following statements are true:

• You are here to discover the truth of who you really are, and to express your truth with the utmost integrity.
• You are here to discover the music you will play, the song you will sing, the dance you will perform, and the friends that will help you create a new world.
• You are a sublime expression of the Life force, the spirit that moves through all things.
• Within you is the wisdom that inspires and informs all religions and sacred teachings, all music and art, all joy and love.

By imagining that these may be true, you are thinking in resonance with the Organic (Both-And) Paradigm, with its basic goal to support the survival of the whole system. Its focus is more about nurturing what is good and loving, and it aims to see the blessed in everyone, in everything.

261

You are the promised kiss of springtime
that makes the lonely winter seem long.
You are the breathless hush of evening
that trembles on the brink of a lovely song.
You are the angel glow that lights a star;
the dearest things I know are what you are.
– Jerome Kern[23]

Life, the Counter-Entropic Force

The forces of entropy, of decay and corruption, of dispersion and violence, of heartlessness and death will continue to pull in one direction, because they must. This is Newton's Second Law of Thermodynamics. Everything physical that exists must decay, energy is on a one-way street becoming more unavailable to do work, molecules continue their unceasing increase in randomness.

Life, on the other hand, is a counter-entropic force. Life organizes, forms organs, and reflects the organic thinking that seeks to create higher order wholes. Life strives to make things less random, and to make energy more available. This is as a result of Life's following the Organic Paradigm. So, to counter that force that would allow you to drop the ball, that would have you doubt yourself, lose interest, or give up, it is essential you have a way of nurturing yourself on an ongoing basis.

Celebrating your successes, especially with your family, friends, and team members, is especially valuable. But even when you are alone, you can give yourself deeply felt appreciation (or, more accurately, give it to your deeper mind).

---

[23] Excerpted from:
Jerome Kern, *All the Things You Are* (Hal Leonard, 2005).

Honoring Your Self – How to Party Hearty

To do this, you must be in a mental and emotional state that is conducive to your being in touch with the depth of spirit that inspired your actions, the honesty, and sincere desire to serve that in which you believe most deeply. I have found the best way to achieve this is to guide yourself to regularly meditate, pray, or enter a deep state of relaxation, to once again touch that place of wisdom within. This place of wisdom, the inner leader, knows how important it is for you to receive praise for caring enough to try as sincerely as you did.

Whether or not you achieved what you wanted or expected, your try was an honest one. You can feel proud to have refused to take rank with those poor spirits who neither enjoy much nor suffer much, because they live in that grey twilight that knows neither victory nor defeat. You honor yourself by appreciating the degree of purity of your intent, and your courage in daring to be yourself.

Similarly, families, teams, communities, and other groupings, up to the national and international level, must also learn to appreciate positive steps forward. This can be accomplished by creating celebrations that are more than just an excuse to get drunk and party; they must provide an opportunity to collectively appreciate the success of the group as a whole. Here, the success of each individual can be shared with the whole group, and the success of the whole can be made available so that each individual can feel it, and feel a part of it.

Whether or not they were the ball carrier, each one of us needs to celebrate the touchdown. The celebration must be guided by wisdom and heartful loving kindness – by the Organic Paradigm. The health and sustainability of the whole must be a central focus, and this must be balanced with the health and sustainability of the subordinate systems, all the way down to the level of the individual: you, and every level within.

Grieving Losses

In addition, at this place of wisdom, you can look honestly at the cost of the venture, and anything that was lost along the way, especially those losses that seem irreversible. This is the time for honest grieving, as if you were grieving for a lost loved one. You honor what you have lost by feeling the inner sadness that comes with that real or imagined loss. This serves to affirm the depth at which you have appreciated, valued, and loved that which is now gone. Feel it, grieve it, let it go …

And as the painful phase passes, and acceptance begins to take over, gradually you begin to feel a certain rightness about things, and a sense that what is most valuable has not been lost.

For it is still part of your soul. Its spirit lives on in your heart. You re-dedicate part of your success, and of who you are, to that which has been lost, in memoriam. And in so doing, this loss leads to an increase in your commitment, energy, and *personal power*.

The message to the deeper mind, to the nervous system, is that when you re-dedicate yourself, the goal you are still pursuing, and your ultimate vision, are even more valuable and meaningful. Now you have let go of what you needed to let go of in a way that has actually made you stronger. And if you wish, it can make you even more dedicated to your future dream, your heart's desire.

Liberty is being free of the things we don't like in order to be slaves of the things we do like.
– Ernest Benn

Remember, you always have the possibility and the permission to seek counsel from that wise place deep within, that inner oracle. Here is where you can inquire: Is this the right time to pause to take stock and reconsider tactics or strategy, beliefs, and values? Most of the time the right thing is to get up, dust yourself off, and get back in the game. Sometimes, however, you will find that life in the "real world" will present certain experiences that will lead you – or force you – to consider making changes in your vision. Sometimes it is a series of unsuccessful experiments, and sometimes it is an extraordinarily successful one.

At such times you may consult that inner advisor and discover that a more compelling vision emerges. If this one resonates better with your deeper values, is more attuned to your purpose, and better expresses the kind of future you want to commit yourself to, then go ahead and allow your vision to morph. In other words, don't "stay the course" if you find a better one.

But don't be too eager to change course. The lack of success in an endeavor may simply be an indication that you are just not taking the time and the care needed to make sure your outer actions and your inner image are fully congruent with your deeper beliefs. Maybe it's time for one of those annoying *reality checks* we all have to do on ourselves every now and then. We have to keep ourselves honest.

Indeed, the waves never cease, and the only constant is change. A healthy life vision is a living thing, and like all living things it tends to grow and change, especially when it is regularly nurtured by love, attention, and passion.

These excerpts from *Awakening the Leader Within* might give you a sense of the kind of attention that should be paid to the "positive" part of your experiences that you want to use as feedback:

First, allowing yourself to see what went well . . . see how you were true to your values, and brought forth energy and focused your attention on those aspects of the situation that seemed most important to address . . . and let yourself feel really good about this . . . this is you, bringing your best to life . . . in support of what you really believe in . . . reinforce your intention to continue to bring this kind of honest effort to bear on those aspects of life that you truly want to

265

have an impact on . . . and breathe into this feeling . . .
letting it grow stronger . . . and spreading it
throughout all the rest of your body . . .
– Awakening the Leader Within

Then, once you've absorbed the above, allow yourself to process those parts that did not go according to plan in such a way that strengthens you:

. . . And making sure you are in touch with that inner voice of wisdom . . . allow yourself to remain relaxed, calm and sober, as you simply see the truth of what happened . . . and breathing out all negative emotion or other distraction . . . permit yourself to accept that things are exactly as they are, and can be no different . . . and realize that the purpose of the past, and of your memory of it, is to allow you to understand better how things work, so that you can make wiser choices and plans now . . . see what happened . . . calmly seeing the errors and miscalculations . . . the hidden traps and obstacles . . . your body breathing comfortably, remaining relaxed . . .
– Awakening the Leader Within

For those who find prayer valuable, this is a time to pray prayers of gratitude, for having been given the opportunity to serve what is most valuable, most precious to you. It is also of great good to have a significant other, a close friend, or team member help you recall these things, especially if you have a tendency to be hyper-critical of yourself or dismissive of your efforts. Having a group that holds many of the same beliefs and life goals in common with you is even better in most cases. The next chapter will introduce some important ways for you to find kindred souls.

If I am not for myself, then who will be for me? If I am only for myself, then what am I? And if not now, when?
– Hillel the Elder

Questions to Ponder

STOP! You are not finished. Reading this chapter is only the beginning. For each step, take at least a few days to go through the suggested experiences. Recall that the essence is to be in touch with your inner feelings, as well as the associated visual and auditory imagery. You could choose, of course, to spend only a tiny amount of time on each and receive some definite positive benefit. How much better, however, if you give each the respect it deserves by fully understanding and embodying its wise guidance.

You may, of course, continue to read on, then return to this chapter from time to time in order to explore these seven steps, taking as much time as you need. A few days to a few weeks is reasonable. You might consider consulting with friends or professionals who may be skillful at helping you understand and experience the messages these steps teach. If you're in therapy, having life coaching, or spiritual counseling, it would be wise to explore these steps in relationship to the work you are doing there.

Start up conversations about these ideas with friends, read books that explore each more fully, write a journal – do what you need to do to fully embody the learnings that each invites.

For each step, after some study and contemplation:

1. State, in your own words, what you understand this step to be.
2. Do you find there are certain challenges or resistance that you must overcome in order to sincerely take this step? What are they?
3. Which of the issues (mental, emotional, behavioral, physical) in your life might be better addressed if you learned more fully what this step teaches?
4. Where have you thought, felt, spoken, or behaved in a way congruent with this step? What was your experience, how did it feel?

5. What music can you listen to or what art can you expose yourself to that would deepen your experience?

6. What kind of interesting conversations with your friends could help illuminate you?

Most people finally get the best results from putting themselves on a somewhat strict schedule, making sure you set aside time on a daily and weekly basis to truly experience each of these steps. You probably are thinking that you have a pretty good idea of how valuable these ideas are – however, you will find that actually guiding yourself through the suggested experiences tends to produce change on a much more profound level.

Ask yourself how valuable these steps might be if integrated into your life. Does your inner wisdom suggest that you make a commitment to follow through here? Why not make that commitment right now?

Then, ask yourself how you'll make sure you follow through on your commitment. This might mean marking it on your schedule, enlisting a friend to participate with you, making a contract with yourself, and so forth. What are the ways you have discovered in your life that you can use to get yourself to do something you really want to do?

Do you really want to do this? Then just do it. Use the following pages to journal the thoughts and images that emerge with each step.

1. How familiar to you is the feeling of "Presence," and how does it differ from your usual state of consciousness? How could you insure that you experience this more often in your life? Do you want to commit to scheduling this into your life?

2. Who are you? What is your deepest sense of yourself? How often are you in touch with this Self? How could you create opportunities to experience this more often? Who are the people with whom you feel most supported in being yourself. Open yourself to these experiences to find the answer to this question.

3. What do you most need to let go of from your inner life (thoughts, beliefs, emotions, reactions)? From your physical world (possessions, relationships, behaviors)? What social roles is to time to let go of? What attitudes? What habits? What beliefs?

There may be physical things you need to let go of such as piles of old magazines, a full garage or clothes you will never wear again. There may be relationships that you need to let go of – you may need to change jobs, disconnect from certain people whose relationship is no longer serving the purposes you've set for yourself. Maybe it's time to let go of certain habit patterns such as alcohol, drugs, overeating, procrastination, etc. Perhaps there are recurring thoughts, automatic ways of thinking about things or feeling that no longer serve you. Make a list, and commit to checking it frequently.

4. In what ways have you, personally, been misled, and by whom (parents, friends, church, teachers, media, politicians)? How has your family, community, parish, or nation been misled? When you revivify your past through imagery, which memories best awaken your sense of personal power? What communal memories would best serve the communities of which you are a member (family, social group, county, nation, planet)? Where can you find power, faith, integrity, and confidence? (In your memories, your teachers, stories you have heard, your heroes, etc.) Expose yourself to them.

5. How have you experienced the "Law of Attraction" in your life? Take the time to answer the questions at the end of Step 5, then ask yourself: Is there a vision or overarching goal towards which I would like to direct my life? Is there a goal towards which I would like my community (family, work team, friends, state, nation, planet) to direct itself?" "What is the most positive vision I can imagine happening?

6. Which relationships would best enable you to contribute your talents, skills, and gifts? What decisions would you make right now if you wanted to commit yourself to establishing, nurturing, develop-

ing, and sustaining these relationships? Where can you look within, and where can *we* look within, and find the courage and moral compass to act in a way that is wise, compassionate, loving, and effective in confronting the challenges we all face?

7. How do you want to change the way you use negative feedback; how can you use negative feedback more wisely in the future? Can you feel that you are here to discover yourself, your role, your connection to the spiritual center, and the wisdom that can be awakened at your core? What are the decisions you would need to make right now, if you really wanted to keep yourself on a path towards healing, transformation, community, peace, freedom, and universal joy and Love? Do you really want to follow this path? When do you want to make those decisions that you should be making right NOW?

Notes to Self

Seven Steps: Take Home Messages

• Those who allow their behavior to be guided by the principles of wisdom tend to emerge from the fray the least damaged and more empowered by it.

• Being present — letting go of illusions and accepting the self and the world as they are — makes possible a peaceful, non-violent solution.

• The time has come to go deeper within and find the self, the soul, the spirit; this is the only way from which to proceed in creating balance in the system.

• Through letting go of what is not essentially ourselves, we become acquainted with the true self and discover our deeper purpose in any situation.

• There is a wise leader within each of us, one who can make the choices that will lead to healing at every level of system.

• Once an individual, community, or society is in touch with their deeper values, they can use this awareness to produce a personal or social environment more congruent with those values.

• As the organs of the body developed the central nervous system to guide the whole, people all over the world can come together to serve what we all hold in reverence, and in doing so create a healthier planet.

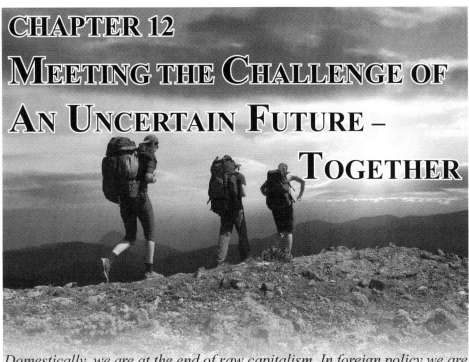

CHAPTER 12
MEETING THE CHALLENGE OF AN UNCERTAIN FUTURE – TOGETHER

Domestically, we are at the end of raw capitalism. In foreign policy we are at the end of raw militarism. Philosophically, we are at the end of simplistic dualism. The old myths that have supported these three pillars of American faith, capitalism, militarism, and dualism, are now diluted, weak and unpersuasive. A revolution in thought will be required to adjust to new realities.
– Craig Barnes

In 1957, historian Arnold Toynbee wrote, "The 20th century will be remembered chiefly by future generations, not as an era of political conflicts or technical inventions, but as an age in which human society dared to think of the welfare of the whole human race as a practical objective." But in the last few decades, this trend towards fairness and inclusiveness seems to have gone underground, as a wave of me-ism swept over us.

Indeed, we have grown so accustomed to the behavior of today's corporations that we have forgotten that in the first half of the previous century we had a very different idea about the purpose

273

of a corporation. The prevailing view was that of Berle, who taught that, contrary to our recent experience, stockholders were merely "stakeholders" in the corporation, and that this new concentration of economic power in corporations must serve not only the owners and management, but also society at large[1].

Dodd, on the other hand, argued that corporations were not public institutions like government bodies, and thus they did not have public responsibility. What ensued was the "Berle-Dodd Debate" concerning to whom the corporate management should be responsible to, the public or stockholders. The Berle position was accepted through the 1950s, and corporations behaved in socially responsible ways (mostly), especially in the treatment of staff.

This all began to change in the 1960s with the gradual shift to the position of Milton Friedman, who believed that any deviation from profit-maximization was mere socialism (the bugaboo of that era) in disguise[2].

By the 1980s his view had become the prevailing one, as exemplified in Michael Douglas' famous line from the 1980s classic movie, Wall Street — "Greed is Good!" The proof of the pudding is in the eating, and the results have been the "bubble economy" of the '90s, in which management attempted to increase shareholder value at all costs, and the current cascade of financial crises, leading to the ethical quagmire that business now is in, to the detriment of society at large.

"Greed is good" became our creed and our business model. And we are now paying the price. Big time!

Wrong Responses

Our inability to respond wisely to a challenge was never more cleary illustrated than during the OPEC oil embargo. The cru-

---

[1]   Adolf A. Berle and Gardiner C. Means, *The Modern Corporation and Private Property* (Transaction Publishers, 1991).

[2]   Milton Friedman, "The Social Responsibility of Business to Increase Its Profits", *The New York Times Magazine* (September 13, 1970).

cial lesson was that we were dangerously dependent on fossil fuels from foreign sources that did not like us very much. At the same time, the problem of pollution and potential global warming was causing deep worries among our scientists. Our response? Instead of creating more fuel-efficient cars, we *relaxed* emission controls and built gas-guzzling SUVs, because this created huge profits for a small group of us, while condemning all of us to the course of events now unfolding.

Central to this has been the continuing increase in our need for petroleum, and thus, the need to control the Middle East. This, in turn, fed Islamic unrest in that part of the world and led to the tragic events of September 11, 2001. And our immediate response to that? To declare the perpetrators "suicidal maniacs" who "do not like our Western lifestyle." My take on it was different.

I wondered why these people were so willing to die in an attempt to disrupt the global financial system. It even occurred to me that perhaps these people might possibly have a point that we needed to pay attention to. Of course, that premise was not a popular sentiment to discuss around the water cooler, especially in those first, tense days. We had to find the evil ones and punish them! Shoot first, ask questions later.

But, having grown up as an African-American in the '40s and '50s, I knew what it was to be in the cultural blind spot, and I had clear recollections of white people treating me as less than human. I knew what it was to be treated with scorn and cruelty. I was tried and convicted by an angry, vindictive society. I was given no chance to speak for myself, and no consideration was given for how much pain I was feeling. I suspect I know something of what the inmates of Guantanamo felt.

What if it had turned out that our country had been abusing the people over there as systematically as we abused the Native Americans and the African slaves, and their unfortunate descendents? What if this decision to demonize and attack these so-called "evildoers" was being made from a similar state of blind prejudice? Discovering that one of the most common nicknames we gave them was "sand niggers" suggested that this might indeed be the case.

Finding an Answer

In our world we've been trained to think that when there's a seemingly unprecedented problem, we expect that the solution is going to be some new invention, probably developed with the use of expensive computers calculating away at very complex computer simulations – like the simulations we have been using to try to predict the rate of global warming. Sometimes, however, as every therapist will tell you, the answer is obvious, once you know how to look at the problem correctly.

When I set out to write this book, my goal was to examine the many ills of our world as a physician might look at a patient, with an eye toward discovering if a major segment, or perhaps even all of them, might be traced to a single deeper cause. Just as most of our physical ailments have their root in our beliefs, thoughts, emotions, and lifestyle, perhaps the problems of our planet/patient (pollution, climate change, violence, genocide, starvation, war, to name a few) could also be traced, systematically and scientifically, to a single underlying issue.

The Systemic Fault

Using the scientific model, I started with the history and physical, and then went on to make a diagnosis, finally settling upon the notion that our system itself has a fault in it. A systemic fault is not a fault that is "here" or "there," but a fault that exists throughout the system. It is everywhere and nowhere. In other words, you may say, "Ah, here is the problem, so I will focus my attention on it." But, "my" attention, "my" way of thinking, is part of the system. What stops me from seeing the solution, then, is that *the fault in my thinking and my attention is exactly what is causing the problem I am trying to solve!* That's like trying to see a red line on a white piece of paper while wearing glasses with red lenses. The unfortunate result is that any solution I find in this way leaves me prone to trying to put out a fire with a bucket of gasoline.

276

I concluded that the paradigm we have been in, attempting to solve problems is actually creating more problems, because it can only look at symptoms. This is similar to the problem we identified in our medical system. We spend billions trying to build artificial hearts and develop drugs to treat premature heart disease, while continuing to eat a wholly unhealthy diet, believing we don't have to take care of ourselves, that we can surgically fix anything that goes wrong as a result. And it is similar to our spending trillions waging war (money that goes into the pockets of a small segment of our population), while dedicating only a pittance to increasing the ability of people to live in peace. And these are but a few of our widespread unethical, unecological and unsustainable practices.

We warehouse those who have broken the law in prisons, where they are placed under enormous stress, trained to become hardened criminals and inducted into street gangs[3]. They break the law, causing loss and suffering to others, and are incarcerated again, which requires more prisons, and more money for the people who run the prisons.

We see the same vicious circle in operation when we put people on welfare, but don't provide jobs that pay enough to get them off welfare. The examples are endless. When at last, we acknowledged the petroleum problem, our response was to spend federal money on subsidizing ethanol, which many believe would create more greenhouse gases than it eliminates[4]. Worse yet, we're creating a planetary crisis by driving up the cost of food as acreage is converted away from growing food crops resulting in starvation and food riots. And on and on.

It might be funny if it were not so tragic. And the most unfunny part is that the system has consistently failed to notice how it is creating the very problems it is supposedly solving. Again, we

---

[3] *Freedom From Within*, a 2-CD program for enabling inmates to find peace, develop meditative skills, use Guided Imagery and Peak Performance skills − www.ShopDrMiller.com
Stephen Leahy, "Ethanol Worse Than Gasoline"
[4] http://stephenleahy.wordpress.com/2008/02/09/ethanol-worse-than-gasoline/

realize Einstein's words of warning: "We cannot solve a problem by using the same level of thinking that gave rise to that problem."

Shifting Paradigms

In our investigation we explored two paradigms (or, more accurately, two types of paradigms). We referred to them as the Either-Or Paradigm and the Both-And Paradigm. The human brain is designed to use both these paradigms in a balanced way, as suggested by the fact that the brain is functionally divided into two main parts. The left cerebral hemisphere is primarily responsible for the analysis, (either-or, black-white, us-them, fragmentation and Violence). Meanwhile, the right cerebral hemisphere concerns itself with *synthesis*, (both-and, integration, creativity, relationship, whole-ness and Love).

There are times when the Either-Or Paradigm seems to work best, as its goal is to try to make things better, to purify, to protect. It is always calculating, manipulating; it is goal- and future-oriented. The goal may be to make money, win a spelling bee, climb the mountain, screen airline passengers for terrorist suspects, or mem-orize a line of Shakespeare. The Either-Or part of the brain/mind is always on the lookout for problems and for danger. The tendency of our culture to rely excessively or exclusively on the either-or mode seems to be an important part of the systemic fault.

The number of choices we perceive life as offering us is limited by two things:

1. The degree that we are open to see the truth of what *is.*
2. The degree that we can free ourselves from the prejudices of the past.

We often find that exactly such prejudices are at the root of our problems. As the old saying goes, "When the pickpocket meets the saint, all he sees are his pockets." We can only see what we've grown an eye to see.

The Law of Unintended Consequences

Empty as a conch shell by the waters cast
The metaphor still sounds – but cannot tell.
And we, like parasite crabs, put on the shell
And drag it at the sea's edge up and down
This is the destiny we say we own.
        – Archibald MacLeish

Even those who really want to do good things often run afoul of the Law of Unintended Consequences when they use the wrong paradigm. Throughout history, we learn of well-meaning people who worked hard to create weapons that would put an end to war. The inventors of the machine gun thought it would put an end to war. They reasoned that wars would become far too costly in human lives, so people would not declare war anymore.

Likewise, Wilbur and Orville Wright thought that the airplane would prevent war because one could fly over enemy lines and see their troop buildups, thus depriving them of the all-important military factor of surprise. How sad they would be to know that theirs was the first step on the way to multiple independent re-entry vehicle (MIRV) missiles.

And Alfred Nobel, the inventor of dynamite, thought it would protect us from war. On reflection, however, it appears the more valuable gift to humanity is probably his Nobel Peace Prize.

There is a lot of talk about "change" these days. Good! I believe the time has come for a change in our thinking. We have been trying to solve our issues at a personal, community, and global (collective) level using a paradigm with a scope that is too limited to accomplish the needs of today's world. Such a blunt instrument cannot help but harm the system we are trying to heal.

A remarkably different set of solutions arises when we approach our challenges – at every level from the personal to the planetary – through the New Paradigm, the lens that sees "black" and "white" not as opposites, but as merely the extreme ends of a

continuum that includes many shades of grey (or even a spectrum of colors).

Where Do We Go from Here?

Should we continue with business as usual? Should we continue to argue about the differences and conflicts in our personal, community, and public lives – or should we start using the tools of healing? Natural systems evolve over millennia via slow chromosomal change.

Now humanity is faced with taking the necessary step of conscious evolution, rather than wait for the snail-paced Darwinian changes to solve our problems. We can't afford to wait. If humanity, as a whole, truly wishes to create health, and continue to sustain itself as a healthy living system, we must begin immediately to apply the principles of healthy living systems – consciously and intentionally – in all of our dealings at every level of system[5].

Beyond Opposition

Of course, when I speak of two different paradigms, our usual worldview (the Either-or Paradigm) tries to seduce us into believing that they are, in some way, opposite, conflicting or opposing views. But actually, they are not. Instead, what we have is a situa-

---

[5]   See the 12 Features of Healthy Living Systems: Appendix page 357

tion very analogous to that point in the development of the science of physics when new discoveries about the subatomic world forced us to expand our understanding beyond the Newtonian-Cartesian model of the universe. Our old way of looking at things was completely incapable of explaining the phenomena of radioactivity and subatomic particles. We needed to shift to a new mode of thinking, as brought to us by such scientists as Einstein and Heisenberg.

Nowadays, Newtonian mechanics is not considered to be "wrong"; it is merely seen as a special case and continues to be quite valuable for most everyday uses. In other words, once our tools for scientifically studying our world became sufficiently sophisticated, it became necessary to expand the model we were using to conceptualize it.

Likewise, the unifying of the world by such phenomena as global climate change, economic globalization, and communications technology requires that we evolve a new way of thinking. There need be no conflict between the Either-Or and Both-And worldviews – they have a natural relationship. The Either-Or Paradigm is merely seen as a special case of the more general Both-And paradigm of integration. Newtonian mechanics works fine for the billiard player or the lumberjack. The process of differentiation is of enormous value in many instances – but we must avoid making the mistake of Aesop's donkey.

The Donkey and the Merchant, an Aesop's Fable

A merchant, driving his donkey homeward from the seashore with a heavy load of salt, came to a river crossed by a shallow ford. Although he had often crossed here without incident, on this occasion the donkey slipped on a wet rock and fell into the water. By the time the merchant helped him to his feet, much of the salt had melted away. When he discovered how light his load had become, the delighted donkey continued the journey with great joy. The following day the merchant loaded the donkey again with salt, a somewhat greater load, to make up for the accident. But on the way home, the wily donkey, recalling the incident at the

---

ford, purposely let himself fall into the water, and again got rid of most of his burden.

But the merchant was no fool. He quickly realized what was happening. He turned around and drove the donkey back to the seashore. Here he loaded him with two huge baskets of sponges. How eager the donkey was to reach the ford, where he gleefully rolled over in the water. But when he at last tried to scramble to his feet, he was in for a big surprise. Indeed, it was a very disconsolate donkey that dragged himself homeward under a load ten times heavier than before.

Moral: The same measures will not suit all circumstances; the wise person will counter old tricks with new ones.

Our Moment of Truth as a Culture and Planet

As a nation and a culture, we have come to a precipice where we have a very important decision to make – whether to try the old tricks one more time, or consider creating a new way to confront our problems. When one looks at the world from the Both-And perspective, it seems clear that the best bet for any of us to prosper and live in peace and health will be to make a sincere effort to create a system where it is possible for all of us to prosper in health and peace.

The luxury of being able to focus solely on the well-being of yourself, your family, or your tribe is not enough anymore. September 11 opened our eyes to the folly of doing only that – and the economic crisis of 2008 added an emphatic exclamation point. We can no longer be like the two men sitting at the stern of a badly leaking rowboat, watching two other men in the front vainly trying to bail out the water – one of them saying to the other, "I'm glad the hole is not in our end of the boat."

Long ago, life developed on this planet. Organic material appeared and life developed as a self-organizing system. It evolved all the way from the single-celled animal to life's crowning achievement, the human being, with our ability to imagine. I believe the time has come to try to imagine something truly extraordinary – that the people of Planet Earth can actually begin to see the possibility of wholeness, fairness, unity, and the possibility of liberty, freedom, and justice for all. And not only imagine it – but believe in it and make it happen.

Imagination is more important than knowledge.
For knowledge is limited to all we now know and understand,
while imagination embraces the entire world, and all there
ever will be to know and understand.
– Albert Einstein

The Development of the Wiser Mind

When I was a child I spoke as a child, I understood as
a child and I thought as a child ...
— 1 Corinthians 13:11

As people mature from childhood, they begin with a simplistic view of the world that becomes ever more complex as they explore and experience life. As our ability to think matures, we transcend the fantasies of childhood and see the world more accurately. In our personal evolution, we confront the unnecessary fears, anxieties, angers, and helplessness we were dragging along within ourselves and let them go. We discover the distorted ways we have learned to see and act in the world. The result is that our lives change for the better.

At some points, deep systemic changes can take place in our thinking – a special kind of growth. This new growth is not simply "more of the same"; it is fundamentally different. Often it appears as a breakthrough, an epiphany, or a *metamorphosis* (the Greek word for *transformation*), as it is similar to the kind of change that occurs when the caterpillar transforms into a butterfly.

The metamorphosis of the caterpillar gives us an interesting model: Within the body of the chrysalis-enshrouded caterpillar, a set of cells begins to conspire. Together, they begin to rearrange the individual living cells of the caterpillar. Although the doomed caterpillar's immune system tries to fight off this invasion from within, it ultimately loses, dissolving into a nutrient broth that feeds the growing cells that ultimately form the butterfly. Interestingly enough, this group of cells is called the *imaginal*, which makes this model so appropriate. The challenge that faces us all is to imagine ways we can transform ourselves so our world becomes coherent, healthy, peaceful, and sustainable.

And in perfect cosmic timing, there is the appearance of a new breed of leader who realizes that there is a very attractive alternative to our behavior of the past. These new leaders believe we can actually hold a new image, one of coherence, wholeness, sustainability. They believe we can guide our world to develop in congruence with this image. Just as an individual can accelerate his or her healing with a mental image, a planet can heal itself with a healthy self-image. Perhaps we are part of an imaginal, and as we grow in number, the result will be the formation of an entirely new entity.

It All Starts With You

The victory belongs to you . . . And above all, I will ask you to join in the work of remaking this nation the only way it's been done in America for two-hundred and twenty-one years – block by block, brick by brick, calloused hand by calloused hand.
– Barack Obama, Presidential Acceptance Speech, 2008

Some might think this an enormous job, and it is. But it may not be as difficult as it seems. Whereas, the Old Paradigm saw a distinct separation between self and other, self and the world, the New Paradigm sees wholes. It sees stepping stones instead of stumbling blocks.

Instead of wondering if someone will come along and change the world out there, we can recognize that there is no "out there" out there. The answer we seek begins right here, right now. It has to do with deciding the lens through which we will see the world. Remember, we cannot see the world "as it really is," in an objective, scientific way, because we do not see atoms and quarks (which is what the world is really made of). All we have are our thoughts and images about ourselves and the world, and the rela-tionship we imagine we have with each other. And it is a very dif

285

Kenyan youth in Obama
shirt - by Nancy Margulies

ferent world when viewed through these different paradigms.

When the relationships we imagine are those that reflect the Old Paradigm, it often leads to failure – to anxiety, anger, abuse, helplessness, and "if only I were the ruler of the world" fantasies, and all the illness and dysfunction that ensue. But there is another way to approach the world, one in which we see a wholeness, a oneness – a world that looks much like that described by revered religious teachers and other wise ones throughout time. Certainly they recognized the value of analyzing the world and of protecting ourselves when need be, but they also strongly urged the use of the Both-And Paradigm as well.

An excellent example of this perennial wisdom appears in the Holy Bible, Matthew 5:38-39. Here it is written: "Ye have heard that it hath been said, 'An eye for an eye, and a tooth for a tooth': But I say unto you, That ye resist not evil: but whosoever shall smite thee on thy right cheek, turn to him the other also." This is certainly not the way most of the world conducts business, yet it is a theme that wise ones among us return to again and again.

Ours is a world of nuclear giants and ethical infants. We know more about war than we know about peace, more about killing than we know about living. We have grasped the mystery of the atom and rejected the Sermon on the Mount.
– Omar N. Bradley

A Rule Better Than Gold

Consider, for example, the Old Testament, Leviticus 19:18, which reads in part, "Thou shalt love thy neighbor as thyself." The concept expressed by this "Golden Rule" is perhaps the most important one in the shift I think we now need to make as a global community. The problem is that in the past, each religion has tended to apply it only to certain people ("our kind"), those of "our" particular religion. The challenge is now to apply this paradigm on a more inclusive basis – perhaps as the Buddhists say, in our treatment of "all sentient beings," and to the earth itself.

The various religions and philosophers may say it differently, but there's a common theme – it means seeing and treating another as oneself – to be sensitive to the deeper oneness that maybe masked by our physical differences.

Loving your "enemies" is the natural result of seeing that they are part of a whole, of which you are also a part . . . If we do not perceive this fundamental truth, we stay in a state of denial, one that also denies us access to important information about the world and about ourselves.

Seeing clearly, you discover that often your enemies represent a denied part of yourself, a part of you that you fear, that you despise, that you refuse to accept and don't want anyone to know about (including yourself). Psychologically, this is called Denial and Projection.

If you don't like what you see in others, take a good hard look at yourself, for others are often your mirrors. Have you ever noticed, for example, how those people who are always concerned about being cheated are often the ones who cheat others, and those who abuse others are the ones most likely to complain of being victims, and those who complain of the anger of others are often the most angry? Funny how they can't seem to see this! And they won't, unless they stop to look.

What is it that you have trouble accepting about yourself? What do you project onto the world around you? Do "things" upset you, do people "make" you angry or anxious?

287

Central to addressing this issue is self-acceptance[6]. As you discover how to accept yourself as you are, you will find it easier to give others the freedom to be the way they are, and to accept them. On the other hand, when you continue to deny aspects of yourself that you don't like, you continually create those same aspects in others until they are resolved within you. The vicious circle again.

When you accept others as they are, and see them as possessing the same essential worth (what some might call the "spark of divinity") as yourself, you realize they deserve the same respect. And you realize how much your habits, prejudices, fears, and resentments have been at the root of your problems in relationships. Suddenly, the frustration and resentment you have felt evaporate, and you no longer complain about the fact that people are exactly the way they are. Then you can begin conversations about things that really matter.

Know Thyself

"Know Thyself" are the immortal words inscribed in the forecourt of the Temple of Apollo at Delphi. The better you know yourself, the wiser your choices will become.

The new paradigm tells us that:

- We are not helpless.
- Our true power lies in our ability to make choices.
- Our choices are crucial.

By making wise choices in our personal lives, and in our relationships, we have the ability to contribute to the transformation of the whole.

---

[6]   I Am: Awakening Self-Acceptance addresses
       this issue experientially
       www.ShopDrMiller.com

Become the change you want to see.
– Mohandas Gandhi

To make the kinds of choices in your life that you will feel good about in the future, it is obviously very important to have a clear and accurate understanding of yourself. You are more likely to make choices that are wise if you know who you are. And if you discover that you have a tendency to resist growth, evolution, and change, you run the risk of being stuck in old ways of thinking and behaving that no longer serve you (if they ever did). Why not explore some different options?

Laws and institutions must go hand in hand with the progress of the human mind as that becomes more developed, more enlightened, as new discoveries are made, new truths discovered and manners and opinions change. We might as well require a man to wear still the coat which fitted him when a boy as civilized society to remain ever under the regimen of their barbarous ancestors.
– Thomas Jefferson

Patience, presence, and appreciative inquiry are important at this stage. This will permit the continuous growth of wisdom and clarity, and as a result, you are more certain to be right when you predict what might be the outcome of the different choices confronting you. Knowing yourself means knowing what you value and what you believe in.

A very important part of who we are results from our living our lives guided by those principles and values that we hold at a deep level, the ways we understand our world. We addressed this in Chapter 11 as an aspect of awakening the leader within.

In addition, you can make wise decisions more consistently if you cultivate integrity, loyalty, reliability, and responsibility. If your feelings, values, choices, and self-image change too much, if you are too dependent on what is going on around you and "flip-flop" often, wise choices are difficult to make. A decision you make today may turn out to be just a capitulation to current social pressures, rather than a thoughtfully developed choice likely to be congruent with your true values and Self.

Integrity: How Well Do Your Thoughts, Words, and Deeds Reflect Your Deeper Values?

Someone once asked the wife of Mohandas Gandhi how it was that he spoke so eloquently, without notes, yet never contradicted himself. Her reply was, "You and I, we think one thing, say another, and do a third; but for Gandhi, they are all the same." This is the essential meaning of integrity.

As humans, we all have needs. Some of these needs may be very specific to an individual – for instance, my friend Frederick needs to listen to classical music for about an hour at the end of the day to wind down from his very demanding workload. Gloria accomplishes the same thing by going for a run. Sam mellows out by playing video games. Although the ways they meet their specific needs are different, the basic need to relax and wind down is one that all three of them share.

Yet there are also needs we humans share in common – the most obvious ones being food, clothing, and shelter. Once these primitive needs are satisfied, we begin to strongly desire certain other things. We might call them higher-level needs, such as:

- We want to feel safe.
- We want to be liked, and even loved, by others.
- We want to be respected and treated fairly in our social environment.
- We want to express the essence of who we are, to actualize ourselves.

So, one challenge we all face is, "How do we go about attempting to get these needs met?" What kind of behaviors should we employ? If we want something, should we try to steal it? Should we try to trick someone out of it? Should we beg for it and try to justify why we think it should be given to us?

Or should we work to earn something that we can trade for it? And after we have it, how do we feel about the behavior we used to get it? How much integrity should we choose to have? We have the possibility of making a choice here – how do we want to interface with the world, and what paradigm do we want to employ?

Community Questions

Just as we can ask these questions at the personal level, it should be clear that exactly the same questions need to be asked at other levels of the system – family, community, national, and global.

The invasion of Iraq by the United States and its allies created a situation that can serve as an excellent example. In 2001, those we had elected to represent our interests concluded that there was a high likelihood that weapons of mass destruction (WMDs) were hidden someplace in Iraq. Most of the rest of the world did not agree. Nonetheless, we allowed ourselves to become convinced that we needed to invade, and we did so. But not many of our allies agreed, and only a few went along with our plan. This gave rise to a question in the halls of Congress, "How should we act towards those allies who happened to disagree with us?"

The public stance we assumed had a dramatic effect on the other countries of the world. We decided that we were so certain of being right that we rejected the notion that others could perhaps have a point worth respecting. The special warmth and respect they had for us seemed to evaporate as they began to experience our behavior as arrogant, haughty, self-centered, and contemptuous.

The contempt with which we reacted was highlighted by the decision by Congress to ban the word "French" from the menu in the congressional dining room. There was no more French dressing, and French-fried potatoes became "freedom fries," and so on. Not only were the French wrong, this seemed to say, but we were unwilling to respect or recognize any contribution they have made to our cuisine, or our culture (e.g., the Statue of Liberty). No wonder they felt insulted!

This represents an excellent example of the inappropriate application of the Either-Or Paradigm, with its focus on differentiation, violence, and competition. The application of the Both-And Paradigm, on the other hand, might be represented by the following response: "We regret you do not agree, but we fully respect your integrity to be true to your beliefs and values – we may not agree with what you say, but we will defend your right to say it. If we are right, we will forgive your error. If wrong, we will admit ours. After all, we are allies!"

So, to learn how to make ever-wiser choices, we must look back with clear eyes, see the results of what we have done, and ask ourselves, "What was the underlying principle that we used to choose the behaviors we employed?" And, "How well is that way of seeing the world and choosing working for us?"

The lame man who keeps the right road outstrips the runner who takes a wrong one. The more active and swift the latter is, the further he will go astray.
– Francis Bacon

How Should We Make Important Choices?

In the final analysis, every decision we make must be based upon:

- The data we have collected.
- The way we interpret it.
- Our underlying beliefs and principles (these beliefs and principles determine how we process that data).

For example, the underlying principle behind the way the U.S. treated other countries when we invaded Iraq seemed, "You don't need road manners if you're an 18-wheeler." And, as we are the world's only remaining superpower, we had the option of choosing to see things in this way. But is this the correct attitude?

At the personal level, we find that when individuals pay conscious attention to the values and principles by which they are living their lives, they find that they gain the valuable ability to shift their thoughts, feelings, and behaviors to ones that reflect health, wellness and high performance. When a person experiences physical, mental, emotional, behavioral, or relational symptoms, the underlying imbalance responsible for these symptoms often turns out to be an attitude – a certain persistent way of approaching the world. The worrier gets a headache, the anxious person stomach and bowel pain, and so forth. The symptoms are related to the kind of thinking, and this is based, in turn, on deeper principles.

So, for example, if a woman who was abused by her alcoholic father has concluded that the following "basic principle" about life is true: All men are selfish, cruel, and willing to abuse you to get what they want – then it is clear how this could lead to uncomfortable and irritable emotions around men, an inability to establish positive working relationships with men, marital difficulties, headaches, and recurrent vaginal infections. Indeed, her beliefs will tend, paradoxically, to lead her into situations with men that will lead to additional experiences of abuse!

With time and experience, on the other hand, she might learn a more nuanced principle — that everyone seeks love and comfort, and that because many men have been abused in their early relationships (by parents, babysitters, peers, coaches, pornography, etc.), they have walled off their vulnerability and lost the ability to have empathy, compassion, and to be caring. As a result, many men, those who have not recovered from this abuse, will be prone to be abusive. On the other hand, not all men fall into this pattern. Some were never abused and are not abusive – and others have recovered from this trauma and are exceedingly kind.

Following this realization – a revision of her worldview – she

293

might find very different kinds of decisions about men are possible, and her experience of men will be markedly expanded. Certainly, it is important to discover whether or not a man is still acting out of his abusive past, but it is equally important to be able to recognize a different kind of man, one who can be soft, gentle, caring, loving. So the new principle leads her to a new way of guiding her choices: Men who have not healed should be avoided, but those who have recovered (or who had not been so abused) warrant a different kind of assessment.

At this point, our hypothetical woman would be likely to make wiser and more rewarding choices in her relationships. Technically, this is often referred to as maturation of one's *cognitive map*.

Principles for Wise and Sustainable Living

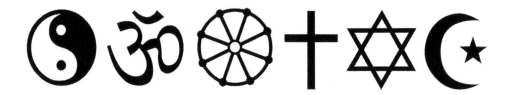

One's philosophy is not best expressed in words. It is expressed in the choices one makes ... the process never ends until we die. And the choices we make are ultimately our responsibility.
– Eleanor Roosevelt

In my work with individuals and groups, I have realized that there is a fundamental set of principles – a set that, when embodied, leads toward balance, peace of mind, high levels of health and wellness, rich, rewarding relationships, and optimal levels of performance – at all levels of system. We have touched on a few of them here: the Golden Rule, integrity, and the principle of selecting carefully the proper paradigm to use in attempting to understand the world and how to act in it.

Furthermore, I have discovered that most of the time people don't need to be convinced that these are the principles they should follow. As soon as they understand them, they realize that they already hold these principles deep within themselves, though they may not have paid attention to them, acted as they prescribe, or realized the importance of doing so. It is as if we are born with the special ability to resonate deeply with this set of principles hard-wired in. In the right childhood home and community, these are easily evoked. When the environment is not supportive, or if there is trauma, or even when there is simply a lack of reinforcement of these principles, they do not emerge, but lie dormant within – much as an enormous musical talent might lay dormant and undiscovered in a person who is never exposed to music, instruments, or a good teacher.

As noted previously, throughout history, these principles for wise living have always appeared whenever the wisest elders of the tribe, community, or culture get together and seek the highest truths. Naturally – because when they are followed, they lead to safety, harmony, peace, security, love, and efficient, effective communication throughout the group.

In my experience, even when applied to very large collections of people, these ways of approaching our world tend to produce healing and efficient functioning. I have been led to the hypothesis that there is a set of basic human principles having the following properties:

• Upon careful examination, they often seem self-evident.
• When they are learned and embodied, they exert a powerful influence on all behaviors, and produce safety, health, wellness and peak performance.
• They are as applicable when applied at the planetary level as when they are applied at the national, community, family, or personal level.
• Though often presented in limited, parochial language, the words can be changed without harming the essence of the

message, thus rendering them universally applicable.

In the practice of medicine and psychology – and as a teacher, author, and publisher of self-healing and training materials – I have come to the following conclusions:

• These clarified principles can be presented dynamically through a variety of products and productions (a variety allows culture-specific references to be used).

• Those who experience this training are often empowered to create changes within their own internal and social lives, and the better they comprehend and embody these principles, the more their behavior will tend to reflect unitive thinking and love.

• The result is more peace, empowerment and the ability to diffuse tense situations and communicate nonviolently.

• People who learn these principles will realize their deeper values and be eager to pass them on to others, thus creating a kind of "paying it forward" – leading to the formation of communities with common values, Internet groups, and so forth.

• Gradually these groups can coalesce, leading to a profound general transformation in thinking throughout our culture and planet.

• The Internet/ World Wide Web is the ideal communication medium to facilitate these changes.

A list of the principles that seem most important to recognize and apply in our lives would have to include:

• Self-awareness, knowing who you are and being in touch with your proper boundaries
• Balance, within the body, with the environment, and with

others in it
• Self respect and self confidence
• Access to high-quality information
• Honesty, a willingness to see, know, and express the truth
• Coordination of parts in harmonious ways
• Integrity, congruence, compassion
• Rationality – the ability to think and reason logically
• Understanding that the source of all suffering is wanting things to be different from what they are at this moment
• The "Golden Rule" – the need to respect others and the environment
• The ablity to express Self in thought, word, and deed

Change Begins with You and Me

The headlines around the world on November 5, 2008, heralded "Change," a marked departure from our usual headline fare. Dominated as they are by persistent stories of hate, greed, domination, violence, and dispersion. It is important to realize that it is the present money and power structure that benefits from this negative approach. Still, it is not difficult to find evidence that the infrastructure of the New Paradigm is already coming into place even as the Old Paradigm crumbles. Prototypes have been created throughout the world by millions of groups. This process is well-highlighted by Paul Hawken in his book *Blessed Unrest* as discussed in Step 6 in Chapter 11.

These groups are generating hope and vision for millions of people. Many feel that this infrastructure, and the ideas and principles that inform it, are the true legacy referred to by Toynbee at the start of this chapter.

Will the forces of love reach critical mass? Only time will tell.

This new-world paradigm suggests that your thoughts, feelings and actions are actually important, that you are a meaningful and powerful part of a whole, and that you have important decisions to make at this very moment in time. In a very real sense, your participation is critical.

Perhaps, as you put these ideas together with other things you have been hearing and reading lately, you may find a message that is meaningful to you. You may be discovering something that inspires you to balance and heal within, and to balance and heal your relationships. Perhaps there is a new hope, or at least a curiosity, as to what might happen if you explore and compare the results you get approaching things according to different paradigms. If so, it may be wise to begin to put these thoughts into action quickly, before the message gets drowned in the distractions of the external world. Now, while you are aware of how crucial it is that you nurture a certain change in your life, make a plan to act.

Act now, and as you do, know that we are at a very important time in the history of the planet. How we husband our resources, balance our usage of our finite capacities, and how we care for each other lies in the balance now.

What If?

What if Gandhi's words, "Become the change you want to be," were not merely metaphorical? What if he were reflecting the truth – that the separation we imagine (and therefore see) between us and other people, and between us and other living things, is just an illusion? What if, as the wise ones have told us, in some really fundamental and important way, we are all part of a seamless whole? The challenge is that it is often not clearly obvious that this is true, and we are distracted by the apparent differences and conflicts.

What if, as Goethe suggests, "All the dragons of our lives are princesses who are only waiting to see us once beautiful and brave"? Our dragons are but a distortion of the world by the emotional state produced in us in the wake of the trauma, abuse, and abandonment we have suffered in our lives. If we honestly address the issues that are out of balance within our lives, and if we improve the balance and performance of those gifts, talents, skills, and creativity within us, might we actually have a direct effect on the fate of the world?

What if, by changing yourself in the direction the whole world needs to change, you are actually actively participating in creating that transformation? What if you trusted what is within, and gave yourself permission to express your truth, had an important positive effect on all those around you? What if really accepting all these possibilities as *true* increases the likelihood that we will actually have this positive effect?

What if your decision to make a change in your life will have powerful and far-reaching effects on a worldwide level? What if, simultaneously, millions of others are making the same choice?

It has been shown time and again, that when enough people are focused on the same outcome, that outcome seems to be favored by the events that ensue. Some who study such phenomenon describe "morphic fields[7]" that are created when we hold an image in our mind, and that as more and more people focus in the same direction, we approach critical mass, which will lead to a sudden transformation of the system as a whole.

What if your participation is all that is needed in order to reach critical mass? And what if, as many have reported, as you begin to see ever more clearly what it is that you need to do in order to help this message spread throughout your own family, neighborhood, workplace, and nation, you will find it easy and enjoyable to share what you are learning about creating peace in your heart and in the environment around you. If so, others will see, and hear, and understand.

The solution we need is not going to be hatched and applied in the halls of congress, or the computer rooms of universities; it is not highly complex, it is elegantly simple. We, you, and I, are the answer to this problem. Can we do it?

Yes, we can!

Always bear in mind that your own resolution to succeed is more important than any other one thing.
– Abraham Lincoln

---

[7]   Morphic field is a term introduced in the 1980s by British biologist Rupert Sheldrake, the major proponent of this concept, through his Hypothesis of Formative Causation. It is described as consisting of patterns that govern the development of forms, structures, and arrangements. Sheldrake's theories have been considered faulty by the scientific community because of his assertions' inability to be falsified or make predictions that contradict current models. The Global Consciousness Project at Princeton, however, is actively studying the phenomenon with some promising results.

Notes to Self

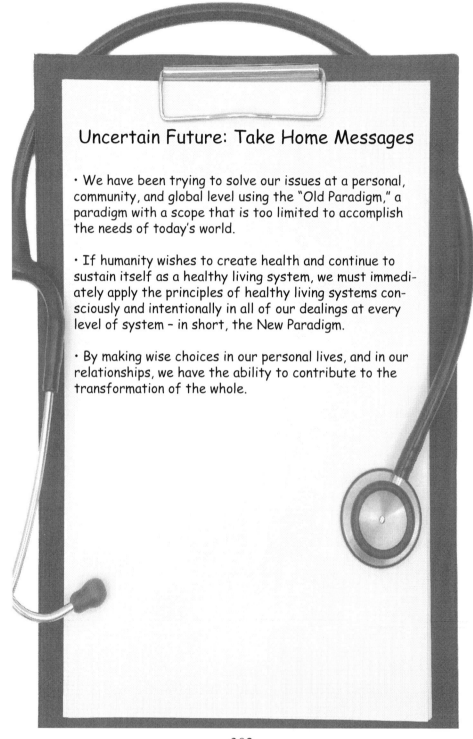

Uncertain Future: Take Home Messages

• We have been trying to solve our issues at a personal, community, and global level using the "Old Paradigm," a paradigm with a scope that is too limited to accomplish the needs of today's world.

• If humanity wishes to create health and continue to sustain itself as a healthy living system, we must immediately apply the principles of healthy living systems consciously and intentionally in all of our dealings at every level of system – in short, the New Paradigm.

• By making wise choices in our personal lives, and in our relationships, we have the ability to contribute to the transformation of the whole.

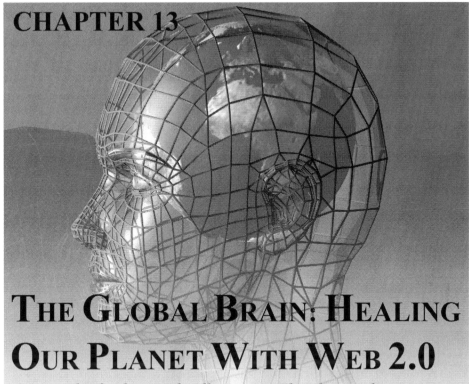

CHAPTER 13

THE GLOBAL BRAIN: HEALING OUR PLANET WITH WEB 2.0

As a result of a thousand million years of evolution, the universe is becoming conscious of itself, able to understand something of its past history and its possible future. This cosmic self-awareness is being realized in one tiny fragment of the universe – in a few of us human beings. Perhaps it has been realized elsewhere too, through the evolution of conscious living creatures on the planets of other stars. But on this our planet, it has never happened before.
– Julian Huxley

In Chapter 12, we examined what might happen if we approached ourselves, our purpose, vision, and who we are as individuals, and as a collective, using the New Paradigm. This meant choosing, instead of focusing primarily on the single problem in front of us, the *symptom*, to examine the system as a whole.

Instead of denying challenges, fleeing from them, or attempting to make them go away, we explored a new approach, starting

303

with deeply relaxing, coming into the present, and accepting things as they are at this moment. Interestingly, this is the same first step we employ when a person wants to use the principles of mind-body medicine to facilitate individual healing of mental, physical, emotional, or behavioral problems.

When we begin to deal with a difficult issue in this way, we are sending a message, in brain language, to the deeper levels of the mind. The message is that we do not have to fight against or resist anything in the world as it is at this moment. The result is that we eliminate distractions and have control of our awareness.

The next step was to guide our awareness, trusting that focusing on the truth of the current moment – rather than fighting or resisting it – would reveal valuable information, wisdom, and guidance from within. One important bit of information from within concerns the nature of our true identity, the answer to the question, "Who am I?".

Who Are We?

In a similar manner, when we are examining a challenging situation from the point of view of a collective (family, team, community, nation, planet), we have the same challenge, "*Who are we?*" What is the nature of this whole that I, as an individual, am part of? And just as it is important at the individual level to do some letting go of distractions, items, and issues that are no longer useful to us, we need to let go of ways of relating with others and the world that are no longer productive so we can make room for changes in the present and in the future.

Next, we opened ourselves to discover and learn from the information, experience, and wisdom within ourselves, from parts of the brain we may not often access. The process of doing this involves the use of the prefrontal cortex of the brain. The prefrontal cortex of the human brain is the seat of the "executive functions" that enable us to see the "big picture," to develop a strategy, to organize a plan, and to keep our attention focused as we systematically complete each task in order.

Similarly, in tapping into the wisdom of the collective, we redirect our awareness to be receptive to information that is present in the collective mind of the group or community. We shift our awareness from looking at ourselves as separate from others, and instead, we focus our awareness on looking within that vast nervous system represented by the individual brains of each of us all networked together by today's incredible communication technology, as exemplified by the Internet/World Wide Web[1].

The Global Brain: Making Connections

In recent years, it has not been unusual to hear people speak of something called the "Global Brain." I take this as being a metaphor for the intelligent network composed of human beings and groups of people, the knowledge and wisdom we have amassed, and the communication systems that connect us to each other[2]. This model sees our society as a living system that expresses itself through our communications media and guides the activities of humans. Ultimately, the Global Brain determines the condi-

---

[1]   The terms Internet and World Wide Web (or Web) are often used interchangeably. Technically, however, the Web is only the most visible – and arguably the most important – part of the much larger Internet.

[2]   Although the term was first coined by Peter Russell, the notion has been around for centuries, dating back as far as Herbert Spencer's "Society as Organism Model."

tions in our society – and thus, the condition of the planet (think global warming) and all life on it.

According to this metaphor, each person is an individual neuron, designed and "programmed" to a certain degree, to react or respond to certain stimuli in certain ways. Groups of individuals – a family, team, or community – can then be thought of as a kind of organ, capable of carrying out a more complex function. An army, or pest extermination service, is a kind of immune system, and an Internet or television network is a kind of visual and auditory organ.

Personal Responsibility

Just as is the case with an individual neuron, each of us has two basic duties:

> 1. To sustain our individual health and optimal performance (body, mind, emotions, behavior)
> 2. To interface well with other individuals (neurons) and groups (organs and organ systems) through the communication technologies that connect us (synapse, relationship)

These two functions are carried out in a manner consistent with our values and beliefs. Some values and beliefs lead to health and high performance, some to illness and dysfunction. In turn, the choices and decisions we make in our interactions with the world around us are always the result of the interplay among three primary factors:

> • Who you think you are, what is your image of yourself: "Who am I?"
> • What you believe about the nature of the world around you: "Where am I and what is happening?"
> • What you believe to be the nature of your relationship to the world around you: "How shall I act or react?"

The challenge for each of us is to identify and live according to our true values, principles, mission, goals, and visions. This allows us to bring about deep healing at the personal level, and to create high-level wellness[3].

Community Responsibility

As we continue the process of balancing at the individual level, we now have the responsibility to discover and play our proper role in the social networks all around us. We must next examine our relationship with other individuals and groups:

- What is the "formula," or paradigm, you use in connecting with others?
- What are your beliefs about the world and the people in it?
- Is the world basically a dangerous place, where we need to be suspicious of everyone or in constant competition?
- Is the world filled with people who have a loving nature, and when treated with patience, respect, and appreciation, might become friends and allies?

Recalling that our beliefs are, in large, the choices we make every day, what we believe has a decisive effect on our experience, and on the kind of impact we have on our social and natural environment.

Relationships Among Individuals

Turning once again to our metaphor of using the individual

---

[3] Emmett Miller, M.D., *Deep Healing,*
    The Essence of Mind-Body Medicine
    Also see *Unlock Your Full Potential Suite*
    www.ShopDrMiller.com

nervous system as a model, we see that there is a certain very common kind of relationship between neurons. Whenever we find a smoothly functioning brain and nervous system, we discover that neurons relate with each other in such a way as to serve the organism as a whole.

For instance, a neuron that detects a sharp pain signal coming from the sole of your foot reliably relays this information up to the level of the spinal cord and the brain. The result is that you become immediately aware that you are stepping on a tack and can take the appropriate action. Likewise, olfactory neurons never fail to alert the brain of the smell of bacon frying, or that of some dog droppings you have stepped in.

In other words, the well-functioning brain is composed of neurons and groups of neurons that are honest with each other, who relate in ways that support the health and proper functioning of the whole, who have integrity and function in a way that is congruent. Similarly, when we study teams, communities, families, and other social groupings that are functioning smoothly and effectively, we find that the individuals relate with each other in similarly congruent and authentic ways.

It follows then, that to best serve your deeper purpose, to fulfill your duty to the deepest part of yourself, you need to strive to connect with others in a manner that is congruent with your deepest values. This means your mission in life must be based on truth and integrity: that what you say and do – and what you think, feel, and believe – are all congruent.

For many people, the notion of relating with others in a manner that is accepting, noncompetitive, nonjudgmental, respectful, and appreciative is an unfamiliar one indeed. Yet, this is the best attitude to have when you recognize that what we share in common is so much more important than that which differs among us, and that serving the whole through our communications with others is a vitally important goal for each of us.

Indeed, such a way of approaching our relationships is dramatically different from what most of us have learned in the process of being socialized in a system that greatly overuses the Either-Or Paradigm.

Clearly, however, if we want to best serve our purpose in the developing global nervous system, we need to develop architectures of engagement that favor the smooth, accurate communication of information to ever-wiser levels of deliberation, thinking and decision-making. And these architectures must facilitate the smooth, accurate communication of effective responses and actions that accomplish the will of the whole (the collective).

Our Bionic Communications Network

Each of us, like individual neurons, is connected to each other person, not only by our face-to-face communications, but also by long axons and nerve bundles composed of telephone lines, wireless cell phone networks, and Internet connections.

According to the Both-And Paradigm, it is in our individual and collective best interest to relate with others more often since this will increase the likelihood of behaviors and relationships that serve the collective, the community as a whole. Of course, if we sincerely want to serve the greater good, we actually need to practice being the kind of person we really want to be. Here's where we can both gain from and contribute to a social network.

Establishing a functioning social network requires that we come out of our hiding places where our fears and helplessness have driven us. Then, empowered by the awareness of our potential as well as our (some would say sacred) duty to ourselves and our higher values and integrity, we can join with like-minded others in a mutual exploration of what we all might accomplish together. This

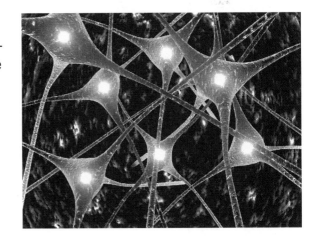

means we must genuinely commit a portion of our life's energy to serve those highest needs that guide us to create honest, open, trusting, accepting, appreciative, supportive, inspiring, empowering, sustaining, healing, creative relationships.

In this environment, we find ourselves empowered and encouraged to allow ourselves to receive valuable information, and to express ourselves openly. As a result, we can gradually, step by careful step, allow ourselves to take certain risks:

1. Revealing our values, visions, and mission to others so as to discover those kindred spirits who resonate with us at the deepest level.
2. Opening ourselves to not just "hear" others, but to really listen to them, and to receive them at all levels, gradually being willing to lower our walls, or at least make them more permeable.
3. Embracing the quality of oneness. This will allow us to discover and create new possibilities, possibilities that express the respect, love, and deep connection we feel with our teammates. What is born will then have a life of its own, having emerged from the harmony of our mutual resonance.
4. Harvesting the collective knowledge, energy, and wisdom we manifest.

Kindred Spirits

If it is your true desire to bring forth the best that is within yourself, as well as from your community, then it is wise to establish your intentional network, beginning with "kindred spirits." By "kindred spirits", I mean those whose deeper values are congruent with yours, whose mission and vision are similar to yours, and whose expression in life is harmonious with yours, people you "vibe" with.

Variety is important, as long as there are substantially similar values – exploring the risks and benefits of varying strategies is ideal for evolving more effective approaches.

Among the important purposes that such "reference groups" serve is that they keep you from getting distracted by all the seductive noise around you, and help you to withstand the slings and arrows of our violent and abusive world. They also reflect back to you your highest qualities, the most beautiful and potent part of yourself – the part you might forget in the midst of some self-critical, insecure snit, or when the world is hurling so much of its negativity at you that it seems the sun no longer shines. Your buddies are there.

They are brothers, they are sisters – they are partners in a very sincere and important enterprise: the healing of our community, nation, and planet.

Sometimes the cause that brings you together is very local, like getting the town to put a stoplight at a dangerous intersection near the grammar school. And sometimes, that which brings you together may be a global goal, such as addressing world peace, genocide, starvation, or global warming. It is up to you – what do you feel called to invest your life's energy in? You get to choose.

You may never know what results come from your actions.
But if you do nothing, there will be no results.
– Mohandas Gandhi

Choosing an Architecture of Engagement

Generally, when groups of people come together, unless they honor certain principles of community functioning, there is a danger of their behaving more like animals or barbarians, rather than rational humans. In such situations (consider the vituperation characteristic of pre-election politics), people are prone to being remarkably disrespectful, contemptuous, and abusive towards each other. A far more effective style of coming together – the "architecture of engagement" as Dr. Juanita Brown[4] refers to it – is one

311

that reflects and is informed by the "organic" (Both-And) worldview. When the principles of healthy living systems are followed, what tends to emerge is a self-organizing system of wise self-guidance, one with enormous energy, creativity, and potential.

The architecture of engagement in use at any given moment can be ascertained by examining the form of the group interaction that takes place. What are the customs and rules – and how are they enforced? For instance, should people be shamed, blamed, punished, or threatened in order to "keep order"? Or, on the other hand, should we strive to protect deeper feelings, and respect individual sensitivities, while seeking that part of each person that is committed to the goals of the group?

Organic styles of interacting are dedicated to honoring, respecting, and sharing fairly with others, and they empower people to accomplish whatever is of greatest value to themselves and their community. Ideally, the interactions are mutually nurturing and inspiring – and evocative of creative energy. The kind of relationships developed with these principles in mind may vary enormously in outward appearances, but they tend to reflect an inner *harmony*. It is this commonality of inner harmony that makes it easy to identify, connect, and network among different groups, thus, in a sense, connecting up as a system of organs.

Principles of Relationships

My experience is that the most successful and enjoyable relationships are characterized by certain principles. They include:

---

[4]   Juanita Brown, Ph.D., co-originator of The World Café, Senior Affiliate withthe MIT Organizational Learning Center, co-author of *The World Cafe: Shaping Our Futures Through Conversations that Matter*, www.theworldcafe.com

- Respect
- Openness
- Honesty
- Generosity
- Compassion
- Trust
- Authenticity
- Intimacy
- Integrity

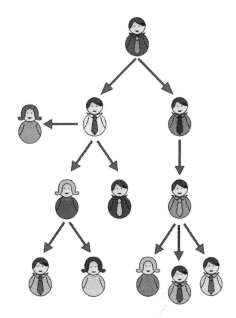

In such relationships:

- You find it easy to give people "the benefit of the doubt."
- You trust that they too recognize the importance of what we are doing at this time in history.
- Everyone recognizes the importance of doing his or her part to help with the shift in thinking that must take place on a wide scale if we are to survive and craft a sustainable future – and a new and more fluid concept of "us."
- You are willing to make a commitment: You care deeply about certain issues, and are willing to devote some energy toward studying them and taking action to create change for the better.
- You understand what Emerson meant by "There is no limit to what can be accomplished if it doesn't matter who gets the credit."

The result of having relationships that are reflective of these ideals is that they are more productive, enjoyable, creative, and self-sustaining. What is needed, then, is a container that can support the architecture of engagement best for your purposes.

Creating (or Finding) the Container

If you search wisely and sensitively, you will find that there are many different kinds of groups that may reflect your inner values and visions.

First, however, you must realize how important it is for you to take those steps to bring forth the leader that is within you, to take charge of your personal life. Many people are becoming aware that, even though each of us feels too small to do anything about it, there is a great need for something to be done about the severely unenlightened path upon which mankind has been leading Planet Earth recently. Many are awakening to the awareness that it is wrongheaded to think someone else is going to do it, and that we need to bring forth our inner leadership. People must begin to believe they can do something to dramatically improve the quality of their own lives – and in the lives of their children, grandchildren, and other loved ones.

The next step is to initiate contact with people with whom you resonate. In addition to the simple joy of being with kindreds, you will find they help you stay on your chosen path, bring you news of the things that interest you the most, and they are available to work with you on meaningful projects. For most of us, the easiest way to find some of those groups that are resonant with your deeper self may be through the Internet/Web.

For many people, the notion of connecting with others in this way is relatively new; the question arises: "What kind of social environment, what kind of architecture of engagement, will support the kind of communication I most want to take place in my relationships?" There are many different approaches that have proven effective in doing this. Most of them tend to reflect essentially the same elements and principles. These principles are eloquently expressed by the concept known as Wisdom Circles.

Wisdom Circles

Wisdom Circles[4] is a term that is used to represent a general style of interacting adopted by many small groups devoted to sustaining and renewing communities, organizations, the environment, and the Earth. An important purpose of such gatherings is to move more deeply into the core of the community, to respond to it, and to nurture it so it will continue to survive, hope, dream, and carry on.

The circle is a universal symbol for unity and wholeness – our ancestors met in circles, around fires, drumming and dancing, telling stories, joining their hearts and spirits, addressing their problems. The politics of our country were shaped by two powerful circle traditions, the British (King Arthur and the Round Table) and the Native American (council circle). The U.S. Constitution was based on the model of the Iroquois Confederacy, tribal councils that met as the Grand Council every five years and were given responsibility for the welfare of the whole. Members of the tribal councils, in turn, were chosen by the Council of Matrons (the oldest women in the tribe) who met in a circle.

In whatever culture or environment, from Quaker Circles to Twelve Step programs, there are certain qualities that are essentially always found to be present. The wisdomcircle.org website calls them the Ten Constants. These constants tend to create a safe container that allows participants to tap their innate capacity to relate to each other in a context of wisdom and compassion. Here is an outline of the Ten Constants. If you can recall a circle in which you have participated, you may recognize at least some of them. If the group failed, you may realize what principle was not sufficiently honored. You can find a more complete description of the Ten Constants in the Appendix page 360.

---

4   www.wisdomcircle.org

1. Honor the circle as sacred time and space by performing simple rituals to mark the beginning and end.
2. Create a collective center by mutually agreeing upon a topic or intention.
3. Ask to be informed by our highest human values such as compassion and truth.
4. Express gratitude for the blessings and teachings of life.
5. Create a container for full participation and deep truth telling.
6. Listen from the heart and serve as compassionate witness for other people in the circle.
7. Speak from the heart and from direct experience.
8. Empower each member to be a co-facilitator of the process.
9. Make room for silence to enter.
10. Commit to an ongoing relationship with all in the circle.

The Power of Good Conversation

Creating a positive future begins in human conversation. The simplest and most powerful investment any member of a community or an organization may make in renewal is to begin talking with other people as though the answers mattered.
– from *Who Will Tell the People*, by William Greider

Consider for a moment the importance of conversation. Virtually every action we take is predicated on a conversation. It is so much a part of our experience that we are rarely aware of its true importance. The conversations we engage in with our families, organizations, and in all portions of our lives give rise to patterns of behavior. Sometimes these are brief conversations whose effects are short-lived, sometimes the conversations are deep and moving, and their effects are stable and long lasting.

By learning to pay attention to our conversation, and acquiring the skills of good conversation, we bring about ever-greater degrees of coherence. As a result, we obtain a high correlation between what effect we intend to have and the effect we actually get. We must always keep in mind that the future is not somewhere we are going; it is a place we are creating in the now with every thought, word, and action.

Modern communication technologies intentionally focus our attention on questions that matter, allowing the emergence and evolution of the knowledge and wisdom that we need to co-create the future we want. We grow what we know, individually and collectively, and are alert to the possibilities for mutual insight, innovation and action that emerge.

High-quality conversations among individuals and within organizations generate meaningful change. Conversations are an important way to actively participate in creating our world and its future through this process of connecting authentically and appreciatively with each other. As we share knowledge, know-how, and creativity, we build relationships. Collaborative conversations among us "neurons" are the synapses of the Global Brain.

> *The intuitive mind is a sacred gift and the rational mind is a faithful servant. We have created a society that honors the servant and has forgotten the gift.*
> – Albert Einstein

For as long as humanity has lived in family groups, tribes and communities, conversation has been a primary medium for making sense of our world, discovering what we value, and imagining our future. Today we are becoming increasingly aware of the power of these networks of conversation and their systemic importance as a core process for large-scale collective learning and transformative change.

New Paradigm leaders recognize that essential learning and knowledge sharing occurs through informal relationships and networks of conversation. The new leadership role focuses on convening and hosting collaborative conversations among diverse stake holders to explore core questions and emerging possibilities. To facilitate this, cafes, community spaces, and offices can be flexibly designed so as to invite individual and collective reflection in addition to the cross-fertilization of ideas.

On the electronic side of things, personal computing is giving way to interpersonal computing. Members across geographic boundaries can assess community knowledge bases, including the resource bank of each person's unique contributions, interests, and areas of expertise. Collaborative technologies enable people to share questions and discoveries, engage in lively exchange, and develop innovative strategies. Shared purpose, courageous conversations, and authentic relationships continually strengthen the organization's identity, focus, and vitality.

So, what if:

• The future is born in webs of human conversation?
• Compelling questions encourage collective learning?
• Networks are the underlying pattern of living systems?
• Human systems – organizations, families, and communities – are living systems?
• Intelligence emerges as the system connects to itself in diverse and creative ways?
• Collectively, we have access to all the wisdom and resources we need?

If this may be so, then what is needed is a way for us to enter conversations around questions that address shared meaning and values and that honor all participants. Some excellent ways to do this have been developed.

The World Café

The World Cafe[5], originally developed and stewarded by Dr.

Juanita Brown and David Isaacs and their associates, is a nonprofit, community-owned venture that is a "conversational process based on a set of integrated design principles that reveal a deeper living network pattern through which we co-evolve our collective future."

I have found The World Café does an excellent job of hosting and facilitating meetings that encourage the practical exploration of questions and principles.

The café model represents an innovative yet simple methodology for gathering

Illustration by Nancy Margulies
http://www.nancymargulies.com/

groups of 12 or more people together to create conversations about questions that matter. These conversations link and build on each other as people move between groups, cross-pollinate ideas, and discover new insights into the questions or issues that are most important in their life, work, or community. As a process, The World Café can evoke and make visible the collective intelligence of any group, thus increasing people's capacity for effective action in pursuit of common aims.

The deceptively simple principles of café groups are nevertheless powerful. The etiquette for a café meeting includes:

---

5   www.theworldcafe.com

> • **Focus** on what matters.
> • **Contribute** your thinking and experience.
> • **Listen** to understand.
> • **Connect** ideas.
> • **Listen together** for patterns, insights, and deeper questions.
> • **Play! Doodle! Draw!**

The World Café website provides complete information that will allow you to apply powerful tools for intentionally harnessing the power of conversation for any purpose, business or social. You will discover useful guidance – ways to foster authentic dialogue in which the goal is thinking together to bring forth collective wisdom and create actionable knowledge. And it is free.

At their website, you will also find a way to begin to network with the thousands of other people, groups, and organizations who are exploring ways to evoke collective intelligence and link it to effective action in pursuit of common aims. Although most of the time The World Café approaches are widely used throughout the world with people meeting in the same physical space. In addition, The World Café is looking forward, beyond the all-important face-to-face conversational environment, and is currently involved in a pioneering use of a variety of experimental platforms to create the optimal conditions for holding meaningful conversation in an online environment.

This is just one of a number of different approaches to addressing the living network of conversations that is continually evolving as we explore questions that matter with our family, friends, colleagues, and community. These invisible webs of dialogue and personal relationships can enable us to learn, create shared purpose, and shape life-affirming futures together. Others include Conversation Cafes and Open Space. Younger networkers

---

6   Conversation Cafe's: http://www.conversationcafe.org; Open Space: http://www.openspaceworld.org/; Youth for Environmental Sanity: http://www.yesworld.org/; Global Youth Action Network; http://www.youthlink.org/gyanv5/index.htm

will find Youth for Environmental Sanity (YES!) and Global Youth Action Network quite stimulating[6].

Practical resources for those who work with communities (in the wider sense of the term) to help them identify and adopt more sustainable practices include Learning for Sustainability, and The Co-Intelligence Institute[7]. An excellent example of how a community has transformed itself using the principles we are exploring here is revealed at Sustainable Connections[8].

A Living Network of Electronic Axons

Beyond discovering the Café movement online, there are many other social networking possibilities offered by Web 2.0[9] that are having a significant impact on the world – and it is just beginning.

There has never, in the entire history of the human race, been anything to compare with this miracle of global connectivity, which Wired magazine has presciently called Renaissance 2.0. The ability to locate such kindred spirits had been very difficult before

---

[7]   Sustainability: http://learningforsustainability.net/; The Co-Intelligence Institute: http://www.co-intelligence.org

[8]   Sustainable Connections; http://www.sconnect.org/

[9]   According to Wikipedia, Web 2.0 is a term describing the trend in the use of World Wide Web technology and web design that aims to enhance creativity, information sharing, and most notably, collaboration among users. These concepts have led to the development and evolution of Web-based communities and hosted services such as social networking sites and blogs.

the Web. We were all limited by default to the people we run into in our neighborhood or at work.

As we have demonstrated again and again, we cannot accurately predict what will arise as more and more people join this planetary network. At first, of course, people approached the Internet using Old Paradigm thinking. Criminals saw new ways to swindle innocents, pornographers saw more ways to exploit women and children by extracting money from lonely men, and terrorists found an insidious way to share information about how to create bombs and biological weapons to more effectively kill those they saw as enemies.

Soon, however, approaches utilizing the New Paradigm began to appear, bringing about changes beyond our imaginings. When people found a way to connect with others, they not only went after what they could get, there was a huge upwelling of the desire to give, to help, and to enter into generative conversation with others.

Now a woman with an autistic child, a man who collects knobs from old Philco radios, and a girl who wants to halt the killing of baby seals can quickly find support groups of others, kindred spirits, interested and invested in the same issues. In a similar manner, sites like Match.com, and eHarmony.com have attracted hundreds of thousands of people looking for a mate, with the result of thousands of relationships and marriages that could never have occurred before. And if you have a rare piece of equipment that needs a certain part, one that has not been manufactured for decades, you may very well find someone who is trying to sell that part on eBay. And the skillful use of the Internet/Web by the 2008 Obama presidential campaign is already legend.

What is fascinating about the new Web culture is that, beyond what people can *get* from the Web, it turns out that a huge number of people want to use the Web to *contribute*. They contribute by writing blogs, answering questions placed by others, donating money, and participating in myriad ways. In a world where everything from the political scene to the competition of the marketplace or the high school football or cheerleader scene is framed in terms of the Old Paradigm, how refreshing to discover the deep desire to give, to share, to be a part of the generosity!

Similarly, MySpace.com, Facebook.com, Hubhub.org and Linkedin.com have amassed millions of subscribers who seem eager to encourage, support and network with each other. And the many self-help support sites give ample opportunity to the millions of people who are eager to share their experiences with others dealing with the same challenges. It appears that a "gift economy"[10] is, indeed appearing.

The following are some of the characteristics that give the Web its remarkable potential:

There's the ability to instantly receive news and messages – and to instantly respond.

- Your questions, responses, and contributions can be completely anonymous, if you wish.
- If what you post on the Web attracts sufficient attention, you can garner a wide audience in an extremely short period of time.
- Through the use of search engines, you can easily find what you're really looking for.
- The Web's social networking capabilities enable kindred spirits to find each other as individuals, and to locate those online groups with which they feel an affinity, to participate. (The word participation is especially important; it's one of the biggest features of the Web.)
- Conversations, participation in chat rooms, and online classes

---

[10] According to Wikipedia, a gift economy is one in which goods and services are given without any explicit agreement for immediate or future quid pro quo. Typically, a gift economy occurs in a culture or subculture that emphasizes social or intangible rewards for solidarity and generosity: karma, honor, loyalty, or other forms of gratitude.

can take place in real time – or over hours, days, weeks. You can ask a question today, I can answer tomorrow, and you pick up the answer on Thursday – or the whole thing might take place over a few hours.

• One person in a small town in a remote corner of a little country can, in a matter of minutes, send a message that will be read or heard by millions, or potentially, billions of people.

Wikipedia

Imagine a world in which every single person on the planet is given free access to the sum of all human knowledge.
— Jimmy Wales, Founder of Wikipedia

Wikipedia, the online encyclopedia, is an excellent example of the kind of power that can be brought into being when people are offered an ability to participate. Think of the encyclopedias of old. Here was a heavy stack of thick books with small print, written at enormous cost by thousands of professional scholars. Impres-

sive, but difficult to use, and, in today's world, partially obsolete by the time they come off the press, in this increasingly high speed world. What would you have guessed would happen if someone created a website and invited people – anyone – to log on and write or edit an entry on any topic? Total mayhem?

Quite the contrary.

Opening to the information and wisdom scattered throughout the world gave rise to an eminently useful, constantly growing and evolving, easy-to-access reference work – that is totally FREE.

In this greed-driven world (Old Paradigm) where our ugliness is paraded before us nightly on the news, one might well be forgiven for expecting chaos. Instead the phenomenally wide-ranging encyclopedia has appeared online with all the articles written by people who have contributed the information, gratis. Even *you* can be one of the authors of Wikipedia – just go to www.wikipedia.com and decide how you would like to make a contribution.

Of course there is a certain amount of disinformational mischief that goes on, and groups of concerned netizens have formed with the intent of reviewing entries, especially in controversial areas, such as those concerning Christianity, Islam, or the Jewish faiths. The result is a kind of open system that learns as it goes along, propelled towards the truth by the consciences of the users of the system. So this is a growing and evolving medium, not a static one, as is print media. Thus, the entry in any given area may be different from day to day, and erroneous or misleading entries, of course, will persist until they are corrected. For everyday use, however, it turns out to be amazingly valuable.

Many people I know now use Wikipedia as their first source of information, using it in a trust-but-verify mode. Think of it, any word, event, place, person, thing – just type it in and Wikipedia usually gives what turns out to be a pretty good and up-to-date response. As I am writing these words, Wikipedia now boasts more than 2.8 million entries!

• There exists in the human community a great tendency towards wholeness and goodness, and great wisdom.
• There are extraordinary possibilities in ordinary people.
• Most of the time the solutions to what we see as problems are already in existence.
• The World Wide Web is simply our way to network and find them.

This is the New Paradigm at work. It suggests that:

Just as we gain insight on a personal basis by refocusing our attention from the outside world and accessing the right cerebral hemisphere, here we open ourselves to the vast unconscious that is available by way of the Internet. Here, just as in the individual, the many neuronal cell bodies are connected by the communication network made up of axons, the Global Brain is composed of individuals, each like a neuronal cell body, linked by an electronic communication system.

The Potential for Social Change and Transformation

In the past, in order for social or political change to happen, people had to get together to converse and be creative together. The situation that pertained at the founding of the United States provides an excellent example. At that time, a group that wanted to think together of necessity had to meet in the same physical place, unless they were patient enough to wait until the postal service got around to delivering their letters to each other. And, as in the case of those who drafted the Declaration of Independence, when the purpose of the gathering was at odds with the desires of an oppressive government, there was always the danger of the meeting being disrupted by police, rioters, or other opposing factions.

But now, with the Internet/Web, it is possible for groups of literally thousands to get together and converse, by means of online newsletters, blogs, chat rooms, and even online audio-video collaborative meetings. The result is an atmosphere of safety and freedom that encourages even the most timid to speak out.

In a sense, your nervous system is the hardware you use to carry out the processes involved in thinking, deciding, and acting. Your beliefs and your worldview in the face of your challenges constitute the "software" you are using in this endeavor. Likewise, the Internet, including the social networking tool of Web 2.0, may be thought of as the hardware that we use as the axons that connect us all together in the software network that is the Global Brain.

All that is needed now is to use the New Paradigm as a way to design the way we will use this incredible new technology. The New Paradigm suggests that – instead of using the Web to amplify differences, debate, criticize, and attack – we can use it to tap into the collective wisdom of humanity as a whole. We can employ it to discover that what we share – like the air, the water, and the global climate, as well as our love for our families and desire for life, liberty, and the pursuit of happiness – is so much more important than those ways in which we differ. Then, together, we can bring forth the "magic in the middle," the collective wisdom that can become available to make this a better world for all of us.

Paying It Forward, The Reverse Ponzi

When I was a child, I recall receiving an odd letter. It contained a list of names and instructions to send a small handkerchief to the first four people on the list and add my name to the bottom of the list. Within a few weeks, the letter went on to say, I would receive 10,000 hankies in the mail. I was a bit bemused by this notion. Why would I want 10,000 hankies, and what was going on here anyway?

My mother explained to me that this was a "chain letter" and that, although those who are first on the list may perhaps get some hankies, sooner or later those who sign up will get no returns on their investment. Later, as an adult, I came up with the idea of a reverse chain letter, as a way of getting people to become aware of the power of money and of our intention in its use.

My idea was to send a letter containing a ten-dollar bill to a group of people with the instructions to take some time and consider that the only value money has is its ability to get people to dedicate time and energy to some purpose. Money given to the cobbler causes him to take the time to mend your shoes. Money given to the museum results in a group of workers adding a new wing and expanding the galleries.

My challenge was to get in touch with your deepest values,

327

and decide what you could invest this money in that would most authentically serve these values. The next step was to send four more ten dollar bills to people you know who would take this task seriously, put ten dollars to good use, and pass on the chain letter. Within a few short cycles 10,000 ten-dollar bills would be being spent wisely – $100,000 would be doing good as a result of your participation! I never sent the letter, but the idea has always intrigued me.

LIGHT

In the 1990s, I began to explore self-organizing systems and the role of wise leadership in facilitating healing change, peak performance and nonviolent communication. It had become clear to me that just as individuals experienced healing through the application of the New Paradigm in their individual, family, and community lives, this same paradigm also needed to be applied at even "higher" levels of system. I then formulated the visions, mission, and strategy for LIGHT, the Leadership Institute for Global Healing and Transformation. The intention was to help apply, on a global scale, the processes of deep healing, the tools for accessing of group wisdom, and the powerful and artistic ways we can purposefully effect spiritually harmonious transformation.

It is clear to me that the time to change the world is now. Now, finally, thanks to the Internet, we can bypass the propaganda of despots and the disinformation of the special interest dominated media. We have the open and free communication that can facilitate the distribution of wisdom, creative solutions, and high quality information to all at little or no cost. The question is, "Will we choose to recognize and take advantage of this startling opportunity?

The mission of LIGHT was formulated as follows:

• Assemble and inspire a "global think tank" of the most creative, enlightened, and empowering healers, thinkers, and leaders.
• Evolve the highest and most appropriate spiritually-informed wisdom and principles from all times and all cultures.
• Develop products and presentations that empower people and nurture healing (the emergence of higher order wholes, holons).
• Make these available worldwide, at little to no cost, along with ongoing support so they can be integrated into the lives of individuals, families, organizations, governments, and religions.
• Identify and evolving coherently with an open "Network of Trust," based on face-to-face as well as Web 2.0 social networking technology dedicated to empowering us to gather and disseminate information, ideas, wisdom, creativity, energy, and support – with the ultimate goal of evolving a more sustainable culture.

My plan was to employ the principles of my "reverse chain letter," but instead of sending a ten-dollar bill, what people would send would be valuable audio and video e-mail attachments. These would be of benefit to the recipient, who would have an opportunity to make positive personal changes, and then pass these attachments along.

LIGHT is now becoming a reality[10] .

---

[10]   for more info, see: http://www.thelightinstitute.com/

Humanity Unites Brilliance (HUB)

One of the interesting new forms of communities that are arising as the intelligence of the global brain increases is Humanity Unites Brilliance, an organization that has attempted to bridge the gap that has always existed between philanthropy and "business-as-usual." I have met members of this network and believe that as a result of such people working together, there is an effort with great heart and great potential.

The principles and approaches that it seems to have incorporated into its structure and function seem essentially identical to the ones we have been exploring here. They have a global, yet very local, focus in the most interesting ways.

In studying this group, I was delighted to find that many of the approaches I had espoused in creating LIGHT were also incorporated into HUB. I was curious, yet cautious. So I arranged to meet Charlie Gay, the prime mover of HUB. I found him to be a sincere and authentic man, who had been quite successful in media and marketing, working with well-known celebrities. He had moved on in his life by shifting his attention to the continent of Africa, where he had authored a number of forays into helping populations who were endangered, in very creative and sustainable ways. Because of this, and the feeling I received in our conversations, led me to feel a growing trust in him and his goals.

I discovered that HUB is an extremely well designed organization that incorporates the principles and values I have outlined above. Forty percent of the membership dues go immediately to creating good works in the world. What's more, the ways this money is being utilized seems far wiser than usual, teaching people to fish, instead of just feeding them. Their focus is on education, training, micro-loans, and other ways of teaching people to fish rather than just giving them fish.

Another mission of HUB is to enrich the lives of those who are part of it. Seeing the need for ongoing input of high-quality learning in ourselves, it states that it is "committed to providing ongoing training in personal growth, wellness, and leadership to its members." In addition, as a bonafide Web 2.0 network, it has the capacity to provide organizational support to subsets of itself, to enabling members to find kindred spirits and to form conversation groups for exploring questions that matter. Worthy goals indeed.

Many organizations led by men and women as committed as these have been formed, but most have faded away – not because the need for their work no longer existed, but because it is very difficult to exist on donations alone. In fact, I have heard that the organizations that specialize in soliciting donations for charities often take as much as fifty cents or more out of every dollar they raise. HUB chose a novel way to overcome this problem: HUB is organized as a profit-making entity. Members invite others to join because they believe in the work the organization is doing, but there is an additional motivation – you can receive money for helping to expand the network with new members.

How successful this model proves to be will rest upon how well they fulfill their mission, how well its behavior fits the founding principles, and whether enough people recognize the importance of the work it is doing. Should it perform well in these ways, I suspect that it will enjoy many more, and larger, successes of the type presented on its website[11], and make a very significant contribution to creating a bright new world.

---

[11]   http://marilynnyborg.hubhub.org

An Opportunity to Choose

And so we come to a pause, here, near the end of our story, one of the fruits that grew from the bitter seed of September 11, 2001. We have stretched the imagination to see the planet as a whole, as the patient, rather than one individual, family, or group. We looked for that deeper cause that might lie at the essence of our global disease, and we have found some interesting perspectives, understandings, and perhaps, wisdom.

Unless, however, you take some pains to make sure that you continue to keep alive the worldview we discovered, it will gradually fade, and you will cease to see it so clearly as you can at this moment. I would highly suggest that you take action now. To this end, I would like to invite you to experience a self-guided program designed to help acquaint your mind and nervous system with the transformative principles and approaches we have been exploring intellectually in these pages, and help you learn a set of techniques that can help enable you to embody them.

At the end of every fantasy, imagination, or imagery experience, you have the opportunity to make a choice. You must now choose what you want to do with all the treasures, insights, and ideas you have encountered on your journey. Was it all just make-believe, simply a distraction that will be soon replaced by another distraction? Or was there something there that you would like to remember, a discovery you would like to keep alive in your life? Sustainability is a quality our thoughts and ideas can have, and, as usual, we need to make conscious, intentional choice to keep them alive, to make a commitment to nurture them [12].

Otherwise, when you return from your heady journey, you will automatically go back to the "default reality" so to speak, and walk away, never visiting these images again.

Why not take a deep breath (literally), and take a few moments to reflect during this pause, and as you let that breath out,

---

[12] See the catalog on page 369 for suggestions on ways to create and sustain your positive momentum.

touch that place of wisdom within you, and decide if, perhaps, you have found something in these pages that has moved or awakened something of value within you. If you wish, you can choose to continue living your life with an ongoing attention to the kinds of issues, perspectives and tools we have been exploring. The story does not have to end here. You can choose to extend your receptivity and learning.

Some people may have refused to participate in this experiment, some may have become uneasy with some of the discoveries. The attractiveness of going back into the state of denial (and subsequent continued victimhood) is understandable upon encountering the enormous difference between what *is* and what *could be* in this world of ours. Feelings of guilt, shame, resentment, despair and helplessness are, at least temporarily, suppressed . . . until next time.

On the other hand, this is an enormous opportunity. I believe that if you take a little care to maintain the perspective offered by the New Paradigm, even for a little while, you will notice unfolding levels of deeper values within, an increasing sense of meaning in your life. You become more aware that you care about something or someone deeply, wholeheartedly and passionately. The maladaptive emotions dissolve, as you connect at these deeper levels.

With a little practice, you will discover how really valuable is the act of becoming more present. As you take the time to clear your mind and become present, you will find that physical symptoms fade, that your emotions are richer and freed from the bondage of anxiety, fear, anger and grief. As a result, you will find the power of your spirit is released to serve that deeper meaning, profound knowing, clear wisdom that is mediated from within.

We are set irrevocably, I believe, on a path that will take us to the
stars – unless in some monstrous capitulation to stupidity
and greed we destroy ourselves first.
– Carl Sagan

Notes to Self

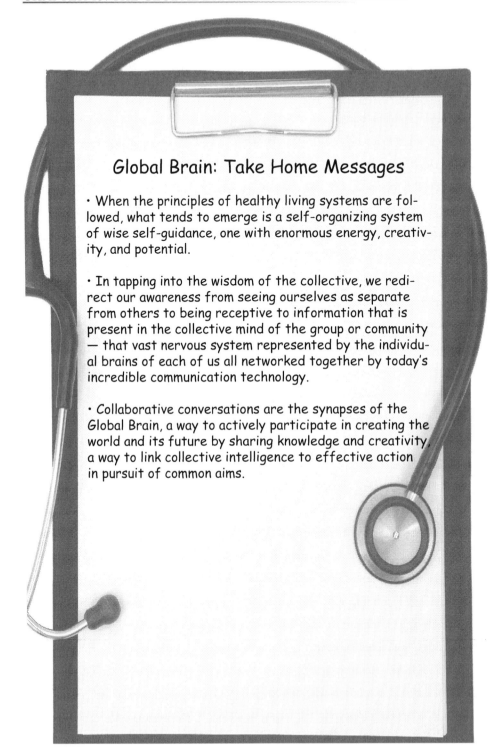

Global Brain: Take Home Messages

• When the principles of healthy living systems are followed, what tends to emerge is a self-organizing system of wise self-guidance, one with enormous energy, creativity, and potential.

• In tapping into the wisdom of the collective, we redirect our awareness from seeing ourselves as separate from others to being receptive to information that is present in the collective mind of the group or community — that vast nervous system represented by the individual brains of each of us all networked together by today's incredible communication technology.

• Collaborative conversations are the synapses of the Global Brain, a way to actively participate in creating the world and its future by sharing knowledge and creativity, a way to link collective intelligence to effective action in pursuit of common aims.

EPILOGUE

How Real is Real?

In a sense, when you come to the end of a book or a movie, you leave the world it has created, a temporary reality you entered by your willing suspension of disbelief and activating your imagination. Now you have a decision to make. If you wish, this can be a conscious, intentional choice.

At the start of this book, you had a certain worldview. I invited you to suspend that worldview for a while, to imagine our planet as a patient, and with an interstellar planetary consultant as guide, and to explore the psychophysiological roots of the great malaise that afflicts us all. Now we have come to a pause in that journey, at which time you may take the opportunity to choose, if you wish, either to return to that same old worldview, or to go forth into the future evolving a new one, one that can include the wisdom, techniques, knowledge, and skill that you have come upon during our voyage. What will you choose for your "reality"?

In truth, it's not as if reality is "there waiting for you" at the end of a dream, a sleep or an imagery experience. There is no "world out there." Or as Sir Roger Penrose famously put it, "The world is an illusion created by a conspiracy of our senses." In other words, the "reality" you experience is, in fact, being created by your mind at the same instant you are experiencing it, although most of us are generally aware of this fact. We create reality with little tiny decisions made in every moment, and have the opportunity to choose which paradigm will dominate our thinking:

> We can choose whether it is the paradigm of differentiation, Black vs. White, Good vs. Bad and Violence, OR we can choose the Organic Paradigm of oneness, wholeness, relationship, sharing, and Love.

The choice is yours in each moment, and all these little choices add up to the big choices you are making in your life – illness, dysfunction, and stress – or health, happiness, and peak performance. Right now is the moment you must choose: will you elect to take with you the fruits of your journey, the insights, and awarenesses you have gained, the confidence, wisdom, and courage you have awakened, and make them part of how you approach the challenges in your life – or not? I believe choosing them to keep these learnings close at hand will keep you much more in touch with your power to choose, consciously and intentionally, to be the person you *really* want to be, and accomplish what you *really* want to accomplish.

Practice, Practice, Practice

But how can you guarantee, right now, that you will follow through on your wise decision to allow your perspective and your life to stay in touch with this wisdom? To insure integrity of your system, so that your intentions mature into actions, the best bet is to take the responsibility of putting activities on your schedule that will help you maintain your awareness and focus on these new perspectives; otherwise, you may not find time for it. The more unlike your usual perspective, the more important to schedule the application of these new principles – otherwise, your nervous system will tend to forget them. New learnings *must* be reinforced!

My suggestion: set up regular, recurring times you will devote yourself to discovering more about yourself and the world you inhabit, times where you can be in silence, perhaps in solitude or with others who have the same intention, reading appropriate literature or appreciating art – and especially by regularly practicing the fascinating and enjoyable techniques of meditation, prayer, and guided imagery[1].

Dharma and Belief in Yourself

The Indian concept of *dharma* speaks to this issue. Dharma is often translated as "Your duty to the deepest part of you, to your soul." (If the word "soul" has no meaning for you, then you might think of it as simply referring to the deepest part of yourself you can be aware of or believe in.)

You have made a vitally important discovery when you realize that it is possible to believe in your Self – to accept as absolutely true, as real to you as the air you are breathing at this moment, your Self – to know the truth of your intrinsic value, the value of your very being, and your personal purpose that expresses your most deeply-held values and commitment. Simultaneously, at that moment you become aware that your beliefs belong to *you* – and that you have the power to change them.

Your choice is whether or not to allow yourself to believe that you *do* have a duty to the deepest part of yourself. And part of that

---

[1]   See www.DrMiller.com

duty is to believe in yourself. In other words, you can choose, right now, to believe deeply that you are a good person, a worthwhile human being – that you are exactly where you are *supposed* to be at this moment in time – indeed, that you are exactly where you *need* to be at this moment in time.

You can choose to believe that you have the power to set yourself free from negativity, stress, and tension, and free your mind, body, and emotions from doubt, criticism, judgment, and comparison. You can release such patterns as worry, resistance and tension, and choose to enter that state of mind where you have the ability to see your life and its challenges from an entirely different perspective, a different worldview, and direct access to your creative imagination.

If these perspectives were familiar to you before, then you may find they are more available now, having been reinforced. Even if you rarely think about paradigms and systems thinking, these perspectives will be reflected in the choices you make, since they are applicable at every level – personal, family, community, and so forth.

If you choose to always take a moment to look from the perspective of the New Paradigm when confronted with a seemingly polarized situation, you will see how quickly conflictual issues dissolve in the light of the greater reality, the higher order truth. You will take the time to return, again and again, to a relaxed focus on the present, with an attitude of complete acceptance, and rid yourself of parasitic thought patterns and the energy-sapping emotions they create.

You may already be feeling the spaciousness that arises as you let go of these burdens from the past and give yourself permission to experience the fullness of your being, your deepest sense of Self. If not, you will find that making a commitment to practicing regularly will soon introduce you to this experience. Why not promise yourself, right now?

Shifting Your Paradigm

The essence of the paradigm shift we have explored lies in the transformation to a way of thinking that tends to give rise to freedom, beauty, wholeness, healing, and Love. It sees the spectrum that spans the seeming chasm between *apparent* opposites, between the black and the white, the red and the blue, the pure and the tainted, the good and the bad. The Old Paradigm, on the other hand, sees only the contrast and interprets it as opposition, seeing black as the opposite of white, right as opposite to and *opposing* wrong.

The New Paradigm, Tao-like, seeks the watercourse way, the path of balance. It is fully cognizant and informed by the central importance of releasing useless and destructive emotions such as unnecessary anxiety, resentment, anger, and despair, emotions, whose only effect has been to chain us to the endless repetition of the chaos of our unwise past. Balance is seen to be the basic principle of life, the sine qua non of sustainability. It guides us to seek the middle way, the source of the wisdom that can enable us to redirect the stress and conflict, so that their energy serves the higher goals of wholeness, mutual respect, harmony, oneness . . . Love. Choosing to believe is an important step.

Namasté

The notion of *oneness* suggests the idea of *namasté*, the expression that people in India and Nepal use to accompany the palms-touching greeting. Those who have been trekking in Nepal, where this is how you greet even the passing stranger on a trekking trail, know what a remarkable experience this is. Gradually you begin to notice a kind of serenity – a sense of connection, of peace, of harmony – a quality of shared value and purpose that transcends skin color, nationality, or religion.

These Nepalis may be browner, but they have that exquisite aura about them that you may recall from paintings or statues of

Christian saints standing with their hands in exactly the same position – a sense of peace and tranquility, of acceptance, of being willing to accept the moment just as it is, without reacting.

The meaning of *namasté* goes far beyond the words, but a rough translation might define *namasté* as: a salute to, an acknowledgement of, a certain deeper identity that we all share, the underlying oneness. Their religion teaches them that there is a place deep within your being, a place of beauty, of peace, of wisdom, a place of love and light, a *sacred* place – and that there is, as well, a deep place of love, light, beauty, and peace within *me*. That:

When you are in that place in you, and I am in that place in me, there is only one of us. Namasté is a salutation to this place.

So, as I wish you namasté, I wish you success in choosing to believe that you are wise, lovable, and deserving of respect and confidence, that you have the courage to be the beauty that you are – and to become the change you seek.

And I wish, as well, when you continue your social explorations at work or home, that you are successful in carrying out Gandhi's dictum, to find in every conflict, an ally – that deeper part of your apparent adversary that knows what is right.

Namasté . . .

APPENDIX PART 1

A BRIEF HISTORY OF SYSTEMS THEORY

Because the notion of *systems* appears so often throughout this book, I would like to offer the following brief review of the development of logical and scientific thought, as an introduction to the concept of systems. It is based on the excellent ideas presented in Peter Checkland's excellent book, "Systems Theory, Systems Practice"[1], which I highly recommend to anyone who would like a fuller treatment of this material. Although the more analytically-minded reader will find this information very fascinating, some may find it overly technical, and choose to skip it.

The central concept "system" embodies the idea of a set of elements connected together, which form a whole, thus showing properties, which are properties of the whole, rather than properties of its component parts. (The taste of water, for example, is a property of the substance water, not of the hydrogen and oxygen, which combine to form it.)

The concern of systems is not a particular set of phenomena

---

[1] Peter Checkland, *Systems Theory, Systems Practice* (John Wiley and Sons, 1999)

(as chemistry and physics), nor does it exist because of a problem area that requires different streams of knowledge — town planning, for example. What distinguishes systems is that it is a subject, which can talk about other subjects. It is not in the same set as the other disciplines, it is a meta-discipline whose subject matter can be applied within virtually any discipline.

The systems outlook assumes that the world contains structured wholes (soap bubbles, for example), which can maintain their identity under a certain range of conditions and which exhibit certain general principles of "fullness."

Systems thinking notices the unquestioned Cartesian assumption: **namely, that a component part is the same when separated out as it is when part of a whole.**

The Cartesian legacy provides us with an unnoticed framework – a set of intellectual pigeonholes to which we place the new knowledge we acquire. Systems thinking is different because it is about the framework itself. Systems thinking does not drop into its pigeonhole, it changes the shape or the structure of the whole framework of pigeonholes.

The Scientific Method

The scientific method is defined in terms of three characteristics: reductionism, repeatability, and refutation. Complexity, in general, and social phenomena in particular, both pose a difficult problem for science; neither has been able to tackle what we perceive as "real world problems" (as opposed to the scientist-defined problems in the laboratory). These are frequent problems of the teleological kind, concerned with ends and means.

The Systems Approach

The core concerns of systems thinking are the two pairs of ideas: **emergence** and **hierarchy**, **communication** and **control**.

The system concept, the idea of a whole entity, which under a range of conditions maintains its identity, provides a way of viewing and interpreting the universe as a hierarchy of such interconnected and interrelated wholes.

Western civilization is characterized by the Judeo-Christian tradition, specific arts and crafts, and technologies. Especially unique is its having developed and organized human activity in a way unknown before – science. The reason for this involvement has social, economic, and intellectual aspects.

The Root of Science and Its Driving Impulse

Science is an invention of our civilization, a cultural invention — it's probably the most powerful invention in the whole history of mankind. Our world in the twenty-first century is essentially the world created by the activity of science: in cities, transportation, and communication systems and in our political and administrative procedures (the way we organize society).

Rationalism and **empiricism**, twin outcomes of the scientific revolution of the seventeenth century, have created enormous changes in all of our civilizations. The fruits of modern science are now all-pervading in their influence. It has provided us with at least the *possibility* of material well-being, even on a planet with finite resources … and it has also given us the means of destroying all life on our planet.

The impulse behind science (scientia, episteme) is the itch to *know* things, to find out how and why the world is. This is different from the drive behind technology (techne), which is the itch to *do* things, to achieve practical ends. **The urge to know and the urge to do are different motives.**

The urge to know came from the Greeks — who gave us the

art of rational thinking.

After the Greeks came the Dark Ages (5th to 10th centuries), then the recovery in medieval times, when scholastic philosophers brought Aristotle's thought within the orbit of Christian faith. The medieval world view, based Aristotelian science, survived until the Renaissance of learning led to its replacement by the new world view created by Copernicus, Kepler, Galileo, and Newton — the worldview that is still recognizably our own.

The Quest for Truth

What is important is the spirit in which Greek speculation was proposed, and the critical debate in which they were discussed. They argued for the sole purpose of arriving at the truth, with argument as to their chief weapon; used deliberately, consciously, and carefully developed into an effective tool.

Newton created a completely new worldview out of Kepler's astronomy and Galileo's mechanics. Urged on by Halley, the astronomer, published "Mathematical Principles of Natural Philosophy," the most celebrated scientific work ever written.

Newton stated the three laws of motion. He proposed a testable mathematical model, with the workings of the universe conceived as an elegant, ingenious, and majestic clockwork. Animistic and teleological explanations were demonstrably no longer necessary, it seemed. (It is an argument out of Checkland's book, *Systems Thinking, Systems Practice*, that in the last 30 years systems thinking has rehabilitated teleology as a respectable concept.)

Francis Bacon (1561-1626), not a practicing scientist, was a prophet of the exploitation of science to transform the physical world.

The Cartesian Influence

Descartes was a lucid exponent of scientific rationalism, the methodologist whose principle of reductionism has deeply permeated science for 350 years. (The Systems Movement may be seen as a reaction against just this principle.)

Descartes emphasized, not the facts of science, but the scientific way of thinking. He rejected the untested assumptions of scholastic philosophy. He sought the truth by deductive reasoning, from basic irreducible ideas.

He starts from the position of extreme skepticism, of absolute doubt. The world he perceived, for example, might be a dream. The one certainty is that I doubt, and this remains true even if I doubt that I doubt. I think, therefore I am. This is the only certainty. He thought that by analyzing the process by which he had become certain of his own existence, he can discover the general nature of the process of becoming certain of anything. In his second discourse, he gives four rules for properly conducting one's reason:

1. Avoiding precipitancy and prejudice
2. Accepting only clear and distinct ideas
3. Orderly progression from the simple to the complex
4. Complete analysis with nothing omitted

The second rule is most significant: to divide each of the difficulties that he was examining into as many parts as might be possible and necessary in order to best solve it. This is the principle of analytic reduction, which characterizes the Western intellectual tradition. The core of his approach to science was reductionist, in the sense that science should describe the world in terms of "simple natures" and "composite natures," and show how the latter can be reduced to the former. He says that finding simple natures in complex phenomena is what he meant by analysis. He excluded any explanation that included terms of purpose.

The reductionist ideal is found in virtually all science of the 18th to 19th centuries. Not until the 20th century have significant challenges to reductionism been made. The Systems Movement is the most serious of these challenges.

The Death of Reductionism

The downfall of Newton's model came in the 20th century through the work of Einstein, which can yield all of Newton's results and more.

Experiments proved Einstein's model better than Newton's, although Newton's is good enough for terrestrial calculations, and even for moon flights.

The results of scientific experiments are not absolute; they may be replaced by later models that have greater descriptive and predictive power. Scientifically acquired and tested knowledge is simply the best *description* of reality that we have *at that moment in time.*

The Method of Science

Science is the human activity which is "the origin of the modern world view and mentality" and within which the systems movement has emerged within the last 30 or 40 years.

Science is a system, an institutionalized set of activities, which embody a particular purpose, mainly the acquiring of a particular kind of knowledge. It is an inquiring or learning system, to find things out about the mysterious world we live in. The Greeks invented rational thought, breaking with the idea of the irrational authority which is not to be questioned; medieval clerics started the conscious development of methodology, providing the beginnings of the experimental approach; the age of Newton united empiricism and theoretical explanation in a way that dealt with necessity and contingency at the same time and made the real world comprehensible through ideas. The 20th century reminds us that knowledge gained is always provisional.

An account of science as an activity: A way of acquiring completely testable knowledge of the world characterized by an application of rational thinking (to experience observations, experiments, concise expression of the laws which govern the regularity of the universe, expressing them mathematically if possible).

Three characteristics define the patterned activity: **reductionism, repeatability, and refutation**. We reduce the complexity of the real world with experiments whose results are validated by their repeatability. We build knowledge by the refutation of hypotheses. These are the three senses in which science is "reductionist." The world is messy. To define an experiment is to define a reduction of the world, one made for a particular purpose. The second way which science is reductionist; much is to be gained in logical coherence by being reductionist in explanation, using the minimum explanation required by the facts to be explained. Thirdly, breaking down problems to analyze piecemeal, component by component. In this sense, scientific is almost synonymous with analytic thinking.

Hierarchy and Emergence

The reductionist ideal is expressed in terms of a hierarchy of the sciences – physics, chemistry, biology, psychology, and social science – each dependent on the preceding. No one would ever argue that the place for psychology is between chemistry and biology. We see here levels of complexity. Laws, which seem to operate at one level, seem to be higher order with respect to those of lower levels. This is the kernel of the concept of **emergence**, the idea that at a given level of complexity there are properties characteristic of that level (emergent at that level) that are irreducible.

The debate of reductionism vs. emergence is a prime source of systems thinking.

The second characteristic of science is **repeatability** of experiments. You might think that D.H. Lawrence or a particular kind of music is good or bad, depending upon the literary or musical tastes of society at a particular time, and ourselves. Knowledge of

349

this kind remains private knowledge in the sense that the choice is ours to accept it or not.

Scientific knowledge is public knowledge. We have no option but to accept what can be repeatedly demonstrated by experiment. The inverse square law of magnetism is the same all over the world. What has to be accepted is the happenings in the experiment, not necessarily the interpretation of the results! It is the repeatability of experimental facts, which places science in a different category from opinion, preferences, speculation (that iron filings are attracted because they are iron, not because of their shape).

Connected with the repeatability criterion for science is the importance of measurement. Measured values can be repeated and recorded more easily than qualitative findings.

Paradigm Shifts

Kuhn (1962) refers to the body of currently accepted knowledge which makes particular experiments as "a paradigm," and describes science as periods of normal science carried out under the influence of a particular paradigm interspersed by revolutionary shifts in the paradigm. He sees a paradigm as an achievement or set of achievements which a scientific community "acknowledges as supplying the foundation for its further practice" achievements which "attract an enduring way from competing modes of scientific activity" and are "sufficiently open-ended to leave all sorts of problems for the redefined group of practitioners to solve."

The Scientist Decides What Section of the World's Variety to Examine

Newton and Einstein were responsible for revolutionary paradigm shifts. This is what happens when a piece of scientific work is planned and carried out: The scientist decides what section of the world's variety to examine. He makes his reduction, designing an artificial situation within which he can examine the workings of a few variables while others are held constant. The experimental design makes sense in terms of some particular view of or theory about that part of the world's variety that he is investigating, and his particular experiment will constitute the testing of a hypothesis within that theory. The question the experiment poses is: Will it pass the test?

In logic, we are more interested in the refutation than corroboration. This is because it is not possible to prove anything by induction. With deductive argument, there is no problem; we can prove that Socrates is mortal. But we cannot prove that the sun will come up tomorrow. Multiple confirmatory observations do not, in logic, get us nearer to truth. **Thus, a hypothesis refuted is a more valuable result.**

Science and the Systems Movement

The present cult of unreason is not a surprising reaction to the astonishing success of the cult of reason as embodied in modern science, especially as to certain fruits of science and technology are to be seen at the material level only. Descartes' dividing of problems into separate parts assumes the components of the whole are the same when examined singularly as when they are playing their part in the whole, or that the principles governing the assembly of the components into the whole are themselves straightforward.

Coping With Complexity

The interesting question: To what extent can the method of science cope with complexity? Where does it fall down and why?

Cursory inspection of the world suggests that it is a giant

complex with dense connections between its parts. We cannot cope with it and are forced to reduce it into separate areas we can examine. Thus we get subjects and disciplines. Because our education is, from the start, conducted in terms of this division, it is not easy to remember that the divisions are man-made and arbitrary.

Nature does not divide herself into physics, chemistry, biology, and so forth. Yet these concepts have been hammered into us, and are so ingrained in our thinking that we find it hard to perceive the unity that underlies them. Our need for coherence, therefore, demands that we arrange the classification of knowledge according to some rational principle. Systems thinking gives us a way to escape this trap and evolve more inclusive paradigms for understanding ourselves and our world.

APPENDIX PART 2

Dr. Harrington[1]

Primum, Non Nocere (First, Do No Harm)

The afternoon was warm, and the chemical disinfectant smell of the hospital corridors mingled with the sour stench of stale vomitus as we entered the room. Dr. Harrington, the British surgeon, wearing his long, white attending physician's coat like a royal gown, strode purposefully to the right side of the room's single metal bed.

One by one, the seven second year medical students filed in and stood silently around the bed. Our focus was on Dr. Harrington. This was our time to spend with this highly-respected abdominal surgeon, and we wanted to learn as much as we could about examining acutely ill patients.

The expression on the face of the middle-aged woman lying beneath the white sheet was one of agony, exhaustion, and despair. Her hair badly needed brushing, and a low moan escaped

---

[1]   Excerpted from *Deep Healing*. This is not his actual name.

her parched lips with each breath that she took.

"This woman is an alcoholic," Dr. Harrington announced in the impatient tone we'd come to expect from our professors. They seemed to want us always to be aware that they had more important things to do than to teach a bunch of *wannabe* doctors things they should have known since birth.

"She has acute pancreatitis, a common sequela to alcoholism," he continued. "This disease can produce one of the most painful abdominal conditions you will ever encounter."

Without any warning, he grasped the bed sheet and abruptly pulled it down to the patient's knees, exposing her naked body, her distended abdomen, and several clear plastic tubes carrying fluids to and from her body. She showed almost no response to this, so depleted was her strength, and so complete was her immersion in her pain.

Dr. Harrington continued, "With acute pancreatitis such as this woman has you will find the most severe rebound tenderness of any disease!"

Dr. Harrington now placed his hands on the woman's abdomen, just below her rib cage, and pressed firmly with the tips of his fingers. Her face contorted in agony; she cried out, and her hands struggled weakly to push him away. My own eyes widened in horror and my mouth went dry. Harrington kept his hands there for a long time.

Then suddenly he jerked his hands away, a maneuver that causes a sharp pain if the peritoneal lining of the abdominal cavity is inflamed. The patient shrieked. Her back arched, and her body went rigid for a few moments as she sobbed. A wave of nausea swept over me, and my breath stuck in my throat.

At last the poor woman's body collapsed back onto the damp sheets, the last of her reserves exhausted. Sweat beaded up on her forehead, her breathing became rapid and shallow, and tears poured from her eyes. The room fell silent except for her weak, whimpering sobs. I felt confused and paralyzed. I wanted to do something, but didn't know what.

Then, quite abruptly, Dr Harrington barked at me, "Doctor

Miller, demonstrate rebound tenderness."

I gasped involuntarily, looked at him, then looked at her. I was speechless. "Sir," I protested, "I've demonstrated rebound tenderness many times in the emergency room, and it's clear that this is the most severe I've ever seen. I don't see why it's necessary for me to do that."

"Dr. Miller, demonstrate rebound tenderness!" Harrington's voice rose to a demanding growl.

I gazed at the woman in the bed. Who was she? Was she the wife of a man killed in the Korean war, whose children had become delinquents? Was she someone's daughter whose songs once warmed the hearts of her family? How did she become reduced to her present state, to mere "clinical material?"

"I think she's suffered enough," I said, shocked by my own brazenness. "I don't feel there's sufficient indication to hurt her again."

"Very well, Dr. Miller," Harrington said in the most clipped British tones, "Please step back from the bed."

I did. But then I watched in horror as he instructed each of the other students to demonstrate rebound tenderness – not just once, but six more times! Harrington's eyes flickered toward my face each time the woman screamed. The message was clear. I was responsible for the torture this woman was enduring. If I had followed Harrington's instructions instead of my conscience, she would have been spared these awful torments.

Even as I write these words, something in me recoils. Could this really have happened? Did I really witness such blatant torture, in broad daylight? Could I have been the only one who felt infuriated, guilty, and ashamed? Am I simply a disobedient, oversensitive wimp? What crime did this poor woman commit to deserve such inhumane treatment? And was this memory the punishment I would forever endure for disobeying the order of my *superior*?

Although I would love to erase this memory, I cannot. Many times over the years, I have relived that moment, standing by helplessly as six medical students inflicted pain on that poor woman, under the steady, searing gaze of Dr. Harrington. Thousands of times I have re-experienced her pain and my own. Part of me always wants to step forward and push the others away, to protect this poor creature as I would my own mother. Another part of me is afraid. I chastise myself: Maybe I don't have what it takes to be a real doctor.

Something changed in me that day. The denial and callousness I had developed to help me endure medical school fell away. I was stunned not only by the utter heartlessness of Dr. Harrington's actions, but by the stark reality that this man was highly-respected throughout the medical community. He was the assistant Chair of the department, and should I choose to complain about what he did that day, my only reward would have been further ostracism by those in power. I might have even been put on probation, or worse, until I had proved myself capable of respectful compliance.

Aside from the hideous incongruity of a physician behaving like a Nazi prison guard, there was an important lesson Dr. Harrington taught me that day. Harrington himself was an exceptionally fine surgeon. He was sought after for his surgical skills and his scientific expertise. He was widely published in the most prestigious medical journals, and he held respected academic appointments. In many ways he reflected a dominant trend in medicine, with technical expertise and scientific knowledge taking the place of our humanity. But certainly there had to be more to the healing profession! Where was the patient's sense of well-being in all this? Where was the *caring* that was once such an important part of the healing process?

The evil in this world is not done only by those who commit it, but by those who stand back and watch it happening.
– Albert Einstein

APPENDIX PART 3

Elisabet Sahtouris

THE 12 FEATURES OF HEALTHY LIVING SYSTEMS

Many thanks to Elisabet Sahtouris[2] and Foster Gamble for their work in helping me integrate into my work these principles and characteristics that are possessed by *healthy* living systems.

Like everyone else who studies biology to any depth, I became aware very early on that all living things share certain basic similar traits; there are certain principles that they must maintain in order to stay healthy. These principles are the same whether we are discussing the life of a streptococcus bacterium, a paramecium, a jellyfish, a crocodile, a herd of zebras, a beehive, a human being, or a tribe of African pigmies.

These have been summarized into 12 basic principles by Dr. Sahtouris. These can be organized into 5 sets. A few moments of thought should convince you of their importance and the universality.

---

[2]   http://www.sahtouris.com/

Self-Regulation

The first three principles have to do with self-regulation. The most basic of these is what we call **autonomics**. It is the automatic response of the organism to protect and nurture itself.

Secondly, there is the well-known "**homeostasis**,"

Thirdly, there is what is called "**self-reflexivity**." Something in the paramecium knows that his actions are designed to help itself.

Coalition (communion) of Parts

The second group of principles has to do with the coalition of parts, it has to do with coordinated functioning of the organelles of a cell, the organelles of a paramecium, the cells of a jellyfish, the organs of a panda bear, or the members of a herd, family, tribe, or nation.

Empowerment has to do with the recognition, nurturance, and support of each of the parts.

Coordination of parts is clearly visible in the sea anemone, or the cheetah capturing prey, or a Superbowl game.

Reciprocity of parts describes mutual contribution and assistance contributing to the harmony and resonance of the system.

Communications among all parts enables the foot to take the mouth to the food the eye has seen.

Guidance

Guidance – so we can get where we want to go and away from unsafe places.

Conservation of what works.

Innovation, which involves creative change of that which does not work well.

Creation

Self-Creation, sometimes called autopoiesis is the result of the fact that every living being is a self-organizing system that organizes and creates itself.

Complexity, or the diversity of parts – the unity among the diversity is crucial.

Embeddedness of each system within a still larger system is characteristic of healthy living systems.

Relationship with environment

Stress response allows the system to detect change within itself or within its environment and respond to it.

Transfer mechanisms are necessary so that matter, energy, and information can be transferred to or received from other holons.

Transformation of matter, energy, and information can be seen, for example, when amino acids absorbed by the intestine must be assembled to create living tissue by the cells of the body.

Balance of interests

Balance of interests, the process of negotiating which enables the self-interest of all holons is balanced with the needs and abilities of others.

APPENDIX PART 4

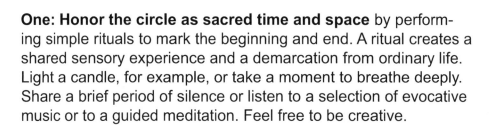

The Ten
Constants
of Wisdom
Circles

One: Honor the circle as sacred time and space by performing simple rituals to mark the beginning and end. A ritual creates a shared sensory experience and a demarcation from ordinary life. Light a candle, for example, or take a moment to breathe deeply. Share a brief period of silence or listen to a selection of evocative music or to a guided meditation. Feel free to be creative.

Two: Create a collective center by mutually agreeing **upon a topic or intention**. This might be visioning the future, choosing a specific focus, healing wounds of the past, or looking within to acquire deeper personal knowledge and wisdom.

Three: Ask to be informed by our highest human values such as compassion and truth, such as the wisdom imparted by those who have preceded us, as well as by the needs of those yet to be born.

Four: Express gratitude for the blessings and teachings of life.

The expression of gratitude has the powerful effect of establishing a very positive, receptive state of mind in relationship to that which is higher, and deeper.

Five: Create a container for full participation and deep truth-telling. Each person is allowed to speak without interruption. A talking stick or some other object that has symbolic value to the group may be passed around the circle, and only the person in possession of it is permitted to speak. Every member's right to be silent is respected, and all is kept confidential.

Six: Listen from the heart and serve as compassionate witness for other people in the circle. Pay attention to what is being shared, without criticism, interpretation, and judgment, without trying to "fix" or rescue the speaker.

Seven: Speak from the heart and from direct experience. The focus is on the communication of personal experience, and abstract, conceptual language is avoided. The experience of feelings and emotions, and their expression is encouraged. The object is to be able to say even difficult things without self-judgment or blaming others.

Eight: Make room for silence to enter to allow for reflection, for meditation, time for feelings to surface and for a sense of the deeper unity of the group to emerge.

Nine: Empower each member to be a co-facilitator of the process. Everyone is encouraged to give voice to feelings of satisfaction or discomfort with the process and progress of the group.

Ten: Commit to an ongoing relationship with each person in the circle. This will encourage the development of trust and caring among members. This caring may also be extended to others not in the group, and as well to all sentient beings, and to the earth itself, by practicing these capacities in evermore aspects of daily life.

APPENDIX PART 5
RESOURCES

Information regarding New Paradigm thinking:

Greater Good Magazine:
>http://greatergood.berkeley.edu/greatergood

The Co-Intelligence Institute:
>http://co-intelligence.org/

Acres USA, resources for commercial scale organic farming:
>http://www.acresusa.com/magazines/magazine.htm

The Archdruid Report:
>www.thearchdruidreport.blogspot.com

Andrew Harvey:
>www.andrewharvey.net/

Peter Russell:
>www.peterrussell.com/index2.php

Global Community Center for Conscious Evolution:
>www.evolve.org/pub/doc/index2.html

David Korten:
>www.davidkorten.org/

Jack Kornfield:
>www.jackkornfield.org/

Support for creating and sustaining group conversation, cohesion and action:

The World Cafe:
>http://www.TheWorldCafe.com

Conversation Cafe:
>http://www.ConversationCafe.org

Margaret J. Wheatley:
>http://www.margaretwheatley.com/

The Berkana Institute:
>http://www.berkana.org

America Speaks: Enaging Citizens in Governance:
>http://www.americaspeaks.org/

Life With Alacrity : Community and team building:
      http://www.lifewithalacrity.com/
My Society : Organizing a local community in the UK:
      http://www.mysociety.org/
Gather the Women:
      www.gatherthewomen.org/gtw/index.htm
Open Space Meeting:
      www.openspaceworld.org/
Further Resources and links:
      http://theworldcafe.com/connections.htm

Online Communities:

Conscious Evolution Network:
      http://interspirit.net/ce.cfm
Alt Globe: dedicated to conscious, sustainable living:
      www.Altglobe.com
Gaia Community:
      http://www.gaia.com/
Esalen's Online Community:
      www.iThou.org
New Heaven New Earth: a community of open thinkers:
      http://nhnecommunity.ning.com/
Freecycle: a site for gifting unwanted things to people in your community:
      http://www.freecycle.org/
Global Ecovillage Network:
      http://gen.ecovillage.org/
Earth Island Institute:
      http://earthisland.us/
Alliance for a New Humanity:
      http://www.anhglobal.org/
Ode Magazine's Online Community:
      http://www.odemagazine.com/groups/
Wiser Earth: Connecting you to Communities of Action:
      http://www.wiserearth.org
Global Youth Action Network:
      http://www.youthlink.org/gyanv5/index.htm

Community Action for ecological change:

Global Family: Shifting Consciousness to Unity and Love:
> http://www.globalfamily.net

Rocky Mountain Institute:
> http://www.rmi.org/

Transition United States: Rebuilding Community and Self Reliance:
> http://www.transitionus.org

SYRCL (South Yuba River CItizens League):
> http://www.yubariver.net/

APPLE (Alliance for a Post Petroleum Local Economy (in Nevada County, CA):
> http://www.apple-nc.org

Support for communities moving towards sustainability:

Sustainable Cities Collective:
> http://www.sustainablecitiescollective.com/Home/

Sustainable Connections:
> http://www.sconnect.org

Transition Towns Wiki: Communities responding to the peak oil crisis and climate change:
> http://transitiontowns.org

The Pachamama Alliance:
> http://www.pachamama.org/

The Awakening the Dreamer Initiative:
> http://awakeningthedreamer.org/

Intentional Communities: Linking ecovillages, communes, cohousing, co-ops, etc.:
> www.communities.ic.org

Yes! Magazine : building a just and sustainable world:
> http://www.yesmagazine.org

Personal health and well-being:

Chris Martenson's Crash Course:
> http://www.chrismartenson.com/crashcourse

Health World Online:
> http://www.healthy.net

Dr. Emmett Miller:
> http://www.DrMiller.com

Social Justice and other organizations:

Humanity Unites Brilliance (HUB):
> http://marilynnyborg.hubhub.org/videofeed.php

YES! Youth for Environmental Sanity:
> www.yesworld.org/

World Health Organization:
> http://www.who.int/en/

EMDR Humanitarian Assistance Programs
> http://www.emdrhap.org/

The Whitehouse's Homepage
> http://www.whitehouse.gov

Whitehouse blog:
> http://www.whitehouse.gov/blog/

Sugguested Readings:

Jack Travis – *The Wellness Workbook*
Lester R. Brown – *Plan B: Mobilizing to Save Civilization*
Peter Russel – *The Global Brain: The Awakening Earth in a New Century*
Dr. Betty Edwards – *Drawing on the Right Side of the Brain*
Patricia Ryan Madson – *Improv Wisdom*
Gabriele Rico – *Writing the Natural Way*
Eckhart Tolle – *A New Earth*
Jim Rough – *Society's Breakthrough!: Releasing the Essential Wisdom and Virtue in All the People*

For up to date information, special offers on *Awakening the Leader Within*, Dr. Miller suites, and for access to all of Dr. Miller's products, visit: http://www.OurCultureOnTheCouch.com

INDEX

367

SOFTWARE FOR THE MIND
Recorded Audio and Video Programs
by Emmett Miller MD

Congratulations on the progress you have made thus far. You may now choose to let these positive learning experiences serve as a basis for further positive change. Below are listed several programs, specially prepared. Dr. Miller has selected from his catalog several different programs to support you in your personal development. Most are highly experiential closed-eye experiences; many are Heart-to-Heart conversations you can listen to anytime. Choose from among them, depending upon your progress so far, and the level of experience you would next like to create.

• To subscribe to Dr. Miller's Newsletter for one year, free, click on Newsletter at www.DrMiller.com.
• Stay in touch with Dr. Miller's views on current events, paradigm shifting, self-healing, and global healing. See his blogs at:www.DrMillerBlogs.com
• For a complete listing of Dr. Miller's products, to listen online, browse products , and to discover more about Dr. Miller's work, go to DrMiller. com. Programs can be downloaded individually from the catalog there.

[signature: Emmett C. Miller MD]

INDIVIDUAL PROGRAMS

Awakening the Leader Within

$16.95 CD $11.98 MP3

This program will help you develop a new kind of leadership. Awaken the power and the desire to become the leader in your life – to change the way you think, the way you feel, and the way you behave, including your personal health habits, how you manage your relationships, and how you participate in your family, your community, and in your world at large.

Healing Our Planet

$16.95 CD $11.98 MP3

Discover how you can make a difference through passion, compassion, and love. In your heart is the future of our planet; learn how to empower your mental imagery to serve your most deeply held values. Experience the wisdom of the ages wedded to cutting-edge mind-body and peak performance technology.

Serenity Prayer

$16.95 CD $11.98 MP3

The Serenity Prayer is perhaps the single most concise and profound guide ever, to wise, healthy, and successful living. The words of wise men and women from many times and cultures, intoned over soothing music, awaken within you, the wisdom to choose well. This program will help you every day, while you drive, exercise, or simply relax, to re-script your unconscious.

Personal Excellence (6 CDs)

$75.00

This extraordinary program helps you achieve Personal Excellence, Peak Performance, and true Self-Esteem. Six Heart-to-Heart talks by Dr. Miller richly enhanced with music, dramatizations, and sound clips of the famous and wise plus six imagery experiences, guide you through the vital stages of personal growth: *I Am, I Can, I See, I Will, I Act, and I Appreciate.*

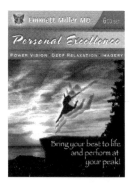

Deep Healing: The Essence of Mind-Body Medicine

$12.95 Book

Dr. Miller's humor, compassion and clinical experience in the hands-on healing of mind, body, emotion and spirit shines through in revealing personal vignettes, thought-provoking fables and profound quotes from wise teachers of all times. Fascinating and illuminating, yet at the same time remarkably user-friendly and entertaining, Deep Healing is for everyone, lay person and health professional alike, who is interested in healing themselves and others.

SUITES

To order suites and for more information on individual products contained within suites, visit Dr. Miller's Online Product Catalog at ShopDrMiller.com, or to request a physical catalog call: 800-528-2737 or write: Dr. Miller, 131 East Placer Street, Auburn, CA 95604.

Awakening the Leader Within Suite

$109.00

This highly entertaining, educational, and satisfying set of tools will enable you to enter a relaxed, stress-free state with *The Ten Minute Stress Manager*, and how to use it to produce the balance expressed by the wisdom of the *Serenity Prayer*.

I Am will guide you to experience your essential Self in a powerful new way, leading to an appreciation and empowerment of your Self. *I Can* builds Self-confidence, and is an excellent preparation for *Empowering Leadership DVD*, and the *Awakening The Leader Within CD*. Your inner leader can then be positively informed with the inspiring images offered by *Healing Our Planet*. And whether the changes you most want are highly personal, or totally global, *Writing Your Own Life's Script* will help you make those changes a reality.

Deep Healing: Your Personal Wellness Suite

$75.00

Healing is derived from an Old English word that is also the root of whole, hale, and hearty. *Deep Healing* presents Dr. Miller's original groundbreaking ideas about how to balance and heal mind, body, emotion, and spirit, and how to use Deep Relaxation and Guided Imagery to "program" your inner bio-computer to create balance, integrity, and peak performance.

Healing Journey, the first program of its kind, provides the experience of applying these remarkable tools to healing, and *Letting Go Of Stress* will show you how they can enable you to eliminate unwanted stress. Since anxiety is at the base of most illnesses, *Abolish Anxiety* will provide you tools to calm fears and quiet inflammation. *Accepting Change and Moving On* offers opportunities to release from your life those things it is time to let go of, be they physical, psychological, relationships, phases of your life – whatever it is time to release. *Easing Into Sleep* is designed to help you get the rest you need for healing, and awaken rested in the morning.

The Heart of Hypnosis and Deep Healing Level One - A Professional Training

$150.00

The study and mastery of Clinical Hypnosis provide an extraordinary set of powerful and fascinating tools for enhancing communication and therapy. Used appropriately, they permit rapid access to deep levels of consciousness, and the potential for deep healing of Mind, Body, Emotions, and Spirit.

The hypnotherapeutic relationship, in its most elegant form, resembles an exquisite dance involving mind, body, emotion, and spirit of both participants – a partnership through which both the guide and the subject are changed. It is a way to be present with each other, to be touched deeply, and to grow through the experience, within clear professional boundaries. Each is part of the experience and grows through it.

The Heart of Hypnosis also focuses on the achievement and experience of therapeutic states of altered awareness by each participant. Expect to complete your lessons feeling relaxed and rested, and in possession of important new avenues for your own personal growth as well. As well as the didactic material, several deep relaxation imagery experiences with beautiful visuals are presented.

You will learn how complementary states of focused concentration through the selective use of words and imagery, tone and timbre of voice, movements, and mirroring, pacing, and leading techniques. You will learn to facilitate your clients in removing barriers to transformation, and in accessing their own inner potentials for deep healing.

This is only a partial listing of individual products and suites. Other Suites that might interest you can be found on Dr. Miller's website DrMiller.com. Prices are subject to change without notice.

About The Author

Although best known for his seminal work in the field of holistic health and Mind-Body Medicine, physician Emmett Miller is also an accomplished musician, scientist, mathematician and living systems specialist. He earned his BS in mathematics at Trinity College, his MD at The Albert Einstein College of Medicine, and has been elected to Sigma Pi Sigma, the national physics honor society. His chief contributions have been his discoveries of how thoughts, emotions, and mental images can be guided to have a profound impact on illnesses, wellness, and performance. Having studied computer systems and programming beginning in 1962, he was able to see in his clinical practice of Family Medicine that the mind functions much like a bio-computer; it perceives, reasons, and feels the way it was programmed, and that self-induced altered states (e.g., deep relaxation, meditation, hypnosis) make it possible to alter this programming through the use of mental imagery.

Miller's first book, *Selective Awareness* – Introduction to the Medicine of Mind and Body (1973), introduced his concepts of guided imagery and software for the mind, and the powerful healing tool he had invented, the guided imagery tape. For the first time the tools of deep relaxation and guided imagery were made available throughout the world. These tools are now the most commonly used of all the approaches of modern complementary or integral medicine. Miller's recordings, distributed on CDs and DVDs, and as Internet downloads, have remained the choice of conventional as well as complementary and alternative health professionals for more than 35 years. In 1977 he co-founded The Cancer Support and Education Center, the world's first training program for cancer support professionals, and served for 20 years as its medical director and imagery instructor.

Often described as a "contemporary hi-tech shaman," Miller is a trainer, coach, speaker, and tireless worker in the service of planetary transformation through his Leadership Institute for Global Healing and Transformation (LIGHT). His most recent book to date : *Deep Healing; The Essence of Mind-Body Medicine*, presenting tools for self-healing and optimal performance.

He maintains a practice in Los Altos and in Nevada City, California, limited to Mind-Body Medicine and Peak Performance Coaching for individuals, leaders, and organizations. His current mission and vision include the development of a web-based global healing center dedicated to catalyzing positive change and wisdom through the electronic distribution of digitized audio and visual media. For more information, visit About Dr. Miller.

Emmett E. Miller, M.D.
P.O. Box 803
Nevada City, CA 95959
530-478-1807
DrMiller@DrMiller.com

Made in United States
Orlando, FL
12 April 2022

16739854R00245